Demystifying the IPsec Puzzle

For quite a long time, computer security was a rather narrow field of study that was populated mainly by theoretical computer scientists, electrical engineers, and applied mathematicians. With the proliferation of open systems in general, and the Internet and the World Wide Web (WWW) in particular, this situation has changed fundamentally. Today, computer and network practitioners are equally interested in computer security, since they require technologies and solutions that can be used to secure applications related to electronic commerce (e-commerce). Against this background, the field of computer security has become very broad and includes many topics of interest. The aim of this series is to publish state-of-the-art, high standard technical books on topics related to computer security. Further information about the series can be found on the WWW by the following URL:

http://www.esecurity.ch/serieseditor.html

Also, if you'd like to contribute to the series and write a book about a topic related to computer security, feel free to contact either the Commissioning Editor or the Series Editor at Artech House.

Recent Titles in the Artech House Computer Security Series

Rolf Oppliger, Series Editor

For a listing of recent titles in the *Artech House Computing Library,* turn to the back of this book.

Demystifying the IPsec Puzzle

Sheila Frankel

Artech House
Boston • London
www.artechhouse.com

Library of Congress Cataloging-in-Publication Data
Frankel, Sheila.
    Demystifying the IPsec puzzle / Sheila Frankel.
        p.   cm. — (Artech House computer security series)
    Includes bibliographical references and index.
    ISBN 1-58053-079-6 (alk. paper)
    1. IPSec (Computer network protocol)   I. Title.   II. Series.
TK5105.567 .F73   2001
004.6'2—dc21   2001018807

British Library Cataloguing in Publication Data
Frankel, Sheila
    Demystifying the IPsec puzzle. — (Artech House computer security series)
    1. IPSec (Computer network protocol)
    I. Title
    004.6'2
    ISBN 1-58053-079-6

Cover design by Igor Valdman

International Standard Book Number: 1-58053-079-6
Library of Congress Catalog Card Number: 2001018807

10 9 8 7 6 5 4 3 2 1

To Mechy, my partner in everything important
and
to the most wonderful results (direct and indirect) of our collaboration,
Benjamin, Shlomit, Chana, Yaakov, Daniel and Eitan,
Sara, Nomi, Shana, and Aryeh

Contents

Preface

IPsec (Internet Protocol Security) has been publicized in the popular computer press; numerous articles have heralded its ready-for-prime-time status; and, of course, numerous standards make up its quintessential and normative definition. But very few books attempt to systematically describe each facet of this ever expanding creature. That is the goal of this book. It is directed at network administrators, informed users, and curious graduate students.

The book is organized as follows. Chapter 1 sets the stage with an introduction to TCP/IP, the basis for Internet communications. Each subsequent chapter discusses a different facet of IPsec

- Chapters 2 and 3 examine the protocols that make up classic IPsec, the Authentication Header (AH) and the Encapsulating Security Payload (ESP).
- Chapter 4 discusses the cryptographic algorithms used in IPsec.
- Chapter 5 looks at the Internet Key Exchange (IKE), IPsec's key negotiation protocol.
- Chapter 6 applies IKE to the road warrior.
- Chapter 7 describes late-breaking additions to IKE.
- Chapter 8 examines PF_KEY, the protocol that enables IKE to talk to IPsec.

- Chapter 9 takes a look at wider-ranging IPsec policy concerns.
- Chapter 10 explains public key infrastructure (PKI) and certificates.
- Chapter 11 discusses extending IPsec protection to multicast communications.
- Chapter 12 gives a summary and conclusions.

Now that it is over, I would like to extend a hearty thanks to Rolf Oppliger, Artech House Series Editor for Computer Security, who recruited me to write this book and who read each chapter within days of its submission. I also would like to thank my editors at Artech House: Viki Williams, who lured me into this and then fled to greener pastures; Ruth Harris, who patiently endured missed deadlines, cracked the whip when necessary, and stretched the schedule (pronounced "shedule") to its limits; and Katie McMenamy, who patiently guided a novice through the prepublication maze. I also would like to thank my colleagues at NIST, Jim Dray, Rob Glenn, Tim Polk, and John Wack; and Paul Hoffman, Director of the VPN Consortium, who took time from their busy schedules to read portions of the book. Their comments were right on target; any remaining errors are mine alone. תושלב"ע

Sheila Frankel
sheila.frankel@nist.gov

1

Introduction

> Railroad carriages are pulled at the enormous speed of 15 mph by engines which, in addition to endangering life and limb of passengers, roar and snort their way through the countryside, setting fire to the crops, scaring the livestock, and frightening women and children. The Almighty certainly never intended that people should travel at such breakneck speed.
>
> *Martin Van Buren*

Back in the old days, when the Internet was young, fire-breathing dragons roamed the earth, and Bill Gates was still working on his fifth billion, the Internet was the plaything of a group of academics and researchers. Its goal was to maximize communication, connectedness, and collaboration and to minimize barriers that would detract from the realization of those goals. The protocols that were defined then—and that still govern the underpinnings of the Internet now—reflect that reality.

When I mentioned to a friend that I was thinking of writing a book on Internet security, he responded, "Internet security is an oxymoron." I found myself reacting in a defensive and somewhat protective manner, although from the perspective of anyone who reads newspapers' daily reports on break-ins and viruses, his response was entirely appropriate.

Once the Internet became the "information superhighway," and the traffic (not to mention the drivers) became more diverse, security blossomed into a major concern. It was as if the inhabitants of a private single-family house were to wake up one morning and discover that each bedroom was inhabited by a group of strangers. If a family member should complain about the lack of privacy or security, one of the interlopers might surely say, "In this house, security is an oxymoron."

Embedded within the complex and rapidly evolving infrastructure, it proved impossible to radically or suddenly alter the Internet protocols, those agreed-on conventions, formats, and rules that govern Internet communications. Thus, two types of solutions have emerged in response to the security hazards that threaten Internet traffic: localized solutions and application-specific solutions. Localized solutions are attempts by computer network administrators to isolate or fortify their particular fiefdoms and take the form of screening routers, firewalls, defensive scanners, and the elimination of known security holes from operating systems and application programs. Application-specific solutions are applied to specific applications, such as electronic commerce or email, and are agreed on by some segment of the user population.

What differentiates IPsec from other solutions? IPsec is an attempt to define a more global solution to the problem of Internet security. Because IPsec will be applied at the Internet layer of communications, it can be used by any or all applications. Rather than requiring each email program or Web browser to implement its own security mechanisms, IPsec involves a change to the underlying networking facilities that are used by every application. It also allows network managers to apply protection to network traffic without involving end users.

The IPsec protocols are like a jigsaw puzzle, consisting of numerous interconnected pieces that, assembled, make a cohesive whole. This book examines the component pieces one at a time; while we are analyzing individual pieces of the puzzle, we shall assume that other, still unexplored components magically appear in an unspecified manner, perhaps through invocations or wizardry.

The impact of each IPsec piece is easier to understand when viewed in the context of a sample communications scenario. Throughout, this book uses three simple but commonplace scenarios for that purpose. The sample scenarios are comprised of two types of building blocks: hosts and gateways.

- A *host* is a system that can initiate messages to be sent across the Internet and receive messages from other systems but cannot act as an intermediary to forward or route messages from one system to another. A host can provide IPsec services for itself but not for other systems. Examples of hosts are a single-user PC, a laboratory computer used to gather and analyze data, and a business data repository.

- A *gateway* is a system that can initiate messages to be sent across the Internet, receive messages from other systems, and act as an intermediary to forward or route messages from one system to another. Routers and firewalls are examples of gateways. A security gateway, in our framework, is a gateway that can provide IPsec services for itself and for other systems.

Scenario 1 is the simplest case: two hosts communicating with each other. Currently, one of the common uses of IPsec is the creation of a virtual private network (VPN). If a company needs to conduct secure communications between scattered locations, a private network can be constructed by leasing or stringing private communication lines. A less expensive and more flexible alternative is a VPN that uses the Internet as the communications medium and employs IPsec to ensure that the communications are indeed private. Although the VPN's traffic crosses the public Internet, IPsec protection prevents unauthorized outsiders from reading or modifying the traffic.

Scenario 2 is a small-scale VPN: two separate networks, each protected from the outside by a security gateway that screens all communications to and from its associated network. This topology can represent a single business with several branch locations or with separate departmental networks in the same location.

Scenario 3 combines aspects of the first two: a single host communicating with another host that resides on a network protected by a security gateway. This commonly occurs when an employee dials into a business network from home or when on a business trip. Scenario 3 is complicated by the fact that the single host, when dialing into the network, may not have a fixed network address. Figures 1.1(a), 1.1(b), and 1.1(c) illustrate scenarios 1, 2, and 3, respectively.

Because you are reading this book, you must have some interest in IPsec. Instead of touting the superiority of the IPsec approach, this book first describes the details of the IPsec protocol itself. Once we have "assembled" the IPsec puzzle, we will compare IPsec to the other leading contenders and contrast their relative strengths and weaknesses.

The information in this book will, we hope, be sufficient to turn IPsec-illiterate readers into informed users of IPsec products or to turn IPsec-aware readers into tweakers of existing IPsec implementations. By

Figure 1.1(a) Communication scenario 1: host-to-host.

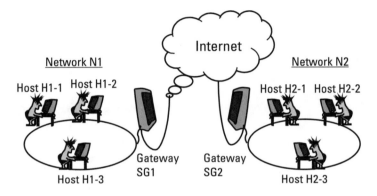

Figure 1.1(b) Communication scenario 2: gateway-to-gateway.

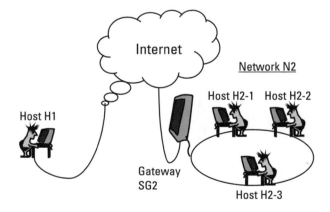

Figure 1.1(c) Communication scenario 3: host-to-gateway.

itself, however, this book is neither sufficiently rigorous nor sufficiently detailed to enable readers to become IPsec implementers from scratch. The technology is complex enough and still in flux so that would-be implementers need to become intimately familiar with the IPsec Requests for Comments (RFCs) and Internet Drafts that are the definitive specifications for this technology.[1]

However, the RFCs and the Internet Drafts do not always present a complete picture. In the spirit of the IETF, the organization responsible for the development of those documents and whose motto is "rough consensus and running code," the documents do not always tell the full story. The details are fleshed out through mailing list discussions, interoperability testing sessions, and hallway discussions at the IETF meetings. Sometimes, the small but essential details are agreed on, but it takes time until that is reflected in the documents. This book attempts to convey the flavor and substance of the finishing details and, in many cases, unresolved disagreements, which are essential to an understanding of IPsec. Because IPsec is still under development, it provides a moving target for any attempt at documenting its features and status. This book attempts to capture the reality of IPsec, presenting a snapshot of IPsec as of October 2000.

The field of computer security embodies a rich and extensive theoretical and historical infrastructure. Although this book cannot cover the theory and practical ramifications of every aspect of IPsec, it does aim to make the IPsec protocols' goals, functionality, and interrelationships understandable to the reader. It also suggests voluminous amounts of extra reading material to those readers with a thirst for IPsec-related knowledge.

1.1 The TCP/IP Protocol Stack

The frame of reference in which IPsec operates is that of the Internet Protocol (IP). IP is one part of a layered suite of communication protocols known as TCP/IP [1–4]. The top layer, the applications layer, consists of protocols that are familiar to users through the applications they use. Internet browsers use the Hyper Text Transfer Protocol (HTTP) protocol to communicate;

---

1. All the Internet protocols, including IPsec, are defined in documents that are developed under the sponsorship of the Internet Engineering Task Force (IETF). An Internet Draft describes a protocol that is in the early stages of development. Once the technology reaches a certain level of consensus and there are multiple vendor implementations of the protocol, it is reclassified as an RFC. All current Internet Drafts and RFCs can be found at the IETF's Web site, http://www.ietf.org. The IETF cautions against citing Internet Drafts as references; because many aspects of IPsec have not yet achieved RFC status, this book does cite Internet Drafts.

email programs use the SMTP, POP3, and IMAP4 protocols; remote terminal programs use TELNET; and file transfer programs use the File Transfer
Protocol (FTP). Those application protocols rely on the Transmission Control Protocol (TCP), the transport protocol that is used to establish reliable
communications sessions, in which data are predictably transferred without
loss, duplication, or other types of errors.

Other applications and their related protocols are not as familiar to
most users but are essential for the smooth operation of the Internet. Network routing relies on protocols such as the Routing Information Protocol
(RIP); the ability to refer to hosts by their names rather than by a lengthy
string of numbers results from use of the Domain Naming System (DNS)
protocol. Those application protocols rely on the User Datagram Protocol
(UDP), a transport protocol that transmits individual packets without checking for loss or duplication. For applications that run over UDP, the applications themselves are responsible for this type of reliability insurance, rather
than the underlying transport protocol. The TCP communications model
can be likened to the phone company: A connection is established, and messages are reliably transmitted and received in the proper order. The UDP
communications model can be compared to the Post Office; messages are
sent out and (one hopes) received, but no checking is done to ensure that
they actually were received or in what order. Both transport protocols, TCP
and UDP, rely on the Internet layer protocol, IP, for the following:

- Transmitting messages from one machine to another;
- Routing the messages so they arrive at the desired destination;
- If the messages are too large to be transmitted by one or more of
  the network links encountered along the way, breaking the messages
  into smaller fragments and, at the other end, reassembling the fragments to reconstruct the original message.

The Internet Control Message Protocol (ICMP) defines special-purpose
messages used by the IP layer to alert other systems to problematic or erroneous conditions and to exchange information related to IP functions.

Figure 1.2 illustrates the layers of a typical system that uses TCP/IP as
its networking protocol. When an outbound message is constructed, each
layer, from the top to the bottom, inserts its own header in front of the
data to be transported and then sends the message to the next (lower)
layer for further processing. When an inbound message is received, the
process is reversed. Each layer, from the bottom to the top, performs its

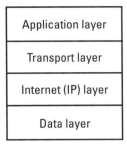

| Application layer |
| Transport layer |
| Internet (IP) layer |
| Data layer |

Figure 1.2 The TCP/IP layers.

layer-appropriate processing, strips off its header, and sends the message to the next (upper) layer for further processing. Each layer views a message as having two parts: the layer's header and "other stuff." The other stuff generally is referred to as "data," although in fact it generally contains a series of upper-layer headers, followed by the message data destined for the application.

1.1.1 IP Packets

The overwhelming majority of packets that traverse the Internet today follow the rules and the format defined by Internet Protocol Version 4 (IPv4) [5]. A new protocol, Internet Protocol Version 6 (IPv6) [6–8], has been defined and is deployed in limited portions of the Internet. The motivation for the development of IPv6 was the predicted depletion of the IPv4 address space due to the unanticipated increase in the Internet's popularity and use. An IPv6 address is 128 bits, as opposed to the 32 bits in an IPv4 address. That is not the only difference between the two versions. The designers of IPv6 took advantage of the experience and lessons learned from the deployment of IPv4 and redesigned many operational aspects, along with the header format. For example, IPsec is a mandatory part of any IPv6 implementation, while it is optional for IPv4. The discussions in this text of the various features of IPsec point out any differences between IPsec for IPv4 and IPsec for IPv6.

The header that is constructed or processed by the IP layer, referred to as the IP header, differs somewhat depending on whether it is an IPv4 header or an IPv6 header. The IPv4 header format is illustrated in Figure 1.3; its composite fields are as follows:

- *Version* identifies the header as an IPv4 header.
- *Hdr Len* is the IP header length.

Version	Hdr Len	Type of service	Total packet length	
Fragment identification value			Flags	Fragment offset
Time to live (TTL)		Next protocol	Header checksum	
Source address				
Destination address				
Options				Padding

Figure 1.3 IPv4 header format.

- *Type of Service* (TOS) specifies whether the packet should receive special delivery treatment as it traverses the Internet.
- *Total Packet Length* is the length of the IP header plus data.
- *Fragment Identification Value* is the unique identifier assigned to all fragments of a packet that must be broken up (fragmented) for the packet to reach its destination.
- *Flags* are specialized control flags, including the DF ("don't fragment") bit, which prohibits intermediate routers from fragmenting the packet.
- *Fragment Offset* is the offset of a packet fragment within the reassembled packet.
- *Time to Live* (TTL) is the maximum number of times a packet can be forwarded within the Internet before it is discarded. Its purpose is to prevent an undeliverable packet from indefinitely bouncing from router to router (possibly in an infinite loop) without ever arriving at its destination.
- *Next Protocol* is the protocol of the next packet header, which for IPv4 generally is TCP, UDP, or ICMP.
- *Header Checksum* is a computed value to ensure that the IP header is not inadvertently changed while the packet is in transit. It is recomputed at each intermediate router.
- *Source Address* is the address of the packet's sender.
- *Destination Address* is the address of the packet's recipient.
- *Options* are used to specify intermediate routing or other special handling for the packet (not used in most IP implementations).
- *Padding* consists of zero-filled bytes that ensure the IP header is a multiple of 32 bits.

A number of features or behaviors can be enabled as options to the IPv4 header. One feature is source routing. Instead of just specifying the source and the destination of a message and leaving the exact intermediate routing up to the routers encountered along the way, a source-routed message specifies the exact route that a message should take, including intermediate destinations. To enable source routing and other optional behaviors, the IPv4 header has a fixed-length options field, which has two disadvantages: (1) a packet that does not need special processing still carries an unneeded options field, and (2) any new types of special processing that might be required have to be retrofitted into the single options field.

The designers of IPv6 took a different approach to options. If needed, one or more variable-length extension headers can be included in a packet. The IPv6 extension headers are special-purpose headers that follow the IP header and describe any intermediate routing or other special handling that is required. That provides more flexibility for special-purpose handling and leaves open the possibility that additional extension headers can be defined in the future. The currently defined IPv6 extension headers are as follows:

- The *hop-by-hop header* defines special processing that needs to be applied to the message at each intermediate router.
- The *routing header* specifies each or some of the intermediate routers to be encountered by the message.
- The *fragment header* identifies each individual piece of a packet that is too large to traverse the path without being divided into multiple segments, called fragments.
- The *destination options header* defines special processing that needs to be applied to the message when it reaches its final destination.

The IPv6 header format is illustrated in Figure 1.4; its composite fields are as follows:

- *Version* identifies the header as an IPv6 header.
- *Traffic Class* specifies whether the packet should receive special delivery treatment as it traverses the Internet.
- *Flow Label* identifies a group of packets as members of a group requiring special processing by intermediate routers.
- *Payload Length* is the IPv6 payload length (extension headers + data).

Version	Traffic class	Flow label		
Payload length			Next header	Hop limit
Source address				
Destination address				

Figure 1.4 IPv6 header format.

- *Next Header* is the protocol of the next packet header, which for IPv6 generally is TCP, UDP, or ICMP.

- *Hop Limit* is the maximum number of times a packet can be forwarded within the Internet before it is discarded. Its purpose is to prevent an undeliverable packet from indefinitely bouncing from router to router (possibly in an infinite loop) without ever arriving at its destination.

- *Source Address* is the address of the packet's sender.

- *Destination Address* is the address of the packet's recipient.

1.1.2   IP Packetization and Fragmentation

Often, the message to be sent by an application (e.g., an email message or a page retrieved by a Web browser) is too large to be sent intact across the Internet, especially after all the requisite headers have been added. How does TCP/IP handle messages that are too large to be sent in a single packet? The packetization routines, which generally are incorporated into TCP or into those applications that run over UDP, divide the message into packets of a reasonable size (what is considered reasonable is a fairly complex matter that will not be dealt with here), and the original message is reconstructed when it is received. In IPv4, the entities that traverse the Internet generally are referred to as *datagrams*; in IPv6, the word *packet* generally is used. This book uses the word *message* to refer to the logical units of data generally sent by an application and the word *packet* to refer to the packetized entity that consists of a series of headers followed by the data that make up all or part of the original message.

What happens if the sender of a packet is unaware that, along the path leading to the destination, one or more segments, or links, are not equipped to handle a packet of the size that was sent? In IPv4, the packet's sender can dictate whether the packet can be further segmented, or fragmented, by a router that the packet encounters. If router R1 attempts to forward a packet that is too large to be accommodated by a subsequent network link, and if the originator of the packet disallowed packet fragmentation by turning on the packet's DF bit, then router R2 on that link will send an ICMP "packet too large" message back to the packet's sender. (Actually, the message is "destination unreachable" with a code that indicates "fragmentation needed and DF set.") That message notifies the sender that the oversized packet should be broken into smaller packets and then resent. If R2 has implemented the Path Maximum Transmission Unit (PMTU) Discovery Protocol, the message will include the size of the largest packet that can be handled by that link; otherwise, the sender will have to determine the PMTU through trial and error. If, however, the sender of the oversized packet did not disallow packet fragmentation, then R2 will break the packet into appropriately sized fragments, which will be reassembled when they reach their ultimate destination. Figure 1.5 illustrates fragmentation performed by an intermediate router. Figure 1.6 shows the situation when intermediate fragmentation is disallowed by the sender.

In IPv6, the approach is somewhat different. On the basis of the experience with IPv4, fragmentation is viewed as a suboptimal approach [9],

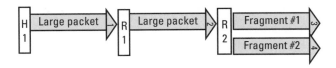

Figure 1.5 Fragmentation performed by an intermediate router.

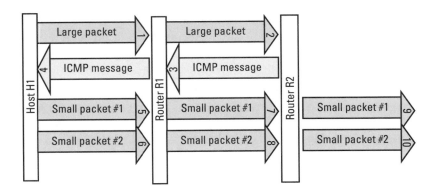

Figure 1.6 Fragmentation avoided by reduction of the packet size.

because it results in releasing larger numbers of packets, some of which are most likely quite small. Unlike IPv4, in which fragmentation is performed and the packets resent by an intermediate router, in IPv6 the packet's source host attempts to reduce the size of all the packets. If that is impossible, the source host fragments the packet into multiple packets, which are identified as individual pieces of the same packet through the use of one of the IPv6 extension headers, the fragmentation header. As in IPv4, reassembly is performed by the host that is the packet's final destination.

IP packetization and fragmentation are very different creatures; the former is the normal operational mode of IP, while the latter is viewed as an abnormal and potentially harmful beast. Ideally, packetization divides a message into packets that are close to the maximum size that can be handled along the path the packets will take. That minimizes the number of packets per message; because small packets require the same handling at each intermediate router as do large packets, avoidance of network congestion and other problematic conditions is best served by the sending of fewer, larger packets. Because each packet contains a full IP header, including all necessary routing and special handling options, each packet can be independently processed by the IP routines once the packet reaches its destination. If portions of a message are not received, only those portions must be resent, rather than the whole message.

Fragmentation is performed by the IP routines. The first fragment contains a full IP header; the subsequent fragments contain only those portions of the header necessary for routing and any special handling that must take place while the packet traverses the route. Thus, the IP routines must reassemble the fragments into a complete packet before the packet can be sent to the appropriate application. Because packet fragments take up space while they are held for reassembly, the IP routines hold them for only a limited amount of time. If all fragments do not show up within the specified time frame, the sender must resend all the fragments, not just the ones that failed to arrive initially. In addition, fragmentation increases the likelihood that numbers of small packets will be traversing the network, since it is unlikely that all of the fragments will be as large as the PMTU.

1.2   Introducing IPsec

Because the format of Internet packets is publicly defined and well known, a packet that traverses the Internet can be captured by any of the routers that lie along its path. Its contents can be read and changed. Even the checksums that are part of the Internet packet format cannot protect a packet from unauthorized alteration. The checksums were intended to guard against data corruption caused by malfunctioning devices. If the data alteration is intentional, the attacker simply can recompute the checksum, and the packet will appear to be perfectly intact. How, then, can Internet packets be protected from attacks by squatters, marauders, and other cybermenaces? The solution lies with a technique loved by children of all ages—secret codes. If the contents of a message are rendered unintelligible through the application of a secret code, then those contents are safe from prying eyes. If a message's contents are left intact, but a secret code is used to compute a value that uniquely characterizes the message, then the message's contents cannot be altered without alerting the recipient that something is amiss. Today's computer-assisted codebreakers, or cryptanalysts, are capable of breaking extremely complex secret codes. Therefore, information that is impossible to guess, even with the aid of today's computing power, must form an integral part of the coded messages. That information, the secret key, must be known only to the communication's participants.

The IPsec protocols are additions to IP that enable the sending and receiving of cryptographically protected Internet packets. Special IPsec headers identify the types of cryptographic protection that were applied to the packet and include other information necessary for the successful decoding of the protected packet. The Encapsulating Security Payload (ESP) header provides privacy and protects against malicious modification, and the Authentication Header (AH) protects against malicious modification without providing privacy. The Internet Key Exchange (IKE) protocol is a mechanism that allows for secret keys and other protection-related parameters to be exchanged prior to a communication without the intervention of the user.

1.3 Summary

This chapter set the stage for an understanding of IPsec by introducing its underlying framework, the TCP/IP networking suite, and by describing IP, the layer in which IPsec operates. This information is critical for an understanding of the puzzle pieces that make up IPsec. We also presented an intuitive, somewhat jargon-free introduction to IPsec. The rest of this book delves more deeply into each facet of IPsec, complete with technical details and the appropriately mysterious vocabulary that generally accompanies such details.

1.4 Further Reading

Two excellent series delve deeply and in great detail into explanations of TCP/IP, *Internetworking with TCP/IP* [1, 2] and *TCP/IP Illustrated* [3, 4]. Each is a three-volume series, in which the first volume describes the architecture of TCP/IP and its numerous protocols, and the second volume explains its implementation, interconnections, and interfaces. The third volume of each series contains a more specialized description of specific protocols, aimed mainly at implementers. The quintessential definition of IPv4 can be found in RFC 791 [5]; IPv6 is defined in RFC 2460 [6]. Christian Huitema, an involved participant in the IPv6 development process, has written a book [7] that describes each aspect of the IPv6 protocol, its motivation, and unresolved issues. The Internet Architecture Board (IAB), a technical advisory group that provides architectural oversight and planning for the Internet protocols, issued a document that presents the arguments in favor of adopting IPv6 [8]. For those who are interested in the issue of fragmentation, [9] presents a detailed analysis of the ills brought into the Internet world through its use.

References

[1]   Comer, D., *Internetworking With TCP/IP. Vol. 1: Principles, Protocols, and Architecture*, 3rd Ed., Englewood Cliffs, NJ: Prentice Hall, 1995.

[2]   Comer, D., and D. L. Stevens, *Internetworking With TCP/IP, Vol. 2: Design, Implementation, and Internals*, 3rd Ed., Englewood Cliffs, NJ: Prentice Hall, 1998.

[3]   Stevens, W. R., *TCP/IP Illustrated, Vol. 1: The Protocols*, Reading, MA: Addison-Wesley, 1994.

[4]   Wright, G., and W. R. Stevens, *TCP/IP Illustrated, Vol. 2: The Implementation*, Reading, MA: Addison-Wesley, 1995.

[5]   Postel, J. (ed.), *Internet Protocol: DARPA Internet Program Protocol Specification*, RFC 791, Sept. 1981.

[6]   Deering, S., and R. Hinden, *Internet Protocol, Version 6 (IPv6) Specification*, RFC 2460, Dec. 1998.

[7]   Huitema, C., *IPv6: The New Internet Protocol*, 2nd Ed., Englewood Cliffs, NJ: Prentice Hall, 1997.

[8]   King, S., et al., "The Case for IPv6," <draft-ietf-iab-case-for-ipv6-06.txt>, June 2000.

[9]   Kent, C. A., and J. C. Mogul, "Fragmentation Considered Harmful," *Proc. Frontiers in Computer Communications Technology*, ACM SIGCOMM '87, Aug. 1987, http://gatekeeper.dec.com/pub/DEC/WRL/research-reports/WRL-TR-87.3.pdf.

2

The First Puzzle Piece: The Authentication Header

> It is a riddle wrapped in a mystery inside an enigma.
>
> *Winston Churchill, 1939*

IPsec is an attempt to enable secure communications at the IP layer. This security protection is furnished through the use of two optional headers, the Authentication Header (AH) and the Encapsulating Security Payload header (ESP). Although the use of these headers is optional, their inclusion in IPv6 systems is mandatory; many implementers of IPv4 systems also furnish IPv4 versions of these headers. This chapter describes the AH, its format, its processing, and the protections it provides.

2.1 Protections Provided by AH

AH provides several types of protection [1, 2]:

- *Connectionless integrity* is a guarantee that the message that is received is the exact one that was sent, and that no tampering has occurred. Why "connectionless"? Because communications at the Internet layer are analogous to the Post Office model rather than the phone company model. Messages are sent from the sender to the receiver, but no attempt is made to ensure that they are received in order or that any (or all) were in fact received. That task is left to the transport layer protocol or to the application that originates the messages.

- *Data origin authentication* is a guarantee that the message actually was sent by the apparent originator of the message and not by another user masquerading as the supposed message originator.

- *Replay protection* (optional) is the assurance that the same message is not delivered multiple times and that messages are not delivered grossly out of order. This capability must be implemented by the sender; the receiver may optionally enable its use.

2.2   Security Associations and the Security Parameters Index

Before two communicating entities can exchange secure communications, they need to agree on the nature of the security to be applied to those communications: which security headers (AH, ESP, or both) will be applied, the cryptographic algorithms to be used, the secret keys, and so forth. A security association (SA) consists of all the information needed to characterize and exchange protected communications. The IETF documents treat the SA and its repository, the security association database (SAD) as hypothetical constructs, because they are entities that are internal to each of the peers. They contain information essential to conducting secured communications via the IPsec protocols, but the SA in its entirety is not part of that communication, so the documents do not dictate its form or location. In practice, the SAD generally is a table that is kept in protected storage by the system process that handles these communications.

Each SA includes various pieces of information that the IPsec-processing routines can use to determine whether the SA is eligible to be applied to a particular inbound or outbound message. Each such item can have a specific value or values, to narrowly define those messages to which the SA applies; or a wildcard value, to indicate that an item is not relevant in evaluating traffic for the SA. These items, called the SA's selectors, include the following:

- *Source and destination addresses* (IPv4 or IPv6). Each of these addresses can be a single IP address: unicast, anycast (IPv6 only), broadcast (IPv4 only), or multicast; a range of addresses; an address plus mask, to specify a subnet. For a single SA, the source address(es) and the destination address(es) all must be either IPv4 or IPv6. If the sole selectors for an SA are the IP addresses of the communicating peers, the SA is called a *host-oriented* SA, because it governs all communications between the two systems, regardless of which users or applications are involved.

- *Name*, either a user ID or a system name. The User ID limits this SA to traffic initiated by or destined for a specific user. If the sole selectors for an SA are the user IDs of the communicating peers, the SA is called a *user-oriented* SA, because it governs all communications between the two users, regardless of which systems or applications are involved. The system name limits it to traffic for a specific system, which can be a host, a security gateway, or any other addressable system. The system name can be specified in one of the following three formats; the user ID can be specified in one of the first two formats:

  - A fully qualified DNS user name (e.g., frankel@artechhouse.com) or DNS system name (e.g., artechhouse.com);
  - An X.500 distinguished name (explained in Chapter 10);
  - An X.500 general name (explained in Chapter 10).

- *Transport Layer Protocol* (TCP or UDP).

- *Source and destination ports.* A single port number generally is used to limit the SA's applicability to a single type of application traffic (e.g., FTP or TELNET). When one or both of the port selectors are used in combination with the Transport Layer Protocol selector and one or both of the address selectors, the SA is called *session-oriented,* because its effect is to limit the SA to one session, or instantiation, of a particular type of traffic between two specific hosts.

Each SA also contains various pieces of information that must be made available to the IPsec-processing routines, including:

- Data used to provide authentication protection: AH or ESP authentication algorithm, keys, and so forth (further explained later in this chapter and in Chapter 4);
- Data used to provide confidentiality protection: ESP encryption algorithm, IV, keys, and so forth (described in Chapters 3 and 4);
- Data used to provide anti-replay protection: sequence number counter and sequence counter overflow flag for outbound SAs,

anti-replay counter and anti-replay window for inbound SAs
(further explained later in this chapter);

- IPsec header mode flag: Tunnel Mode, Transport Mode, or both
  (further explained later in this chapter);

- SA lifetime, measured in elapsed time or number of bytes protected
  (SA expiration and replacement are discussed in Chapter 5);

- Data used to perform message fragmentation: PMTU information
  for outbound SAs (further explained later in this chapter).

The granularity of an SA is a rough measure of the SA's selectivity. An
example of an SA with a coarse granularity could be a host-to-host SA or
even a network-to-network SA, one that applies to all traffic between the two
hosts or networks, regardless of application or user. An SA with a moderate
granularity might be limited to a specific type of traffic between two hosts,
such as FTP, or to all traffic between two hosts conducted by a specific user
on each host. An example of an SA with a fine granularity is one that could
be limited to a specific session between two hosts, such as a single FTP file
transfer session.

It is highly likely that multiple SAs will be established between a pair
of communicating hosts. For example, one set of security features might be
required for email or Web communications and a different, more stringent
set for a remote payroll application. When protected messages are sent, the
sender needs to indicate which SA was used to encode the communication,
so the receiver can use the same SA in decoding the message. That is the
function of the security parameters index (SPI). Because each SA is unidirectional, protected two-way communications between two peers requires the
establishment of two SAs: an inbound SA and an outbound SA. The SPI, in
conjunction with the destination address and the security protocol (AH or
ESP), is sufficient to unambiguously select a unique inbound SA from the
SAD. To ensure the SPI's uniqueness, each peer selects the SPI for its own
inbound SA.

Another hypothetical database, the security policy database (SPD),
reflects more general policies governing the treatment of various classes of
protected and unprotected traffic. Each SPD entry can result in the creation
or negotiation of one or more SAs. The SPD is discussed in excruciating
detail in Chapter 9; for now we simply assume that there is a magical policy
mechanism that is used to determine which SA (if any) applies to an

incoming or outgoing message; we also assume that the applicable SA has been added, *deus ex machina* (more on that in Chapter 5), to the SAD.

2.3   AH Format

Figure 2.1 illustrates the AH format. The header comprises six fields. Five of the fields have a fixed length, for a total length of three 32-bit words; the sixth field is variable length. The individual header fields are as follows:

- *Next header* is the type of the header that follows the AH. It might be the other IPsec header, the ESP header; a TCP header if the application that originated the message runs over TCP (e.g., email or Web access via HTTP); a UDP header if the originating application runs over UDP (e.g., the troubleshooting program traceroute); or an ICMP header, if this is an IP error or informational message. In IPv6, it could be one of the extension headers.

- *Payload length* is the length of the total AH in words, minus 2 (or the length of the authentication data portion of the header, plus 1). This elegant calculation is a legacy of the former version of the AH, defined in RFC 1826, which did not include a mandatory Sequence Number field. The intent is to transmit the length of the authentication data, which is a variable-length field, to the receiver. Initially, an optional sequence number was included in the authentication data, and the Payload Length field conveyed the length of that combined field. Once the Sequence Number field was made mandatory and was separated from the Authentication Data field, a graceful description of the Payload Length field became impossible.

- *RESERVED* is a field currently set to 0 but reserved for future use.

- *Security parameters index* (SPI) is the index into the receiver's SA database.

Next header	AH payload len	Reserved (set to zero)
Security parameters index (SPI)		
Anti-replay sequence number field		
Authentication data (ICV + optional cipher-dependent data)		

Figure 2.1   AH format.

- *Sequence Number field* is the number of messages sent from the sender to the receiver using the current SA. By keeping track of this quantity and sending it to the receiver, the sender enables the receiver to perform replay protection, if desired.

- *Authentication Data field* is a variable-length field that fulfills the AH's main purpose. It contains the integrity check value (ICV), which is a cryptographic version (more on this in Chapter 4) of the message's contents that can be used by the receiver to check the message's authentication and integrity. This field is padded, if necessary, so that the total length of the AH is an exact number of 32-bit words (IPv4) or 64-bit words (IPv6).

2.4   AH Location

Figure 2.2 illustrates AH's placement for both IPv4 and IPv6. In IPv4, it follows the IP header, preceding the next header (ESP, TCP, UDP, or ICMP). Nothing else intervenes between the AH and its preceding IP header or its trailing next header. In IPv6, the positioning of AH is similar, but the optional IPv6 extension headers can either precede or follow AH. The IPv6 extension headers that can precede AH are the hop-by-hop header, the

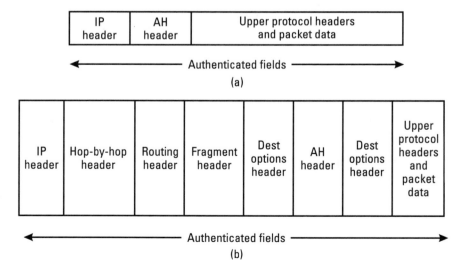

Figure 2.2 AH placement in Transport Mode: (a) IPv4 and (b) IPv6.

routing header, and the fragment header. The destination options header can either precede or follow AH. Its position relative to AH is dependent on whether the special processing should take place before or after authentication processing occurs.

2.5 AH Modes

An additional factor governs the placement and processing of AH. Figure 2.2 illustrates the placement of AH in what is known as Transport Mode. This mode is used primarily for end-to-end authentication between two hosts. However, when a security gateway is used to provide protection for multiple hosts on a network, Tunnel Mode is used. An additional (outer) IP header, whose source address is that of the security gateway, is placed at the beginning of the packet; the original (inner) IP header, whose source address is one of the network hosts protected by the gateway, is left intact. The new IP header's destination address can be the same as the original IP header's destination address, or, if the destination is also protected by a security gateway, the new IP header's destination address can differ from the original IP header's destination address. Figure 2.3 illustrates AH's placement in Tunnel Mode. In IPv4, AH follows the new IP header and precedes the original IP

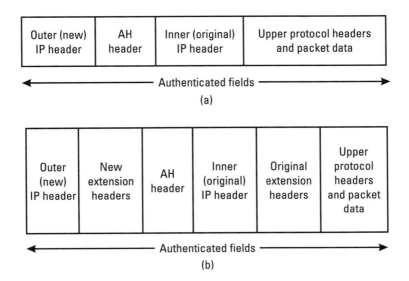

Figure 2.3 AH placement in Tunnel Mode: (a) IPv4 and (b) IPv6.

header. In IPv6, AH follows the same extension headers (if present) that it follows in Transport Mode and precedes the original IP header.

Tunnel Mode also can be used for host-to-host communications, in which case the addresses are the same in both the original IP header and the additional IP header.

In scenario 1, to provide AH protection between hosts H1 and H2, either Transport Mode or Tunnel Mode could be used. In scenario 2, if gateways SG1 and SG2 are to provide AH protection for their hosts, a Tunnel Mode SA will be established between SG1 and SG2. Figure 2.4 illustrates the Tunnel Mode communication. Traffic from H1-1 to H2-1 will traverse the leg from SG1 to SG2 inside a Tunnel Mode packet whose outer header has source address SG1 and destination address SG2, but whose inner header has source address H1-1 and destination address H2-1. In scenario 3, if gateway SG2 is to provide AH protection for its hosts, a Tunnel Mode SA will be established between host H1 and SG2. Traffic from H1 to host H2-1 will traverse the leg from H1 to SG2 inside a Tunnel Mode packet whose outer header has source address H1 and destination address SG2, but whose inner header has source address H1 and destination address H2-1. Figure 2.5 illustrates the Tunnel Mode headers for each of the three scenarios.

2.6 Nested Headers

More than one SA can be applied to a single message. If both endpoints of both SAs are the same, the AHs are referred to as adjacent AHs; if one or both sets of endpoints differ, the AHs are referred to as nested AHs. Adjacent

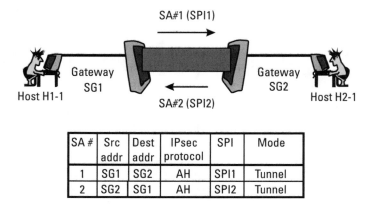

SA #	Src addr	Dest addr	IPsec protocol	SPI	Mode
1	SG1	SG2	AH	SPI1	Tunnel
2	SG2	SG1	AH	SPI2	Tunnel

Figure 2.4 Tunnel Mode SA between gateways.

Outer IP header	AH header	Inner IP header
Source: H1 Destination: H2		Source: H1 Destination: H2

Outer IP header	AH header	Inner IP header
Source: SG1 Destination: SG2		Source: H1-1 Destination: H2-1

Outer IP header	AH header	Inner IP header
Source: H1 Destination: SG2		Source: H1 Destination: H2-1

Figure 2.5 Sample tunnel headers.

AHs do not provide extra protection, and their implementation is not mandated. (Adjacent IPsec headers are discussed in Chapter 3.) Nested AHs do make sense in certain contexts. In scenario 2, if host H1-1 and host H2-1 require end-to-end authentication, but each is protected by a security gateway that demands to authenticate all traffic transiting the gateway, nested AHs are a reasonable approach to fulfill both requirements. A Tunnel Mode SA can protect traffic between SG1 and SG2, and a Transport Mode SA can protect traffic between H1-1 and H2-1. When a message is sent from H1-1 to H2-1, it will have a single Transport Mode AH from the time it leaves H1-1 until it arrives at SG1; as it travels from SG1 to SG2, it will incorporate nested AHs, an inner Transport Mode AH, and an outer Tunnel Mode AH; and traveling from SG2 to H2-1, it will once again have a single Transport Mode AH. Figure 2.6 illustrates the four unidirectional SAs, each with its own SPI, that provide this protection.

2.7   Implementing IPsec Header Processing

Generally, one portion of the operating system, or kernel, is responsible for networked communications. For outbound messages, the networking routines add the IP header to the message, fragment messages when needed, and

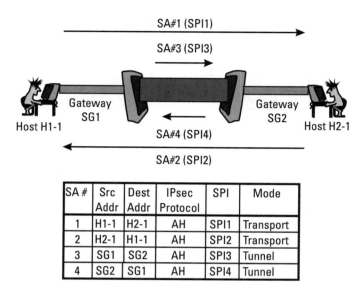

Figure 2.6 Nested AH SAs.

forward the message to the network access or physical layer to be sent out. For inbound messages, the routines accept messages from the network access layer, reassemble fragmented messages when appropriate, strip off the IP header, and forward the message to the transport or application layer for further processing. How do the IPsec-processing routines fit in relative to the operating system networking logic? There are three common approaches:

- Modifying the networking (IP stack) code. This is the most direct approach, but it involves a change to the kernel code, so it would normally be the solution of choice for developers of operating systems. It is applicable to both hosts and gateways.

- Separating the IPsec code from the networking code. This approach does not involve changing the kernel code, but it can necessitate reimplementing portions of the networking code (e.g., fragmentation and reassembly of messages). It generally is referred to as a "bump-in-the-stack" (BITS) implementation, because the IPsec code is placed between the Internet layer of the stack and the network access layer. A BITS implementation is applicable to hosts and gateways, but it is more commonly found on hosts with legacy operating systems.

- Placing the IPsec code outside the machine. This external crypto-processor, referred to as a "bump-in-the-wire" (BITW) implementation, is the least intrusive option, in terms of the kernel code. The IPsec code can be integrated with router or firewall code and placed in a router or firewall, or it can be implemented in a standalone "IPsec box." It can be attached to a single host or gateway or to multiple machines.

2.8 AH Processing for Outbound Messages

Once it has been determined that an outgoing message needs the protection afforded by AH (more on that in Chapter 9), and the outbound SA governing the protected communication has been found (more on that in Chapter 9) or negotiated (described in Chapter 5), the message is passed to the IPsec-processing routines, which perform the following steps.

1. Insert an AH template in the proper place (as described above).
2. Fill in the Next Header field.
3. Fill in the SPI field with the SPI of the selected SA.
4. Compute the Sequence Number field. This field has a length of 32 bits, which means it can hold a maximum value of 4294967295 (hex FFFFFFFF, or 2^{32-1}). If the selected SA has been used to protect less than that number of messages, the Sequence Number field is simply incremented by 1; the new value is placed in the AH and also saved in the SAD. However, if the Sequence Number field has reached its maximum value, meaning that this SA has already been used to protect the maximum allowable number of messages, there are several possibilities. If the SA's secret keys were negotiated by the peers (more on that in Chapter 5), it is time to negotiate new keys, whether or not the message recipient has enabled replay protection. This message is set aside or discarded until that can take place. If the SA's keys are manually established keys that were agreed on by the peers in some unspecified manner (e.g., over the telephone or through the use of couriers), and if the sender knows that the recipient is not enabling replay protection, the sequence number is simply reset to 1. For manually established keys, in the case where the recipient does require replay protection, new keys

must be agreed on. Until that happens, this message cannot be sent, and the AH processing comes to a halt.

5. For a Transport Mode SA, change the preceding IP header's Next Header field to AH.

6. Add a tunnel header, if required. If the SA specifies Tunnel Mode, the additional (outer) IP header must be constructed and added to the message. The source and destination addresses of the outer header are the tunnel endpoints, as specified by the SA.

    If both headers are IPv4 headers, the following fields are copied from the inner header to the outer header: Version, Type of Service, Protocol, Fragment Identification, MF (More/Last Fragment) Flag, and Fragment Offset. The following fields are recomputed for the outer header: Header Length, Total Length, and Header Checksum; the recomputation is necessary so that these fields incorporate information from both the inner and outer IP headers and from the AH. The Next Header field is set to AH. The Options field is not copied. The TTL is set to the system's default value. The local system's policy also determines the value of the DF (don't/may fragment) Flag: It can be copied from the inner header, set to 1 to prohibit fragmentation, or set to 0 to allow fragmentation. The fields of the inner header are left intact, with the following exception: If the source addresses of the inner and outer headers differ, that means the inner packet has traveled to reach the tunnel's source address. In this case, the inner header's TTL field is decremented and the inner header's Header Checksum is recomputed to reflect that change.

    If both headers are IPv6 headers, the following fields are copied from the inner header to the outer header: Version and Traffic Class. The Payload Length field is recomputed for the outer header; the recomputation is necessary so that this field incorporates the lengths of both the inner and outer IP headers and the AH. The Next Header field is set to AH or to the header type of the extension header that precedes the AH. The extension headers themselves are not copied. The hop limit is set to the system's default value. The fields of the inner header are left intact, with the following exception: If the source addresses of the inner and outer headers differ, that means the inner packet has traveled to reach the tunnel's source address. In that case, the inner header's Hop Limit field is decremented.

If the inner header is an IPv4 header and the outer header is an IPv6 header, or vice versa, the processing is slightly different: The Version field is set to 4 for the IPv4 header and to 6 for the IPv6 header; the Traffic Class field is transformed into TOS; and the source and destination addresses are converted to the appropriate format, if necessary.

7. Compute the authentication data. The authentication data consist of the output of a keyed message hash. An algorithm (more on this in Chapter 4) is used that takes a message of any size and generates a fixed-length output, with the property that it is infeasible to modify a message in such a way that the resulting hash of the modified message would be equivalent to that of the original message. Incorporating a secret key into the hash computations makes it impossible for a user not privy to the key to fake an authenticating hash.

The entire message is not protected by the AH, because IP headers can contain three classes of data: immutable data, which never changes in transit; mutable but predictable data, which can be modified during transit, but whose final value, on arrival at the destination, is predictable; and mutable unpredictable data, whose value can change during transit in an unforeseen manner. Table 2.1 lists the fields of the IP header that fall into each category. Only the message data and those header fields that will not change in an unpredictable manner in transit are used as input to the authenticating hash, so the final recipient of the packet can verify the hash. Thus, in Transit Mode, the message data and the predictable fields of the IP header are protected. In Tunnel Mode, the entire original IP header and the message data are protected, but only the predictable fields of the added header are protected. When the hash is computed, zeroes are used in place of the contents of the unprotected header fields.

The mandatory keyed hash algorithms for IPsec AH are HMAC-MD5, which generates a 128-bit hash, and HMAC-SHA-1, which generates a 160-bit hash. In AH, to ensure proper byte boundaries for efficient processing, the authenticating hash is truncated to 96 bits. Expert cryptographers have ascertained that truncating the hash does not lessen its uniqueness or the properties that ensure cryptographic safety. Once the hash has been placed in the Authentication field, along with any other data required by the specific hash algorithm, the message is ready to be sent on its way.

Table 2.1

Classes of IP Header Fields

	IPv4	IPv6
Immutable	Version	Version
	Internet header length	Payload length
	Total length	Next header (AH)
	Identification	Source address
	Protocol (should be value for AH)	Destination address (without routing extension header)
	Source address	—
	Destination address (without source routing)	Destination and hop-by-hop extension headers option type/data length
	Option type/data length/data (classified as immutable)	Destination and hop-by-hop extension headersoption data (option type classified as immutable)
Mutable but Predictable	Destination address (with source routing)	Destination address (with routing extension header)
	—	Routing extension header
Mutable Unpredictable	TOS	Class
	Flags	Flow label
	Fragment offset	Hop limit
	TTL	Destination and hop-by-hop extension headers: option data (option type classified as mutable)
	Header checksum	—
	Option type/data length/data (classified as mutable)	—

8. Fragment the message, if necessary. If the message, enlarged by the AH and possibly by an additional IP header for Tunnel Mode, is sufficiently large that it needs to be fragmented before it is sent, fragmentation takes place at this point. In Transport Mode, the message's source address is always the initiator of the message, so the total message can be authenticated before fragmentation occurs. In Tunnel Mode, the source address of the original header

is the actual initiator of the message; if that source address differs from the outer header's source address, the message may already have been fragmented after it exited the original host. In that case, the tunnel header's authentication was performed on a message fragment, which at this point may have to be further fragmented. Figure 2.7 illustrates the Transport Mode case and Figure 2.8 the Tunnel Mode case.

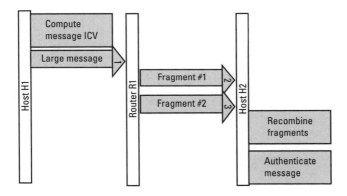

Figure 2.7 Fragmentation and authentication: Transport Mode host-to-host SA.

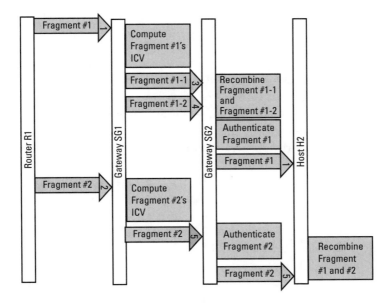

Figure 2.8 Fragmentation and authentication: Tunnel Mode gateway-to-gateway SA.

2.9   AH Processing for Inbound Messages

When a message is received that contains an AH, the IP processing routines first ensure that all fragments of the message have been received and reintegrated to form a complete message. The routines also ensure that the fields that identified each piece of the message as a fragment are reinitialized: The offset field is reset to zero and the "more fragments" flag is turned off, so the IPsec processing routines do not erroneously identify the reassembled message as a message fragment. The message is then passed to the IPsec processing routines, which perform the following steps.

1. Locate the inbound SA governing this protected communication in the SAD. This step is initially accomplished through the use of the three identifying indices: the SPI, the destination address, and the AH protocol. The SA's indices are compared to those found in the packet's outmost AH, whether it is Tunnel Mode or Transport Mode. The packet must also conform to any other selectors that limit the SA's applicability (e.g., port or protocol). If this is a tunnel header, the SA selectors are compared to those found in the packet's inner header, because these fields are not copied into the tunnel header. Once a matching SA has been found, processing can continue. If no such SA is found, the packet is dropped.

2. If replay protection is enabled, perform the replay protection check. The originator of a packet with AH will always increment the replay protection counter; the recipient is free to either ignore this counter or use it to ensure replay protection. However, because IP does not guarantee delivery of packets in the same order in which they were sent (that is the responsibility of the Transport Protocol or the application), this counter cannot be used to ensure exact ordering of the packets, but only a relatively correct order within a window that is a multiple of 32.

   For each inbound SA, the SAD includes a replay window. The size of the window determines how greatly out of order a message can be without being rejected; the size is a multiple of 32, with 64 recommended as a default. A replay window of size N keeps track of the sequence numbers of the last N messages received. Any message with a sequence number so low that it is outside the window's range is dropped. A message within the window's range whose sequence number is a duplicate of a message that was already received is also dropped.

A bit mask (or some equivalent structure) can be used to track the sequence numbers of the last N messages received for this SA. Initially, a 64-bit mask could keep track of the receipt of messages with sequence numbers between 1 and 64. Once a message with a sequence number greater than 64 (e.g., sequence number 70) is received, the bit mask would keep track of messages with sequence numbers from 7 to 70; it would then drop any arriving messages with a sequence number less than 7. This check ensures that each inbound message has not been previously received and that it is not grossly out of order. Figure 2.9 illustrates how the sliding replay window works.

3. Verify the authentication data. The authentication hash is computed, in exactly the same manner as for an outbound message. If the computed hash does not match the authentication data found in the message, the message is discarded and no further processing takes place.

4. Strip off the AH and repeat the IPsec processing for any remaining IPsec headers. If there are other nested IPsec headers that terminate at the current destination, each successive header must be processed

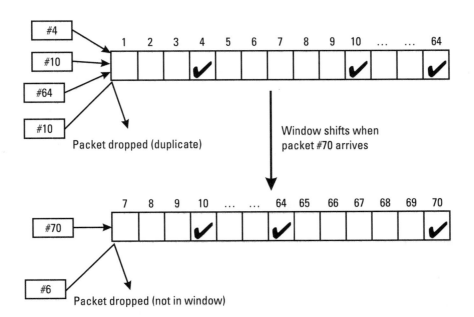

Figure 2.9 The sliding replay protection window.

until one of two conditions is met. Once the last IPsec header is successfully processed, and an upper layer protocol is encountered, the packet is sent to the IP processing routines so it can proceed up the IP stack. Alternatively, if a tunneled IP header is encountered that is not destined for the current host, the packet is forwarded to that destination, where further IPsec processing takes place.

5. Check the SPD to ensure that the IPsec protection applied to the incoming packet conforms to the system's IPsec policy requirements (more on this in Chapter 9). This critical step is difficult to illustrate using only AHs. More impressive examples are possible once we add the other type of security header, the ESP, into the brew in Chapter 3.

2.10 Complications

Two somewhat interrelated aspects of IP networking behavior have the potential to cause severe heartburn for IPsec implementations: packet fragmentation and ICMP [3, 4] error messages.

In scenario 2, let's assume that a Tunnel Mode SA has been established between SG1 and SG2 that protects all traffic between networks N1 and N2. If a packet from host H1-1 to host H2-1 is fragmented before it gets to security gateway SG1 (case 1), either by an intermediate router (IPv4) or by the originating host (IPv6), SG1 computes separate ICVs, one for each fragment. When the fragments reach security gateway SG2, each is authenticated separately, prior to packet reassembly. The reassembled, authenticated packet is then forwarded to its final destination, H2-1. Now let's assume that the packet fragmentation is performed by an intermediate router that lies between SG1 and SG2 (case 2, IPv4 only). SG1 has already computed an ICV for the whole packet. When the fragments reach SG2, they must be reassembled before the packet can be authenticated, because the ICV was computed before fragmentation occurred.

Now let's change the scenario slightly. Assume that SG2, knowing that some segments of the path contain bottlenecks in terms of packet size, decides to do away with the Tunnel Mode SA, thus shortening the size of each packet by avoiding the addition of the outer IP header. This approach, although it does not conform to the prescribed IPsec architecture, has at times been adopted by some implementations. Let's also alter the topology slightly. Unknown to SG2, there is another router or security gateway SG3 (perhaps a back door) serving N2, as illustrated in Figure 2.10. If the SAs

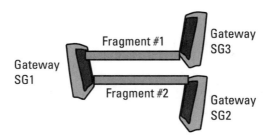

Figure 2.10 Pitfall of (illegal) Transport Mode gateway-to-gateway SAs.

between networks N1 and N2 are all Tunnel Mode SAs, negotiated by SG1 and SG2, all the packet fragments will be routed to the appropriate gateway and the messages properly processed. However, if SG1 and SG2 decide to economize on packet size and establish Transport Mode SAs, problems can ensue. SG2 establishes a Transport Mode header with SG1, under the assumption that it is the only entry point into N2, so that it can grab any protected packets and perform the authentication before the packet reaches H2-1. If any of the fragments are routed via SG3, proper reassembly cannot occur. In case 1, SG2 authenticates each fragment it receives and attempts reassembly. Because all the fragments will not arrive at SG2, the partially reassembled packet is discarded once the reassembly timer expires. Meanwhile, the fragment that arrives at SG3 is either discarded by SG3 or forwarded to H2-1, which, finding no appropriate SA for the fragment, discards it. In case 2, SG2 attempts to reassemble the packet before performing authentication, but otherwise the results are the same as for case 1. This is definitely a worst-case scenario, but in networking worst-case scenarios seem to occur with alarming frequency.

These cases illustrate why the IPsec security architecture requires Tunnel Mode SAs between two gateways, if the SAs protect traffic between hosts other than the two gateways themselves. This also applies to a gateway-to-host SA, in which the gateway protects traffic for other hosts behind the gateway. They also show the complications that fragmentation can cause in the IPsec context.

To avoid fragmentation, gateways must communicate to their protected hosts the size of the headers that the gateway will add to packets sent by the hosts. The originating host generally attempts to send packets that are as close as possible to the PMTU [5–7]. Only by first subtracting the size of the tunnel headers to be added by the security gateway can packet fragmentation be avoided.

There is another way to avoid fragmented packets: The source host can probe the network to ascertain the maximum PMTU for the packet and then adjust the packet size accordingly. In IPv4, this technique also requires that the source host turn on the DF bit, to prevent fragmentation by intermediate routers. This approach can also present problems within the context of IPsec. If a packet is too large to traverse the entire route, an intermediate router sends the ICMP message "packet too big" back to the originating host. In the case of a Tunnel Mode SA, the message is sent back to the security gateway that is the source address of the outer header. It is also significant that the ICMP "packet too big" message used to convey the maximum transmittable packet size (the PMTU) is sent to the packet's source not from the packet's ultimate destination but from an intermediate router. This fact can be very important in an IPsec context, in which we may want to accept only authenticated messages. The gateway then has a problem: Should it believe this unauthenticated message? If it chooses to accept the message as valid, it then has to communicate the message, along with the new PMTU (if included) to the packet's originating host, the source address of the inner header. If the gateway chooses not to relay the message to the host, a black hole situation can occur: The host keeps resending packets with the DF bit on; because it never receives a PMTU message, it does not reduce the packet size. Thus, the packets are continuously resent, adding to network congestion, but they never arrive at their final destination.

The same ICMP messages used to relieve network congestion through the elimination of packet fragmentation can also be used to mount a denial-of-service attack on the network. An attacker can send bogus PMTU messages, with a smaller-than-necessary PMTU. If the gateway accepts unauthenticated PMTU messages and passes them on to the originating host, the host will decrease the packet size for all packets traversing that path. That leads to the transmission of an increased number of small packets, an increasing number of computationally expensive IP-related operations, possibly causing network congestion and a degradation of service.

Several proposals have been advanced to handle the PMTU problem. One possible suggestion involves cooperation between SG1 and SG2. SG1 allows fragmented packets from H1-1 to proceed on their way. To ensure that, if H1-1 sets the DF bit in the inner header, SG1 does not set it in the outer header. When SG2 receives the fragmented packets, it sends a PMTU message to SG1, informing SG1 of the largest fragment size that has successfully traversed the path from SG1 to SG2. Because there is an IPsec tunnel between SG1 and SG2, the PMTU message is protected. This solution differs from the standard PMTU message usage, because the PMTU message is sent after receipt of a fragmented message; the normal PMTU message results from an unsuccessful attempt to forward an unfragmented message. Alternatively, SG2 can save a PMTU as part of each SA and periodically inform SG1 of the latest PMTU value. If H1-1 attempts to send too large a packet, SG1 can communicate the current PMTU to H1-1. As yet, there is no consensus on the solution to this issue.

Another increasingly common complication is the use of network address translation (NAT) boxes [8–13]. A NAT box can be a separate entity or it can be co-resident with a security gateway. NAT is employed in two different situations. The first is a private network, in which the hosts' addresses must be kept secret for the purposes of security and privacy. The second is a network that uses private addresses that may duplicate addresses used elsewhere on the Internet, because the installation was not assigned enough unique addresses to cover every host. In such a case, a pool of public, globally unique addresses is used for communications with destinations outside the private network. When such messages cross the NAT box, the private source address of an outbound communication is converted to a public address and the public destination address of an inbound communication is converted to the corresponding private network address. That effectively rules out the end-to-end IPsec protection afforded by scenario 1. Because AH authenticates both source and destination addresses, the revised address introduced by the NAT box causes authentication to fail once the message reaches its destination. If the NAT transformations are performed before the IPsec processing for outbound messages and after the IPsec processing for inbound messages, the gateway-to-gateway protection afforded by scenario 2 still is possible. Figure 2.11 shows a workable network configuration incorporating NAT boxes and security gateways.

An IPsec-friendly alternative to NAT, Realm-Specific Internet Protocol (RSIP) [14–16], is emerging. With RSIP, traffic from a host with a private address does not need to use the private addresses for messages intended for destinations outside the private network. The host, acting as an RSIP client, can request a public address from an RSIP server. That way, the message's source address is a globally unique, public address that can be used for end-to-end IPsec protection.

2.11   Auditing

The IPsec documents do not mandate auditing of anomalous or erroneous behavior, because auditing is a process internal to one of the peers and does

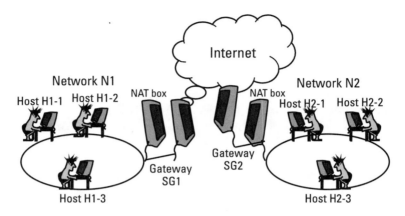

Figure 2.11 Configuring NAT boxes and security gateways.

not change the "bits on the wire." However, events are mentioned that may trigger auditing. If an event is recorded in an audit log, the entry should include the date and time, the source and destination addresses, and the SPI; for IPv6, the flow ID also should be included. In addition, if the system hosting an IPsec implementation does have auditing capabilities, the IPsec implementation is required to support auditing and to allow the system administrator to turn the auditing capability on and off. A warning message is not required to be sent to the peer, because that could start a hailstorm of exchanged messages that could lead to denial of service on one or both machines.

Among the events that can trigger an audit log entry are:

- An attempt to use an outbound SA whose replay counter has reached its maximum value to a recipient that has enabled replay protection;

- An attempt to perform inbound IPsec processing on a message fragment;

- Receipt of an inbound message for which no current, applicable SA can be found;

- Receipt of an inbound message for which verification of the authentication data fails.

In each of those cases, the message is discarded and no further IPsec processing occurs for the discarded message.

2.12   Threat Mitigation

What real-life threats [17, 18] are prevented through the use of the AH? Unauthorized packet alteration can take several forms. The packet content can be altered. The source address can be altered so that the packet appears to come from a sender other than the actual sender; this is called "address spoofing." The packet destination can be altered, in effect rerouting a packet to an unintended recipient. An end-to-end AH, which protects the packet's data, source address, and destination address, protects a packet from all those unauthorized alterations. Unfortunately, if the AH protection is not end to end, and an "unfriendly" user is present on the same network as the source host, that user can capture and alter packets before they reach the gateway that performs the outbound AH processing. Even if the destination address is not altered, a packet can be effectively rerouted if a bogus, unauthenticated DNS message reassigns the destination address (e.g., charlie.org) to the numeric address (e.g., 1.2.3.4) of another host. DNS spoofing can be avoided by accepting only authenticated DNS messages.

AH's replay protection feature can be used to prevent delivery of grossly out-of-order packets, stemming from network problems, an attacker attempting repeated delivery of a significant message (e.g., an electronic funds transfer), or disruption of service via network flooding. The effects of an attacker attempting to bring down a host by flooding it with messages that require expensive cryptographic processing can be mitigated through the use of replay protection, because duplicate packets are discarded before the inbound AH processing takes place.

However, AH does not provide privacy. Even if the packets safely traverse the Internet and arrive intact at their destination, the packets can be read by any of the intermediate nodes that forward the packet on its way. In particular, an attacker can exploit the source routing header option to divert a packet and route it past an evil, information-gathering router. The router can then restore the source routing header to its original form, and the tampering will not be noticed by the recipient.

2.13   Summary

The AH provides several types of critical protection at the network layer. It ensures that messages traversing the Internet arrive at their destination unchanged, that the apparent sender of the message is in actuality the message's originator, and that messages are not erroneously or fraudulently retransmitted. However, AH does not provide confidentiality to its protected messages. That is the function of the other security-related header, the ESP header.

2.14 Further Reading

AH is definitively described in RFC 2402 [1]. The generalized IPsec architecture, of which AH is an integral part, is defined in RFC 2401 [2]. Two excellent books [17, 18] describe the nature of various security threats and solutions, as well as general security-related information. ICMP for IPv4 is defined in RFC 792 [4]; ICMP for IPv6 is defined in RFC 2463 [3]. The PMTU protocol for IPv4 is described in RFC 1191 [6]; PMTU for IPv6 in RFC 1981 [5]. The interaction of PMTU and security gateways is explored in [7]. NAT is a hotly debated and much analyzed topic; it is defined in RFC 2663 [10] and [12]. The interaction between NAT and IPsec is discussed in [8] and [13]; the interactions between NAT and other protocols are discussed in [19]. An approach to enable NAT to coexist with Tunnel Mode IPsec is defined in [11]. The IAB has issued a report [9] that analyzes NAT's relationship to the Internet's generalized infrastructure and offers guidance on minimizing its negative impact on Internet communications. RSIP is defined in [14] and [15], and its relationship to IPsec is described in [16]. The IPsec email list archive can be found at http://www.vpnc.org/ietf-ipsec.

References

[1]   Kent, S., and R. Atkinson, *IP Authentication Header*, RFC 2402, Nov. 1998.

[2]   Kent, S., and R. Atkinson, *Security Architecture for the Internet Protocol*, RFC 2401, Nov. 1998.

[3]   Conta, A., and S. Deering, *Internet Control Message Protocol (ICMPv6) for the Internet Protocol Version 6 (IPv6) Specification*, RFC 2463, Dec. 1998.

[4]   Postel, J., *Internet Control Message Protocol*, RFC 792, Sept. 1981.

[5]   McCann, J., S. Deering, and J. Mogul, *Path MTU Discovery for IP Version 6*, RFC 1981, Aug. 1996.

[6]   Mogul, J., and S. Deering, *Path MTU Discovery*, RFC 1191, Nov. 1990.

[7]   Richardson, M., "Path MTU discovery in the presence of security gateways," <draft-richardson-ipsec-pmtu-discov-02.txt>, Aug. 1998.

[8]   Aboba, B., "NAT and IPsec," <draft-aboba-nat-ipsec-02.txt>, July 2000.

[9] Hain, T., "Architectural Implications of NAT," <draft-iab-nat-implications-09.txt>, Aug. 2000.

[10] Srisuresh, P., and M. Holdrege, *IP Network Address Translator (NAT) Terminology and Considerations*, RFC 2663, Aug. 1999.

[11] Srisuresh, P., *Security Model With Tunnel-mode IPsec for NAT Domains*, RFC 2709, Oct. 1999.

[12] Srisuresh, P., and K. Egevang, "Traditional IP Network Address Translator (Traditional NAT)," <draft-ietf-nat-traditional-05.txt>, Oct. 2000.

[13] Stenberg, M., et al., "IPsec NAT Traversal," <draft-stenberg-ipsec-nat-traversal-00.txt>, July 2000.

[14] Borella, M., et al., "Realm Specific IP: Framework," <draft-ietf-nat-rsip-framework-05.txt>, July 2000.

[15] Borella, M., et al., "Realm Specific IP: Protocol Specification," <draft-ietf-nat-rsip-protocol-07.txt>, July 2000.

[16] Montenegro, G., and M. Borella, "RSIP Support for End-to-End IPSEC," <draft-ietf-nat-rsip-ipsec-04.txt>, July 2000.

[17] Cheswick, W. R., and S. M. Bellovin, *Firewalls and Internet Security: Repelling the Wily Hacker*, 2nd Ed., Reading, MA: Addison-Wesley, 2000.

[18] Kaufman, C., R. Perlman, and M. Speciner, *Network Security: Private Communication in a Public World*, Englewood Cliffs, NJ: Prentice Hall, 1995.

[19] Holdrege, M., and P. Srisuresh, "Protocol Complications With the IP Network Address Translator (NAT)," <draft-ietf-nat-protocol-complications-06.txt>, Oct. 2000.

3

The Second Puzzle Piece: The Encapsulating Security Payload

I couldn't tell if the streaker was a man or a woman, because it had a bag on its head.

attributed to Yogi Berra

AH arms a message with several crucial security services, but it does not provide the quintessential form of cryptographic protection, that of hiding message contents "in plain sight," otherwise known as encryption. That leaves AH-protected messages vulnerable to the Internet's version of eavesdropping: An interested observer along the message's delivery path can read its contents and header information. Preventing such loss of privacy is the domain of the other security mechanism, the Encapsulating Security Payload (ESP) [1, 2]. Like the AH, the ESP header is required for IPv6 implementations but is optional for IPv4.

3.1 Protections Provided by ESP

The ESP header can be used to provide two separate sets of security features, the first of which is unique to ESP and the second of which duplicates those services provided by AH. Either set or both sets can be furnished through the use of an ESP header.

The following types of protection can be provided through the use of ESP but not by AH:

- *Confidentiality.* A guarantee that, even if the message is "read" by an observer, the contents are not understandable except to the authorized recipient.
- *Traffic analysis protection* (Tunnel Mode only). An assurance that an eavesdropper cannot determine who is communicating with whom or the frequency and volume of communications between specific entities.

The ESP header can provide the following types of protection that are also covered by AH:

- Connectionless integrity;
- Data origin authentication;
- Replay protection.

There is a distinction between the authentication and integrity provided by the AH and that provided by the ESP header. A Transport Mode AH protects both the IP header and packet data, while a Transport Mode ESP header protects only the packet data. In Tunnel Mode, both types of headers protect the original header, but only AH protects the outer header. However, as Chapter 5 shows, SA establishment can indirectly authenticate the IP addresses, effectively closing the gap between the two headers' levels of protection. Using a single header to provide multiple types of security protection lessens both the packet processing and the packet size, which contributes to increased network effectiveness and performance.

Thus, the ESP header is used to furnish confidentiality and/or a combination of connectionless integrity and data origin authentication for the communications to which it is applied. If confidentiality is provided in Tunnel Mode, traffic analysis protection can also be provided. If integrity and authentication are provided, the recipient can optionally select replay protection.

3.2   Security Associations and the Security Parameters Index

The SAD and the SPD are used to keep track of AH SAs and ESP header SAs. The SA selectors are the same for both types of headers. Some of the SAD information differs for AH entries and for ESP entries, because the type of protection offered by the two headers differs and, thus, the identifying pieces of information differ as well. Because three pieces of information—the SPI, the destination address, and the header type—are sufficient to pinpoint a unique inbound SA, theoretically the same SPI can be used to identify both a unique AH SA and a different, unique ESP SA.

If the ESP header is being used to provide confidentiality, those portions of the IP packet following the ESP header are encrypted and thus unintelligible to the SA selection routines. That means the SA selectors located in that portion of the packet cannot be used to distinguish ESP-protected traffic. In particular, the transport protocol (UDP or TCP) and the source and destination ports are unavailable as selectors for packets protected by such an ESP header.

3.3   ESP Header Format

Figure 3.1 illustrates the ESP header format. The header comprises seven fields, two of which are optional. The individual header fields are as follows:

- *SPI:* The index into the receiver's SA database.
- *Sequence Number field:* The number of messages sent from the sender to the receiver using the current SA.
- *Payload Data field:* A variable-length field that fulfills the ESP header's main purpose. If the message is to be afforded confidentiality protection, this field contains an encrypted version (more on this in Chapter 4) of the message's contents, replacing the initial, unencrypted message. In addition to the data portion of the packet, the three ESP header fields following the data (the padding, the pad length, and the next header) also are encrypted. This field can also hold special unencrypted data that is required as input to the encryption process. (This, too, will be explained in Chapter 4.)
- *Padding* (optional, with a maximum length of 255 bytes). Padding can be added for three distinct purposes:
  - If an encryption algorithm performs its magic on blocks of a specific size, padding may be required to ensure that the data's length is an integral multiple of the algorithm's block size. In that case, the relevant length is the sum of the lengths of the unencrypted data that are to be encrypted, the padding, the Pad Length field, and the Next Header field, but it does not include the special data that will not be encrypted.

- • If the message is to be authenticated, padding is needed to ensure that the Authentication Data field begins on a 4-byte boundary. In that case, the relevant length is the sum of the lengths of the unencrypted data that are to be encrypted, the special data that will not be encrypted, the padding, the Pad Length field, and the Next Header field.
- • If traffic analysis protection is desired, padding may be added to disguise the message's length. Because this type of padding adds uninformative baggage to the transmission, extreme caution is recommended in its use.

- • *Pad length:* Total number of bytes of padding (of all three types) contained in the previous field.

- • *Next header:* The type of the header that follows the ESP header. It might be a TCP header, if the application that originated the message runs over TCP (e.g., email or Web access via HTTP); a UDP header, if the originating application runs over UDP (e.g., the troubleshooting program traceroute); or an ICMP header, if this is an IP error or informational message. In IPv6, it could be one of the extension headers.

- • *Authentication Data field:* An optional, variable-length field that contains the ICV, if this packet is to be afforded authentication and integrity protection.

The ESP header is considered to consist of four distinct parts (Figure 3.1):

- • The *initial ESP header* consists of the SPI and the sequence number.

Security parameters index (SPI)		
Anti-replay sequence number field		
Payload data (special unencrypted data + encrypted data)		
Padding (0-255 bytes)	Pad length	Next header
Authentication data (ICV + optional cipher-dependent data)		

Figure 3.1 ESP header format.

- The *data* consist of the special unencrypted data (if any), any destination extension headers that follow the ESP header (IPv6 only), the TCP or UDP header, and the message data.
- The *ESP trailer* consists of the padding (if any), the Pad Length field, and the Next Header field.
- The *ESP authentication data* consist of the authentication data (if any).

What can be confusing is that the term *ESP header* is usually applied to the total entity, but at times the same term is used to refer to the initial ESP header.

3.4   ESP Header Location and Modes

The ESP header can be used in either Transport Mode or Tunnel Mode. Figure 3.2 illustrates the placement of the ESP transport header for both IPv4 and IPv6. In IPv4, it follows either an IP header or an AH, preceding the next header (TCP, UDP, or ICMP). In IPv6, zero or more extension headers (hop-by-hop, routing, fragment, or destination options) can precede

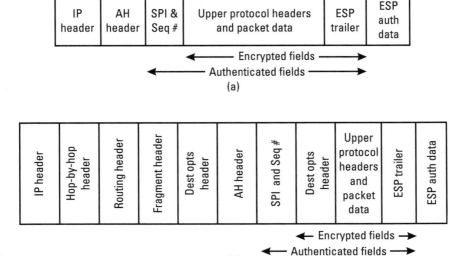

Figure 3.2 ESP header placement in Transport Mode: (a) IPv4 and (b) IPv6.

the ESP header; in addition, a destination options header can follow the ESP header. The position of the destination options header relative to the ESP header depends on whether its special processing should take place before or after the ESP processing occurs. If the packet is encrypted, a destination options header following the ESP header cannot be viewed at any intermediate destination; it will only become visible once more following ESP processing and decryption at its final destination.

Figure 3.3 illustrates the placement of the ESP header in Tunnel Mode. In IPv4, the ESP header follows the new IP header and precedes the original IP header. In IPv6, the ESP header follows the same extension headers (if present) that it follows in Transport Mode and precedes the original IP header.

3.5   Nested and Adjacent Headers

With two types of security headers, the application of more than one SA to a single message makes more sense. If adjacent authentication and ESP headers

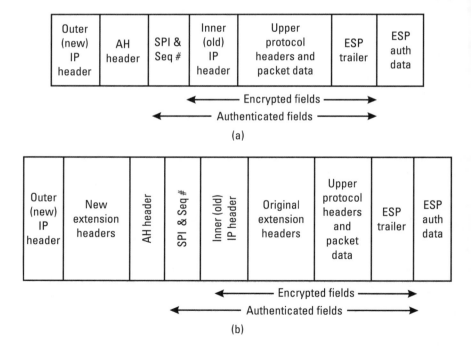

Figure 3.3 ESP header placement in Tunnel Mode: (a) IPv4 and (b) IPv6.

are desired (i.e., both endpoints of both SAs are the same), the AH will precede the ESP header. That means the packet is encrypted first and then authenticated; in that way, the encrypted packet is protected from tampering. However, that goal can be more efficiently met by using a single ESP header to provide both authentication and encryption.

Nested headers are a common and useful phenomenon. In scenario 2 (presented in Chapter 1), if host gateways SG1 and SG2 require all gateway-to-gateway communications to be encrypted and authenticated, that could be provided in one of two ways: through an ESP SA that furnishes both authentication and encryption or through adjacent AH and ESP SAs. For the gateways to protect traffic between hosts H1-1 and H2-1, the SAs would have to be Tunnel Mode SAs. But that leaves communication between host H1-1 and its security gateway SG1 unprotected. If H1-1 does not trust its security gateway to reliably transmit its traffic, or if there are untrustworthy users or hosts on H1-1's local network, host H1-1 might want to authenticate local traffic as well. For that purpose, nested SAs would be ideal: a pair of Tunnel Mode ESP SAs between SG1 and SG2 and a pair of Transport Mode AH SAs between H1-1 and H2-1. Figure 3.4 illustrates the use of nested SAs. In this case, when a message is sent from H1-1 to H2-1, it has a single Transport Mode AH from the time it leaves H1-1 until it arrives at SG1; as it travels from SG1 to SG2, it incorporates nested AH and ESP

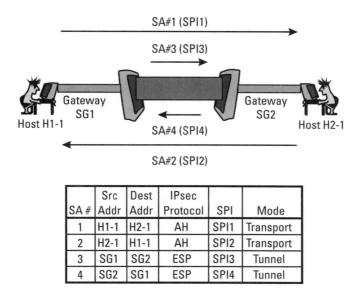

SA #	Src Addr	Dest Addr	IPsec Protocol	SPI	Mode
1	H1-1	H2-1	AH	SPI1	Transport
2	H2-1	H1-1	AH	SPI2	Transport
3	SG1	SG2	ESP	SPI3	Tunnel
4	SG2	SG1	ESP	SPI4	Tunnel

Figure 3.4 Nested headers for end-to-end IPsec protection.

headers, an inner Transport Mode AH, and an outer Tunnel Mode ESP header; and traveling from SG2 to H2-1, it once again has a single Transport Mode AH.

3.6 ESP Header Processing for Outbound Messages

A number of the processing steps for ESP and for AH are identical. Those steps are not described in detail here (they were dealt with in Chapter 2). Once it has been determined that an outgoing message needs the protection afforded by the ESP header, and the outbound SA governing this protected communication has been found or negotiated, the message is passed to the IPsec-processing routines, which perform the following steps:

1. Insert an initial ESP header template in the proper place (as described above).

2. Fill in the SPI field with the SPI of the selected SA.

3. Compute the Sequence Number field.

4. If encryption is to take place, and the relevant encryption algorithm calls for any additional special data that will not be encrypted, add those data to the packet. All the encryption algorithms currently defined for the ESP header (more on that in Chapter 4) are chained block algorithms. These algorithms encrypt one fixed-length block of the message at a time. The encrypted blocks are chained together by using the encrypted form of each block as one of the inputs when the following block is encrypted. Because there is no block preceding the first message block, a special block-sized number, the initialization vector (IV), is used instead of the encrypted previous block. The initialization vector is placed in the packet, unencrypted, so the recipient can properly decrypt the message.

5. Add a tunnel header, if required.

6. Append the remaining packet data.

7. Compute the length of any required padding and pad the packet with the requisite number of bytes of data. The padding contents should be as specified by the encryption algorithm or, if no such specification exists, the padding should contain a series of increasing single-byte integers with the values 1, 2, 3, ...

8. Fill in the Next Header field.

9. Encrypt the message, if encryption is mandated by the SA. The packet data, padding, pad length, and Next Header fields will be encrypted, along with the tunnel header for a Tunnel Mode SA. The mandatory encryption algorithms for IPsec ESP are DES-CBC and the null encryption algorithm. The latter does not provide encryption protection. Because an ESP header must provide confidentiality, authentication, or both, when the null encryption algorithm is used for encryption, the null authentication algorithm must not be used for authentication.

10. Compute the authentication data, if authentication is specified by the SA. The authenticated data includes the initial ESP header, as well as the data covered by encryption. The mandatory authentication algorithms for IPsec ESP are HMAC-MD5, HMAC-SHA-1, and the null authentication algorithm. The last algorithm does not provide authentication protection. Because an ESP header must provide confidentiality, authentication, or both, when the null authentication algorithm is used for authentication, the null encryption algorithm must not be used for encryption.

11. Fragment the message, if necessary.

3.7 ESP Header Processing for Inbound Messages

When a message is received that contains an ESP header, the IP-processing routines first ensure that all fragments of the message have been received and reintegrated to form a complete message. The routines also ensure that the fields that identified each piece of the message as a fragment are reinitialized: The offset field is reset to zero and the "more fragments" flag is turned off, so the IPsec-processing routines do not erroneously identify the reassembled message as a message fragment. The message is then passed to the IPsec-processing routines, which perform the following steps.

1. Locate the inbound SA governing the protected communication in the SAD.

2. If replay protection is enabled, perform the replay protection check.

3. Verify the authentication data. The authentication hash is computed in exactly the same manner as for an outbound message. If the computed hash does not match the authentication data found in the message, the message is discarded and no further processing

takes place. Performing the authentication verification prior to decryption is efficient. If the message has been altered, the computationally expensive decryption process is avoided.

4. Decrypt the encrypted portion of the packet. If decryption is not successful or results in garbled header information, the message is discarded and no further processing takes place.

5. Strip off the padding, if any was added.

6. Strip off the ESP header and repeat the IPsec processing for any remaining IPsec headers.

7. Check the SPD to ensure that the IPsec protection applied to the incoming packet conforms to the system's IPsec policy requirements.

The successful authentication or encryption of an incoming packet as specified by an existing SA does not ensure that the SA should have been used to protect this particular type of traffic. In scenario 1 (presented in Chapter 1), let's assume that hosts H1 and H2 have established several SAs to provide end-to-end security coverage for their communications. SAs 1 and 2, which ensure that HTTP messages are not tampered with, are AH SAs. SAs 3 and 4, which protect FTP data transmissions, are ESP SAs. When a packet comes into H2, and the SPI, protocol (ESP), and destination address tie in the packet to SA 3, that SA will be used to decrypt the packet. What would happen if H1 mistakenly used SA 3 to send HTTP traffic to H2? The inbound packet's destination address, SPI, and protocol (ESP) would all point to SA 3. The port number, which would show that the packet is not an FTP message, cannot be interrogated before the packet has been decrypted. The packet will successfully decrypt, because it has used a valid SA. It is only a policy check, after decryption, that will show that the packet has been sent under the umbrella of the wrong SA. This erroneous usage is demonstrated in Figure 3.5.

A more dramatic example is the case in which H1 and H2 use an SA bundle, a grouping of several related SAs, to protect a single packet. Perhaps the hosts have established two end-to-end SAs: SAs 1 and 2 are ESP encryption-only SAs, and SAs 3 and 4 are AH SAs that will authenticate the encrypted traffic and its IP header. What would happen if H1 mistakenly used only SA 1 to send an FTP request to H2? The inbound packet's destination address, SPI, and protocol (ESP) would all point to SA 1. The packet would successfully decrypt, because SA 1 is perfectly appropriate for this traffic. However, a policy check would reveal that the packet should have had

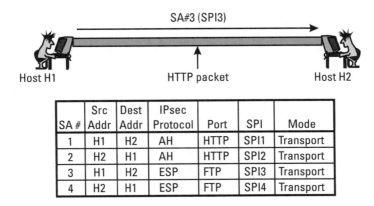

SA #	Src Addr	Dest Addr	IPsec Protocol	Port	SPI	Mode
1	H1	H2	AH	HTTP	SPI1	Transport
2	H2	H1	AH	HTTP	SPI2	Transport
3	H1	H2	ESP	FTP	SPI3	Transport
4	H2	H1	ESP	FTP	SPI4	Transport

Figure 3.5 Erroneous SA usage.

two security headers, and the packet would be dropped. Figure 3.6 demonstrates this erroneous case, as well as the correct usage of SAs 1 and 3.

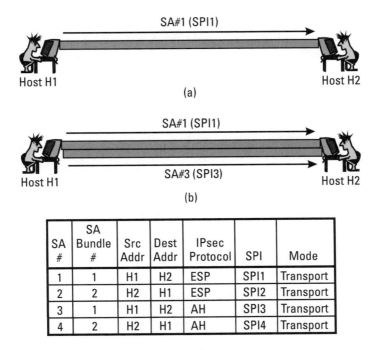

SA #	SA Bundle #	Src Addr	Dest Addr	IPsec Protocol	SPI	Mode
1	1	H1	H2	ESP	SPI1	Transport
2	2	H2	H1	ESP	SPI2	Transport
3	1	H1	H2	AH	SPI3	Transport
4	2	H2	H1	AH	SPI4	Transport

Figure 3.6 SA bundle applications: (a) erroneous application and (b) correct application.

3.8 Complications

Although encryption of the upper-layer headers is desirable for security purposes, it eliminates the transport header fields, including the Transport Protocol and ports, as SA selectors. It also poses problems for certain specialized uses of Internet traffic. A number of fields in the transport header can be used for purposes other than transport layer processing, including network traffic analysis, management, and performance enhancement; intrusion detection; and preferential treatment for specified types of traffic, resulting in several different classes of quality of service (QOS). A new protocol, called transport-friendly ESP (TF-ESP) [3], has been proposed, but the details have not yet been fully hammered out. There are two possible approaches: (1) defining a special TF-ESP header that would duplicate the critical fields in an unencrypted form and (2) beginning the encryption at a later point in the packet, leaving the desired header fields unencrypted. One downside of the first solution is the fear that security would be compromised by providing potential attackers with unencrypted header information, which is also present in its encrypted form in a well-known location within the packet. Another potential drawback is the duplication of information, resulting in increased packet size. The second solution could complicate an already complex protocol, requiring additional specialized processing. Whether the advantages provided by TF-ESP would outweigh the negative considerations has not yet been determined.

3.9 Criticisms and Counterclaims

The well-known and well-respected cryptographer Bruce Schneier co-authored, with his colleague Niels Ferguson, an extremely critical analysis of IPsec and IKE [4]. Ferguson and Schneier begin by stating that complexity is the sworn enemy of security. Of course, they are correct; unfortunately, the problem that IPsec is attempting to attack is an extremely complex and multifaceted area. IPsec not only has to secure IP traffic; it has to coexist with numerous existing protocols, cope with open-ended network topologies, and, one would hope, accommodate future networking developments as well.

In the name of simplification, Ferguson and Schneier suggest the elimination of the AH protocol and of Transport Mode. Many IPsec developers agree that AH should be abolished, and it is possible that that will happen in the next version of IPsec. On the other hand, there may be other protocols that require the use of AH and would protest its demise. As far as limiting all

SAs to Tunnel Mode, they also suggest a somewhat complex header-minimization scheme to compensate for the extra baggage of Tunnel Mode when it is not really needed. The authors admit that they are not networking experts. Those who are expert in that arena vociferously declare that the inclusion of both Transport and Tunnel Modes is dictated by the nature of the network architecture [5, 6].

Ferguson and Schneier are not happy with the order of operations performed in ESP processing; they believe that outgoing packets first should be authenticated and then encrypted. That order was selected intentionally, so that incoming packets that did not authenticate properly would not progress to the more computationally demanding decryption stage. The authors present a scenario in which the authentication and encryption keys are decoupled, so that successfully undergoing authentication does not guarantee that the packet will decrypt correctly. To solve the problem without reversing the order of the operations, Ferguson and Schneier suggest authenticating the decryption key and any other data used in the encryption, along with the packet data. On the other hand, the cryptographers who participated in the IPsec development appear to be comfortable with this order of operations, without requiring authentication of additional information. In addition, as discussed in Chapter 5, when IKE is used to negotiate the keys, the ESP's authentication and encryption keys are part of an integral whole.

The authors view unidirectional SAs as unnecessary baggage, causing SAD bloat. They propose bidirectional SAs, reducing the size of the SAD and simplifying matters. However, a single SAD entry would not allow each peer to select its own inbound SPI; a dual entry, each with its own SPI, would restore the SAD's larger size. Moreover, there may be uses of IPsec, such as multicast (more on this in Chapter 11), in which traffic actually does flow in only one direction.

Ferguson and Schneier also are uncomfortable with affording users and system administrators too much leeway in security decisions. With regard to the SPD, they feel it is dangerous enough to allow users to choose which types of traffic should or should not be IPsec-protected. Selecting specific algorithms and levels of protection is fraught with more peril than they can bear. It is true that the specification of security-related parameters is a tricky business. However, it is an area in which individual implementations can distinguish themselves in terms of the interplay of ease of use and the level of security controls.

One of their major criticisms is the difficulty of comprehending the documentation. Aside from the number of documents involved, the failure to include background, goals, and rationale is a major stumbling block. They suggest that the documents should include explanations, discussions of trade-offs, and the reasoning behind the ultimate solution. That could be included in a nonnormative portion of the document. It also would mitigate another problem faced by every consensual standards body: the replaying of ancient, already solved issues as new members join the group. That is, of course, an excellent suggestion. The problem in a voluntary standards body is that each member writes his or her own position description. If no one leaps forward to undertake this major effort, it does not get done. In addition, the IETF culture is one of the experts working together toward a goal. In spite of the wide range of the participants' backgrounds and experience, a certain level of knowledge is assumed.

Protocol development occurs over time in an iterative, give-and-take process. It is easy to criticize the final product, ignoring the realities that gave rise to it. Ferguson and Schneier unfavorably compare the IPsec/IKE development process to that of the Advanced Encryption Standard (AES) by the National Institute of Standards and Technology (NIST), in which a competition was held to select the cryptographic algorithm that will replace DES. However, an encryption algorithm is an atomic entity. A protocol is much broader and encompasses a larger, more amorphous problem space.

Once IPsec had reached a critical stage of definition and numerous implementations had been fielded, there was a reluctance within the IPsec developers' community to change the protocol definition in such a way as to "break" compliant implementations. However, just as the current incarnation of IPsec is the second version and is incompatible with the previous round of IPsec RFCs, there undoubtedly will be another leap forward. The next round of RFCs will have the chance to address those criticisms and to incorporate a significant amount of operational experience with IPsec. Another well-respected world-class cryptographer, Hugo Krawczyk, sums it up:

> It could have been better, it could have been simpler, it could have been more elegant, it could have been better documented, it could have included some better design decisions, it could have corrected known weaknesses. But, in spite of all these "could have[s]", ipsec/ike IS a very valuable protocol. Not just the best available alternative but a good protocol in many senses. [7]

3.10 Threat Mitigation

What real-life threats are prevented through the use of the ESP header? The ESP header with encryption provides privacy. Even if the packets are captured and read by any of the intermediate nodes that forward the packet on its way, the packet data are not understandable to an eavesdropper who does not possess the secret encryption/decryption key.

However, an encrypted packet whose data are not also afforded integrity protection can be subject to a number of cut-and-paste attacks [8]. That sounds like a benign kindergarten activity, but in an attacker's toolkit they can be devastating. For that reason, authentication of encrypted data is strongly recommended. That can be accomplished through the use of an ESP header with both encryption and authentication or through the use of adjacent or nested ESP and AH headers.

When the ESP header is used in Transport Mode, the packet's data are encrypted, but the source and destination addresses are not hidden. Any node along its path can determine the packet's source and destination; this information, as well as the packet's size and contents, can be used for traffic analysis. If a business has an internal network and wants to prevent outsiders from performing this type of analysis, the use of scenario 2 can provide a limited type of traffic analysis protection. A Tunnel Mode ESP SA between SG1 and SG2 will encrypt the actual source and destination addresses as part of the inner header. The outer header will contain the unencrypted gateway addresses. That allows Internet eavesdroppers to surmise the general source and destination of the packet from the gateway's location, but the exact addresses of the communicating peers and the nature of the traffic are hidden. If SG1 and SG2 are not local to a particular business but instead are provided by a regional Internet server provider (ISP), a greater level of traffic protection is provided.

3.11   Why Two Security Headers?

Because ESP can provide the same protections as AH, as well as privacy, why are two distinct security headers necessary? The answer lies in the dual realms of history and politics. A number of countries forbid the export of software that enables or incorporates encryption. The initial round of RFCs (RFC 1826 and RFC 1827, both now obsolete) split off the undeniably exportable AH from the more problematic (in terms of exportability) weapons-grade[1] ESP header. In its original form, the ESP header provided only encryption; if authentication was required, both headers had to be applied. Because an

---

1. Several countries define encryption software to be munitions, and its export is legally tantamount to trafficking in weapons.

encrypted, unauthenticated packet is vulnerable to several types of modification attacks [8] (more on that in Chapter 4), every encrypted packet also should be authenticated, which would have required two distinct SAs and a fair amount of unnecessary processing for each protected packet. Therefore, in the second round of RFCs (RFC 2402 and RFC 2406), authentication was added to the ESP header. Initially, the new, improved ESP header always provided encryption and, optionally, authentication. The definition of the null ESP encryption algorithm (more on that in Chapter 4) allowed the ESP header to provide authentication without encryption, thus duplicating the AH.

It is true that the AH protects header fields not protected by the ESP header, in particular the source and destination addresses. However, an authenticated exchange of secret keys can inextricably bind the participants' addresses to the keys (more on that in Chapter 5), effectively providing source and destination address protection. In addition, the AH processing, faced with the necessity to distinguish between mutable and nonmutable IP header fields, is more complex than that required for ESP. The AH was left intact for the original political reasons, as well as through a desire not to radically alter the IPsec protocols, which were beginning to be implemented and used. It is possible that at some time it may be either eliminated or converted into an optional component of IPsec.

3.12 Summary

The two IPsec headers, the AH and the ESP header, can be used separately or together to provide the critical security protections of authentication, integrity, and confidentiality. Now that we understand the purpose, format, and processing of those headers, it is time to focus on the mechanisms that actually furnish the protection: the cryptographic algorithms.

3.13 Further Reading

The ESP header is definitively described in RFC 2406 [1]. The generalized IPsec architecture, of which ESP is an integral part, is defined in RFC 2401 [2]. A description of the dangers of encryption without integrity protection can be found in [8]. Steve Bellovin has presented several talks on TF-ESP, including [3]. Ferguson and Schneier's critique of IPsec is presented in [4];

responses from IPsec members can be found in [5–7] and on the IPsec mailing list archive, http://www.vpnc.org/ietf-ipsec.

References

[1]   Kent, S., and R. Atkinson, *IP Encapsulating Security Payload (ESP)*, RFC 2406, Nov. 1998.

[2]   Kent, S., and R. Atkinson, *Security Architecture for the Internet Protocol*, RFC 2401, Nov. 1998.

[3]   Bellovin, S., "Transport-Friendly ESP, or, Layer Violations for Fun and Profit," NDSS '99, Feb. 1999, http://www.research.att.com/~smb/talks.

[4]   Ferguson, N., and B. Schneier, "A Cryptographic Evaluation of IPsec," http://www.counterpane.com/ipsec.{pdf,ps.zip}, Feb. 1999.

[5]   Bellovin, S., "Bruce Schneier on IPsec," communication to the IPsec mailing list, Jan. 19, 2000, http://www.vpnc.org/ietf-ipsec/mail-archive/msg00066.html.

[6]   Kent, S., "Counterpane Comments, ASCII Version," communication to the IPsec mailing list, Jan. 25, 2000, http://www.vpnc.org/ietf-ipsec/mail-archive/msg00123.html.

[7]   Krawczyk, H., "Re: Bruce Schneier on IPsec," communication to the IPsec mailing list, Jan. 20, 2000, http://www.vpnc.org/ietf-ipsec/mail-archive/msg00075.html.

[8]   Bellovin, S., "Problem Areas for the IP Security Protocols," *Proc. 6th Usenix UNIX Security Symp.*, July 1996, pp. 205–214.

4

The Third Puzzle Piece: The Cryptographic Algorithms

> To each man is given the key to Heaven. The same key unlocks the gates of Hell.
>
> *Tibetan Buddhist saying*

The algorithms used to afford IPsec protection, both those used for authentication and those used for encryption, ideally would fulfill two incompatible goals: to provide maximal protection against a variety of mathematical, cryptanalytical, and brute force attacks, and to require minimal processing on the part of each participant in the communication. The algorithms that were chosen as the standard IPsec algorithms constitute a best-guess, reasonable compromise. We know the capabilities of today's computers and if we extrapolate to forecast the capabilities of computers in the next decade, those algorithms are believed to provide a reasonable amount of protection for most computer applications. The computations that make up the IPsec algorithms are well known, because they are defined in public specifications. Rather than relying on keeping the algorithms' definitions a deep, dark secret, the security provided by the algorithms is enhanced by allowing expert cryptographers to attempt to break them. Furthermore, the algorithms have been implemented on today's computers and gateways, and (one would hope) their widespread use will not demand a level of computation that would bring electronic commerce and communications to a standstill.

This chapter explains the cryptographic algorithms and mechanisms used by IPsec and the Internet Key Exchange (IKE). It is not a general-purpose introduction to cryptography and cryptographic mechanisms [1, 2] but tries to give the user an understanding of the purpose and operation of the cryptographic services essential to IPsec and some of the tradeoffs involved in their selection. It also presents a high-level algorithmic description of IPsec's mandatory authentication and encryption algorithms, HMAC-MD5, HMAC-SHA-1, and DES. Although the IPsec documents mandate specific algorithms to provide standard-grade, interoperable security, consenting parties are free to implement additional algorithms, either selected from the public domain, or private or proprietary algorithms.

4.1 Underlying Principles

The details of the algorithms used in the AH and the ESP header [3] differ, but a number of generalities apply to all the algorithms currently defined for both headers.

All the algorithms are block algorithms; starting at the beginning of the message, each block is processed one at a time. The blocksize is part of the definition of each algorithm; currently, the most common blocksize is 8 bytes (64 bits). Each block undergoes some sort of repetitive processing; each iteration of that processing is known as a *round*. The number of rounds is sometimes used as a rough characterization of the cryptographic strength of an algorithm. Each round, in turn, consists of a *round function*, which is the processing that constitutes each round of the cipher. The round function can be simple and straightforward, or it can be extremely complex. Some algorithms have multiple round functions, each of which is applied to one or more rounds. In many algorithms, the whole secret key is not used to hash or encrypt each block; instead, the secret key is used to generate multiple *subkeys*, or *round keys*. Each round can incorporate one or more subkeys.

If each block were hashed or encrypted separately, it would make an attacker's job much easier, because the contents of some portions of an Internet packet are known. In the case of a hash function, the final hash must reflect every bit of every input block, not just the last block. In the case of an encryption algorithm, if each block could be decrypted separately, without reference to any other block, the predictable blocks could be more easily attacked. Once the key was known, every block could be decrypted. For this reason, every mandatory IPsec algorithm incorporates within its definition a feedback mechanism; the encryption or authentication of each block has, as one of its inputs, the cryptographically computed output of the previous block.

A number of the operations commonly used in the algorithms may not be included in the mathematical repository of some readers: the circular shift operation, the exclusive OR (XOR) operation, and modular arithmetic. A circular shift operation, illustrated in Figure 4.1, shifts all the bits in a numerical entity in the prescribed direction, to the left for a circular left shift and to the right for a circular right shift. The bits that "fall off" the end are appended, one at a time, to the other end of the entity, thus qualifying it as a circular shift. To a 32-bit number, a shift from 1 to 31 bits can be applied; a 32-bit shift would reproduce the original number.

An XOR, illustrated in Figure 4.2, consists of a bit-by-bit comparison of two numerical quantities. The result of the XOR will contain "0" bits in the positions in which both input numbers had the same value (either 0 or 1), and "1" bits in the positions in which the input numbers had differing values.

Modular arithmetic (addition, subtraction, multiplication, and exponentiation) often is used in cryptographic algorithms. For example, when we perform an addition modulo 2^{32}, if the result contains more than 32 bits, only the last 32 bits are used, in effect dividing the result by 2^{32} and keeping only the remainder. Operations modulo 32 are commonly used, because the word size in bits of most computers currently is 32. Figure 4.3 illustrates arithmetic modulo 16 (or 2^4), which is more intuitive to people.

The security provided by a cryptographic algorithm obviously depends on the cryptographic complexity and robustness of the algorithm itself, as

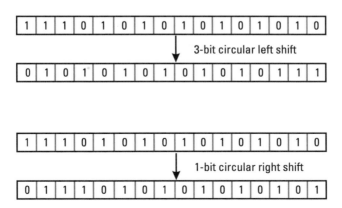

Figure 4.1 The circular shift operation.

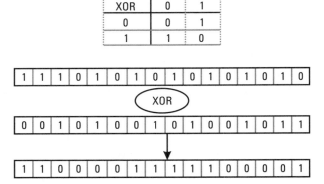

Figure 4.2 The exclusive OR (XOR) operation.

well as the algorithm's resistance to known attacks. However, a secure algorithm is not sufficient to ensure the security of the communications protected by that algorithm. Several other factors come into play as well. The algorithm must be implemented, whether in hardware or software, in an accurate and secure manner. The secret keys must be the appropriate length for the algorithm and must be generated, exchanged, managed, and stored in a secure manner. If a pseudo-random number generator is used to generate the key or to generate values that will be used in the key's computation, it is critical that the outputs of the pseudo-random number generator meet generally accepted criteria for randomness; if that is not the case, the keys will be more easily subject to discovery through guessing, which will compromise the security mechanisms that rely on the pseudo-random number generator.

4.2   Authentication Algorithms

A one-way hash is an algorithm that computes a characteristic value, or hash, for a message in such a way that it is not feasible, given only the hash, to

$$7 + 8 = 15_{\text{modulo } 10} = 15_{\text{modulo } 16}$$

$$7 + 18 = 25_{\text{modulo } 10} = (25 - 16)_{\text{modulo } 16} = 9_{\text{modulo } 16}$$

$$7 + 28 = 35_{\text{modulo } 10} = (35 - 2 * 16)_{\text{modulo } 16} = 3_{\text{modulo } 16}$$

Figure 4.3 Modular arithmetic: addition module 16 (2^4).

reconstruct the original message. Although in theory an infinite number of messages could result in a given hash, it should not be computationally feasible to find two messages with the same hash or, given a message and its hash, to find a second message with the same hash. A collision-resistant hash adds the characteristic that it is highly unlikely that two different messages would result in the same hash. One way of increasing the collision resistance of a hash is to compute the hash not only over the message but over the concatenation of the message and the message's length. That decreases the probability that two messages of different lengths will result in the same hash.

Computing this type of hash and transmitting it with the original message would be sufficient to alert a recipient to transmission errors that are a result of equipment malfunction or transmission "noise." It does not protect a message from purposeful tampering, because the entity that tampers with the message can simply recompute the hash so that it matches the newly changed message. What is required is a keyed hash, one that permeates every bit of the hash with information from a secret key. That type of hash, which is called a message authentication code (MAC), can be computed only by an entity that possesses the secret key. If that key is known only to the sender and to the recipient of a message, the sender can compute the MAC before transmitting the message, and the recipient can recompute the MAC to verify that the message as received is identical to the message that was originally sent. This also serves to provide data origin authentication.

The original AH [4] identified keyed MD5 and keyed SHA-1 as its default authentication algorithms. In 1996 [5], a successful attack was mounted on MD5. It was demonstrated that, by solving a series of simultaneous equations, it was possible to find two messages that differed in only one word and resulted in the same output hash. That made it inadvisable to plan on the continued use of MD5 for an open-ended time period. The current, revised AH [6] instead specifies HMAC-MD5 and HMAC-SHA-1. HMAC can be viewed as a cryptographic wrapper; it uses an existing one-way hash function but iteratively applies the hash function twice to the message and to the secret key. The iterated application of a cryptographic primitive serves to strengthen a suspect hash function like MD5, because attacking iterative applications of the algorithm is a problem of considerably greater complexity than the original attack on plain MD5. To understand the operation of HMAC, it first is necessary to explain the underlying hash functions and then to show how HMAC is superimposed on the hash.

4.2.1   The MD5 Algorithm

MD5 [7] is the latest hash in a series invented by Ron Rivest. It has a block-size of 64 bytes (512 bits) and a key length of 128 bits and generates a hash of 16 bytes (128 bits). The MD5 hash of a message is computed as follows.

1. Pad the message so its length in bits is 64 bits less than the blocksize of 512 bits. Padding is always added; the pad length will always be between 1 and 512 bits. The first pad bit is set to 1, and the remaining pad bits are set to 0.

2. Following the padding, append the original message length (without padding) as a 64-bit number.

3. Initialize four 32-bit buffers with specially selected constants.

4. Process each block of the message in turn. The processing consists of four rounds, with each round consisting of 16 complex computations. Each computation replaces one of the four buffers with the sum (modulo 2^{32}) of its current contents plus:

    a. The contents of one of the other buffers.

    b. One of four predefined functions performed on the other three buffers. Each of those functions has the characteristic that independent input (input in which each bit has no predefined relationship to the other bits) will produce independent output.

    c. One word of the current message block.

    d. A one-word element of the sin function (a constant).

    Before the sum of those four quantities is added to the buffer, it is first shifted left a specified number of bits.

5. After each block is processed, a feedback mechanism is included. Each buffer is incremented by the value that it contained at the end of the previous block's processing.

6. The output of MD5 is the concatenation of the final values of the four buffers. Thus, the output hash is 128 bits.

The MD5 definition specifies, for each round and each computation within that round, the specific values to be used in that computation, which include the buffers used, the function, the message word, the sin table entry, and the number of shift bits.

4.2.2   The SHA-1 Algorithm

SHA-1 [8] was originally defined by The National Security Agency (NSA), and was adopted by NIST as the one-way hash prescribed for use with the digital signature algorithm (DSA). It has a blocksize of 64 bytes (512 bits) and a key length of 160 bits and generates a hash of 20 bytes (160 bits). The SHA-1 hash of a message is computed as follows.

1. Pad the message so its length in bits is 64 bits less than the blocksize of 512 bits. Padding is always added; the pad length will always be between 1 and 512 bits. The first pad bit is set to 1, and the remaining pad bits are set to 0.

2. Following the padding, append the original message length (without padding) as a 64-bit number.

3. Initialize the five buffers (H_0, H_1, H_2, H_3, and H_4) with specially selected constants.

Perform steps 4 through 8 for each block of the input message.

4. The block consists of 16 words (512 bits). Compute an additional 64 words, each of which consists of a 1-bit circular left shift of the XOR of four of the other words.

5. Set each intermediate buffer (A, B, C, D, E) to the contents of the corresponding H buffer (H_0, H_1, H_2, H_3, H_4).

6. For each of the 80 words (the 16 message-block words plus the additional 64 words), compute the sum (modulo 2^{32}) of its current contents plus:

    a. The contents of intermediate buffer A, circular-left-shifted 5 bits.

    b. One of four predefined functions performed on intermediate buffers B, C, and D. Each of those functions has the characteristic that independent input (input in which each bit has no predefined relationship to the other bits) will produce independent output.

    c. The contents of intermediate buffer E.

    d. One of four specified constants.

7. Shift the intermediate buffers' contents, as follows.

    a. Place the contents of buffer D in buffer E.

   b. Place the contents of buffer C in buffer D.

   c. Place the contents of buffer B, left-circular-shifted 30 bits, in buffer C.

   d. Place the contents of buffer A in buffer B.

   e. Place the results of the new calculation in buffer A.

8. This step incorporates the feedback mechanism. Each H buffer (H_0, H_1, H_2, H_3, H_4) is set to the sum (modulo 2^{32}) of its current contents and the current contents of the corresponding intermediate buffer (A, B, C, D, E).

9. The output of SHA-1 is the concatenation of the final values of the five H buffers. Thus, the output hash is 160 bits.

The SHA-1 definition specifies, for each of the 80 words, the specific function and the additive and initialization constants to be used in that computation. Although SHA-1 shares a number of computational constructs with MD5, the expansion of each block from 16 words to 80 words, in which each of the new words contains portions of several of the original words, makes SHA-1 less susceptible to the type of attack that jeopardized MD5's security.

4.2.3   The HMAC Algorithm

The HMAC algorithm [9, 10], which was defined by Hugo Krawczyk, Mihir Bellare, and Ran Canetti, adds a secret key and additional computational robustness to an existing hash function, without significantly increasing the level of required computational resources. Its purpose is to further strengthen well-known, well-understood hashes; to allow the continued use of the original hash's code; and to facilitate an easy transition from one underlying hash function to another, if necessary. The blocksize and output MAC size are those of the underlying hash function. However, for use with AH or ESP, the MAC is truncated to 96 bits.

   The generalized HMAC definition does not specify the key length. If the key length exceeds the block length of the hash (64 bytes/512 bits for MD5 and SHA-1), the key is first hashed with the underlying hash function to yield a new key that is the output size of the hash. For proper security, the secret key's length should be no smaller than the output size of the underlying hash (16 bytes/128 bits for MD5, 20 bytes/160 bits for SHA-1). However, a key length greater than the hash output does not appreciably increase security. Therefore, for use in IPsec, a key of 16 bytes is mandated for HMAC-MD5 [11] and a key of 20 bytes for HMAC-SHA-1 [12]. The HMAC computation is as follows.

1. The key is padded with zeroes, if necessary, to the hash's blocksize.
2. The key is XOR'd with a special constant (ipad).
3. The message data are appended to the expanded, XOR'd key.
4. The underlying hash is applied to the result of step 3 (the expanded XOR'd key + message data).
5. The expanded key is XOR'd with another special constant (opad).
6. The output of step 4 (the hash output) is appended to the expanded, XOR'd key from step 5.
7. The underlying hash is applied to the result of step 6 (the expanded XOR'd key + hash output).

Figure 4.4 illustrates the steps of the HMAC computation, using MD5 as the underlying hash.

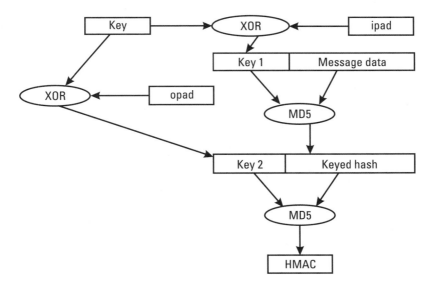

Figure 4.4 The HMAC-MD5 algorithm.

4.2.4 Other Authentication Algorithms

One other authentication algorithm, RIPEMD-160 [13], is defined for use with the IPsec headers. It is a five-round hash with a blocksize of 64 bytes (512 bits) and a key length of 160 bits, and generates a hash of 20 bytes (160 bits). RIPEMD's inventors, Hans Dobbertin, Antoon Bosselaers, and Bart Preneel, originally intended it to be a more secure version of MD4, the predecessor of MD5. RIPEMD-160 is a reengineered version of RIPEMD, with a similar structure but additional security features. It consists of two parallel MD5-like computations, which differ from each other in the order of application of the functions, the message words selected for the hash, and the additive constants. After the final round, the two resulting hashes are added to produce the final hash.

A number of attempts have been made to discover encryption algorithms that can provide both encryption and authentication in the same operation. In such a case, the required computations would be greater than those required for encryption alone but less than the computational requirements of encrypting and authenticating with distinct algorithms. So far, security weaknesses have been discovered in all such schemes. The latest proposal for such a dual-purpose algorithm, integrity-aware plaintext-ciphertext block chaining (iaPCBC) [14, 15], appears secure, but has not been around long enough to be subjected to the rigorous cryptographic analysis necessary for an operational, trusted IPsec algorithm.

4.3 The ESP Header Encryption Algorithms

The ESP header encryption algorithms are all block-oriented algorithms. Each block of input text, or *plaintext*, is transformed, through the use of the encryption algorithm in conjunction with a secret key, into its encrypted counterpart, known as *ciphertext*. The chaining mechanism used by the ESP encryption algorithms is called the Cipher Block Chaining (CBC) Mode. In CBC Mode, prior to encryption, each unencrypted block is XOR'd with the encrypted text of the previous block. An analogous value is also needed for the first block; that value is referred to as the *initialization vector* (IV). Because the first encrypted block of text generally contains multiple fields (e.g., TCP header fields) whose values are known and that are invariant from one packet to the next, the use of an IV ensures that identical fields that are encrypted with identical keys will vary from one packet to the next.

A common approach, and the one that is mandated for IPsec, is to generate a random IV for each packet. When generating IVs for a series of packets, it is essential that each IV is a random value and that the IV generation does not follow a predictable pattern. In particular, the IPsec documents caution against IVs that have a low Hamming distance. The *Hamming distance* between two values refers to the difference, in the number and placement of bits with a value of 1, between the values. Because an IV is XOR'd with the packet's first block, it is the IV's 1-bits that actually mask, or hide, the block's data. The IV's 0-bits preserve the value of the bits with which they are XOR'd, but the 1-bits flip 1-bits in the data to 0. Thus, IVs whose 1-bits are similarly placed, applied to similar data, yield results that are not significantly dissimilar.

Many of the IPsec encryption algorithms belong to a class of ciphers known as *Feistel networks*. These ciphers divide each input block into two sections. The round function is applied to one section of the input block. The encrypted output of that step then is XOR'd with the other section of the input block, and the two halves are swapped. The beauty of a Feistel network cipher is its reversibility: The same algorithm that is used to encrypt the plaintext can be used, unaltered, to decrypt the ciphertext. Generally, the only difference between encryption and decryption is the order in which the individual subkeys are applied. That enables efficient, compact implementations in both software and hardware. The round function itself does not have to be reversible.

A significant issue related to encryption algorithms is whether a particular algorithm has known *weak keys*. Weak keys do not provide the level of security generally ascribed to the algorithm in question. For instance, two successive encryptions with a weak key may reproduce the original plaintext, or a single encryption may result in ciphertext that is more vulnerable to a known attack. IPsec SAs are not supposed to be established with known weak keys for the selected encryption algorithm.

Currently, the mandatory ESP encryption algorithm is the Data Encryption Standard (DES) [16]. DES and its stronger variant, Triple DES, are the most commonly used ESP encryption algorithms today. There are a number of other encryption algorithms whose use is described in the ESP documents. This chapter includes a detailed description of DES and Triple DES, brief descriptions of the other currently used ESP encryption algorithms, and a summary of the Advanced Encryption Standard (AES), which will replace DES as the U.S. government's encryption standard.

4.3.1 The DES Algorithm

DES [17], originally defined by IBM, was adopted by NIST as the government's standard encryption algorithm for unclassified data [18, 19]. It consists of 16 rounds, has a blocksize of 8 bytes (64 bits), and generates an encrypted version of a message that, at most, increases the message's size so that it is an exact multiple of the blocksize.

The DES algorithm, as originally defined, has four modes. Plain vanilla DES, which encrypts each input block separately, constitutes the Electronic Codebook (ECB) Mode. The other three modes, CBC Mode, Cipher Feedback (CFB) Mode, and Output Feedback (OFB) Mode all incorporate some form of feedback. Each block's encrypted text is a function not only of that block's original text and the secret key, but of the encrypted text of one or more other blocks. The DES Mode required by IPsec is the CBC Mode. Chaining the encrypted blocks affords some limited protection against cut-and-paste attacks, protects against replay attacks, disguises repetitive information, and increases the cryptographic robustness of the output.

DES requires a secret key that is 64 bits long, but only 56 of those bits are actual key bits; the remaining 8 bits are parity bits that ensure the internal consistency of each byte of the key. The DES algorithm consists of 16 rounds, each one of which uses a different 48-bit key to work its wonders. The original 56-bit key is transformed into sixteen 48-bit keys as follows.

1. Using a table, the 56 bits of the key are permuted, resulting in two 28-bit values, the lefthand key source and the righthand key source.

2. To obtain the key for each round, the lefthand key source and the righthand key source are each circularly left shifted 1 or 2 bits, yielding a new lefthand key source and righthand key source. The current round's key is obtained by performing a permutation on the concatenation of the current lefthand key source and the current righthand key source, yielding a 48-bit round key.

DES is an extremely complex algorithm. After the key for each round has been computed, the real fun begins. For CBC Mode, each block is XOR'd with the previous block's ciphertext or, for the first block, with the IV. The XOR'd output is permuted and then divided into a lefthand half and a righthand half. The righthand half and the round key are used as the inputs to a complex numeric manipulation; its result is then XOR'd with the lefthand half. The XOR'd output becomes the new righthand half, the old righthand half becomes the new lefthand half, and the next round begins.

After 16 of these rounds, the final lefthand half and righthand half are swapped and concatenated, permuted once again, and ciphertext exists. In more detail, the processing of each block is as follows.

1. To conform to the CBC Mode, the current block's to-be-encrypted text is XOR'd with the previous block's encrypted text. In the case of the first message block, its text is XOR'd with the IV, which for IPsec is a randomly generated 64-bit value. The output of that operation becomes the current DES input block.

2. The bits of the input block are then rearranged in a complex permutation; the permuted block is then divided into two halves, the initial lefthand half and the initial righthand half.

3. Each of the 16 rounds consists of the following steps.

   a. The previous round's righthand half (or, for round 1, the initial righthand half) is stored in the lefthand half.

   b. The bits of the current 32-bit righthand half are permuted, and some of the input bits appear more than once in the output, resulting in a 48-bit output.

   c. The 48-bit output from step 3(b) is XOR'd with the current round's 48-bit key.

   d. The 48-bit output of step 3(c) is divided into eight 6-bit values. Each of those eight values is used as the index into one of eight tables, each with 4 rows and 16 columns. The first bit and the last bit of each value constitute the row, and the middle 4 bits are the column. Each of the eight 6-bit values is replaced by the 4-bit table entry referenced by the row and column index derived from the 6-bit value. The output of this step is the concatenation of the eight derived 4-bit values, resulting in a 32-bit output. The eight tables used to transform the 6-bit values into 4-bit values are referred to as S tables or S boxes.

   e. The 32-bit output of step 4(d) is permuted, resulting in the new, updated righthand half.

   f. The updated righthand half is XOR'd with the previous round's lefthand half, and the result is stored in the righthand half.

4. After the completion of round 16, the lefthand half and the righthand half are switched. The concatenation of those two values (righthand half followed by lefthand half) is then subjected to

the inverse of the permutation performed in step 2. The output of that permutation is the DES encryption of the current block.

The DES definition contains tables that define the initial and intermediate key permutations; the number of shift operations to be applied to each round's key; the initial block permutation and its inverse; the permutation that expands each block's righthand half from 32 bits to 48 bits; the eight S tables; and the permutation applied to the output of the S tables. Figure 4.5 illustrates the general DES logic necessary to encrypt the *N*th message block. Figure 4.6 shows the round function as applied to the righthand half of the *N*th message block; intermediate calculations are labeled Val-1, Val-2, and so forth.

A message that has been encrypted with DES is decrypted using the same algorithm, with just one change: the subkeys are used in the opposite order; in other words, the last pair of encryption subkeys is used for the first decryption round. That is easily accomplished by reversing the order of application of the permutations and by subjecting each key to a right circular shift, rather than a left circular shift, to obtain the next subkey.

The portions of the DES algorithm that rely on permutations of the message text conceivably could be vulnerable to analysis and solution using a series of simultaneous equations. It is the S tables that protect DES from that type of attack. The values in the S tables were carefully chosen to maximize the diffusion of each message bit and each key bit throughout the encrypted output and to protect the output from analytic attacks. In the end, DES succumbed not to any new, analytic, or elegant attack but to brute force and the upward creep of technology [20]. In 1997, in response to a challenge from RSA Security Inc., thousands of ordinary PCs divided up all potential keys that could have been used on a specific message, and after 4 months, one of the computers found the actual key. In 1998, that feat was duplicated on a $250,000 machine in 56 hours. In the face of those successful attacks, DES is not considered fit for encryption of important communications. Although DES still is the official default algorithm for the ESP header, a reinforced version of DES, called Triple DES, is more commonly used. In October 1999, NIST declared Triple DES a government standard [17], allowing DES to be used only by legacy systems and recommending that even those systems upgrade to Triple DES as soon as possible.

4.3.2   The Triple DES Algorithm

Because it depends on DES, Triple DES also has a blocksize of 8 bytes (64 bits). Its key size is nominally 192 bits long, but, like DES, 1 bit out of

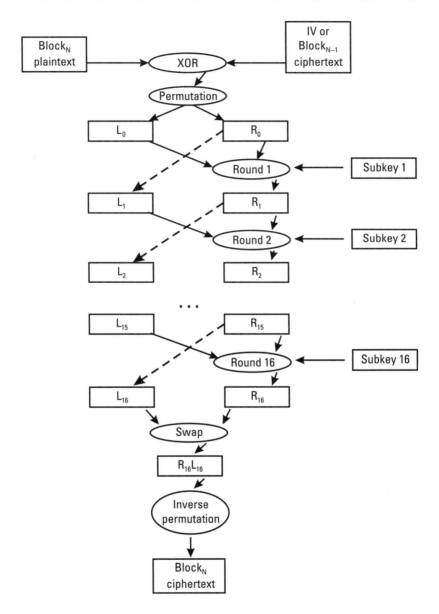

Figure 4.5 DES encryption: overall logic.

every 8 is a parity bit that ensures the internal consistency of each byte of the key. That results in a secret key that is actually 168 bits long. Operationally,

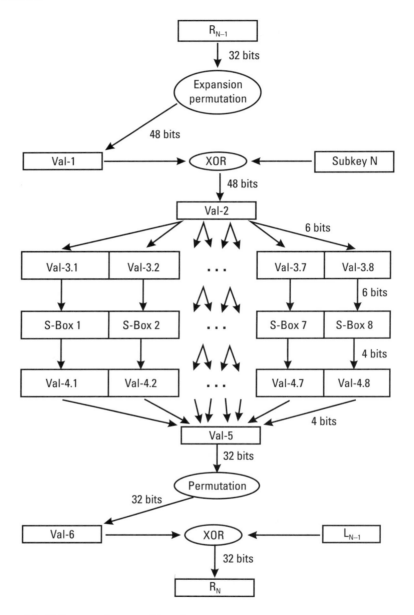

Figure 4.6 DES encryption: round function.

the key is broken down into three DES-sized keys of 56 bits each. For IPsec, the CBC Mode of Triple DES is the default mode.

Each block of the input message is processed as follows.

1. To conform to the CBC Mode, the current block's to-be-encrypted text is XOR'd with the previous block's encrypted text. In the case of the first message block, its text is XOR'd with the IV, which for IPsec is a randomly generated 64-bit value. The output of that operation becomes the current Triple DES input block.
2. Use DES to encrypt the output of step 1 with the first 56-bit secret key.
3. Use DES to decrypt the output of step 2 with the second 56-bit secret key.
4. Use DES to encrypt the output of step 3 with the third 56-bit secret key.

Figure 4.7 illustrates Triple DES encryption. The application of three successive DES operations to each block results in a considerably increased level of security that is resistant to brute force key-guessing attacks generated by

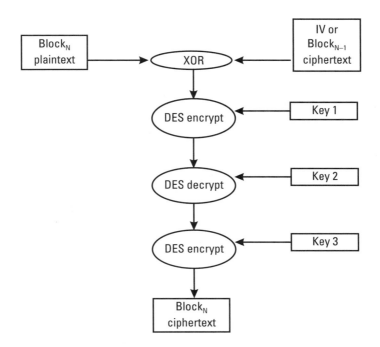

Figure 4.7 The Triple DES algorithm.

current computers. However, if either the first two subkeys or the last two subkeys are identical, the application of Triple DES would be equivalent to plain single DES. Thus, such keys should never be used for an IPsec SA. As is the case for DES, Triple DES messages are decrypted by applying the same series of operations that were used for encryption, but reversing the order of key usage.

4.3.3 Other Encryption Algorithms

Currently, DES is the only algorithm designated as mandatory for IPsec. The most commonly used encryption algorithm, however, is Triple DES. A number of other encryption algorithms are also defined for use in the ESP header. Practically speaking, two communicating peers can use any encryption algorithm on whose use they reach consensus; however, without prior knowledge, it would be foolish to assume that a potential recipient can handle any algorithms other than the most common ones.

The Blowfish [21, 22] algorithm was invented by the well-known cryptographer Bruce Schneier. It is a 16-round Feistel cipher, capable of handling a variable-length key; for IPsec, a 128-bit key is defined as the default. Blowfish's subkey computations are quite complex, but the encryption portion of the algorithm is extremely straightforward. Like DES, the prototype of Feistel ciphers, Blowfish consists of permutations and a round function that contains multiple S-box substitutions. Unlike DES, the permutations are key dependent, as are the four S-boxes. The S-box outputs, which are 32 bits in length, are combined using XORs and modular addition.

The CAST [23] algorithm is named after its original inventors, Carlisle Adams of Entrust Technologies and Stafford Tavares of Queens University in Canada. The generalized CAST algorithm has a variable key size and consists of either 12 or 16 encryption rounds, depending on the size of the key. The version of the algorithm selected for use with the ESP header is known as CAST-128, uses a 128-bit key, and has 16 rounds. The cipher uses eight S boxes, four for the computation of the keys used for the individual rounds and four for the actual encryption. There are actually two keys for each round, a "masking key" and a "rotation key." The masking key is combined with the block's data through either modular addition, modular subtraction, or an XOR, then shifted the number of bits dictated by the rotation key. Each round uses one of three encryption functions; the functions combine the output of the S-boxes through the use of modular addition, subtraction, and XOR, with the order of the three operations dictated by which function is to be applied to the particular round.

The International Data Encryption Algorithm (IDEA) [24, 25] is the brainchild of Xuejia Lai and James L. Massey of the Swiss Federal Institute of Technology. It is an eight-round cipher with a blocksize of 64 bytes (512 bits) and a key length of 128 bits. It differs from the other ESP ciphers in several particulars: it is a non-Feistel cipher, and its use is patented. Each of the eight rounds uses six subkeys and involves a series of XORs, modular additions, and modular multiplications, combining the subkeys with portions of the input block or results of previous round calculations. Following the final round, an additional step uses four more subkeys. Although it is not a Feistel cipher, it is designed so that the encryption and decryption operations are the same; the decryption is accomplished using different subkeys, generated from the encryption subkeys.

RC5 [26], which is the creation of Ronald Rivest of MIT, is a straightforward and elegant cipher that can be used with a variety of key sizes, blocksizes, and number of rounds. The version of RC5 specified for use with ESP has a key of 128 bits, a blocksize of 64 bits, and 16 rounds. A hallmark of RC5 is data-dependent rotation, which is the left circular rotation of one data element by a variable number of bits, according to the value of another data element. The round functions combine those data-dependent rotations, XORs, and modular addition.

The NULL encryption algorithm is the means through which the ESP header can be used to provide authentication without encryption. It is defined in a tongue-in-cheek manner in RFC 2410, which describes its history, performance (stellar, naturally), and potential usage unencumbered by patents or other intellectual property limitations.

4.3.4 The AES Algorithm

The DES algorithm is approaching the end of a long and glorious career. To select its replacement, the Adanced Encryption Standard (AES), NIST conducted a multiyear competition, first announced in January 1997. Of the 15 ciphers that were submitted as AES candidates in August 1998, 5 were designated as finalists: MARS [27], RC6 [28], Rijndael [29], Serpent [30, 31], and Twofish [32, 33]. All the finalists have a blocksize of 128 bits and can handle key sizes of 128, 192, and 256 bits. Public analysis, discussion, and comparison of the candidates continued until the final selection was made.

Rijndael was chosen as the AES on October 2, 2000. It has a variable key size and consists of either 10, 12, or 14 encryption rounds, depending on the size of the key. Each round consists of four steps: byte substitution using a single S box; column mixing; shifting rows over a variable offset; and

XORing with the round key. The choice was made on the basis of security; computational efficiency and memory requirements on a variety of software and hardware, including smart cards; flexibility; and simplicity. The AES will be the government's designated encryption cipher for sensitive, nonclassified information. It undoubtedly will be widely adopted for use by businesses and financial institutions. The IPsec working group most likely will declare the AES [34] to be a mandatory encryption algorithm for the ESP header.

NIST has also defined three new hash algorithms that are appropriate for use with the three key sizes required for AES and that will replace SHA-1 as the government's standard hash. They are SHA-256, SHA-384, and SHA-512 [35, 36]; each generates a hash whose length in bits is commensurate with the hash's name. NIST is also considering whether to define new chaining modes to replace or supplement those defined for DES [37]. Federal Information Processing Standards (FIPS) will be issued for AES, the updated SHA hashes, and the modes of operation.

4.4 Complications

The block ciphers used for ESP, other than DES, generally are considered to be safe from brute force attacks and other known attacks. However, there is one attack that can be applied to messages that are encrypted but not authenticated [38, 39]. If a message is sent from host H1 to host H2, under certain circumstances an attacker can devise a cut-and-paste attack that results in the attacker's ability to retrieve the unencrypted message. Three conditions are necessary for such an attack: the hosts are multiuser machines, the attacker has user accounts on both hosts, and there is a host-oriented SA between the hosts. In such a case, an attacker can retrieve an outgoing, encrypted message from H1 to H2 and insert the encrypted portion of the message into a new message to be sent from the attacker's account on H1 to the attacker's account on H2. Each block of a message that is encrypted with a block cipher needs three pieces of information to be successfully decrypted: the encrypted block itself, the secret key, and the preceding encrypted block. Thus, every block of the compound message sent by the attacker will decipher correctly, except the first block of the purloined message.

Figure 4.8 illustrates the cut-and-paste attack. The only block of the attacker's compound message that will not decipher correctly is the first block of the original user's TCP header. The data portion of the original message is intact and will decipher perfectly. Cut-and-paste attacks can be prevented if all encrypted messages are also authenticated. The newly

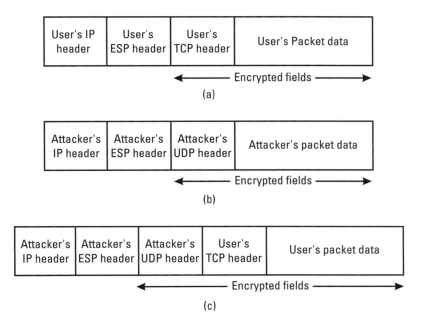

Figure 4.8 The cut-and-paste attack: (a) user's original message; (b) attacker's original message; (c) attacker's compound message.

constructed message will not authenticate correctly on receipt at host H2; therefore, the IPsec routines will not even attempt decryption. The authentication can be applied as part of the ESP SA that provides the encryption, or it can be applied through the use of a separate AH SA. Another way to frustrate a cut-and-paste attack is through the use of user-oriented, rather than host-oriented, SAs on multiuser machines.

4.5 Public Key Cryptography

The cryptographic algorithms that have been presented so far all depend on the use of a single shared or *symmetric key* by both parties involved in the communication. That necessitates the sharing or exchange of the key, which is a tricky business (more on that in Chapter 5). Other algorithms, known as *public key* algorithms, involve two mathematically related keys, the public key and the private key. Public-private key pairs can be used for a number of purposes: for digital signatures, for encryption, and for the exchange or transport of symmetric keys. Why not use public key algorithms in AH and ESP headers and simplify the key distribution nightmare? Unfortunately, public key algorithms are significantly more resource intensive than symmetric key algorithms, so they are not a practical alternative in today's technology.

However, public key cryptography is used for several different purposes by IPsec's key negotiation protocol, IKE.

4.5.1 Digital Signatures

A written signature can be used to prove that a communication was authorized by the signer. Similarly, if an entity, E1, wants to prove that it actually sent a specific communication, E1's digital signature can be used for that purpose. E1 hashes the contents of the message and signs the hash with E1's private key. The peer, E2, verifies the signed hash using E1's public key; the verification constitutes proof of E1's identity. One of the methods used by IKE to authenticate the communicating peers to each other is digital signatures. If E2 can verify a hash signed by E1, then E2 is assured that the communicating peer is indeed E1. If E1 and E2 exchange digitally signed hashes, then they have mutually authenticated each other's identity. The digital signature algorithms that can be used with IKE are RSA [40] and DSA [41].

4.5.2 Other Public Key Operations

Public-private key pairs can be used for encryption and decryption. Besides transmitting the encrypted value in a secure and private manner, the encryption/decryption operations can also constitute proof of the sender's or the recipient's identity. E1 encrypts a message, or a portion of a message, with E1's private key. If E2 can successfully decrypt the message with E1's public key, the decryption constitutes proof of E1's identity. Thus, another method used by IKE to authenticate the communicating peers to each other is through the use of public key encryption. If E1 can use E2's public key to successfully decrypt a message that was encrypted with E2's private key, then E1 is assured that the communicating peer is E2. If E1 and E2 exchange messages, each of which is encrypted with the peers' private key, then they have mutually authenticated each other's identity. The public key encryption algorithms that can be used with IKE are RSA [40] and El-Gamal [42, 43].

4.5.3 The Diffie-Hellman Exchange

Another technique closely allied with public key technology and used by IKE is the Diffie-Hellman exchange. In this ingenious method, two peers, E1 and

E2, can send information across an unprotected public network. If E1 and E2 each sends its public values to the other, E1 can then combine E2's public value with a private value known only to E1, and E2 can combine E1's public value with a private value known only to E2. The results of the two peers' computations are identical, with the result that E1 and E2 have used a public channel to compute, in a perfectly secure manner, a shared secret value.

A Diffie-Hellman exchange can be based on one of two types of computations: modular exponentiation or elliptic curves. In the case of modular exponentiation, the peers' computations involve exponentiation of extremely large numbers, modulo another very large number. In the case of elliptic curves, the computations involve the addition of two points on the curve, which yields another point on the curve. In both cases, the reason an attacker cannot use the publicly available information to compute the shared secret rests on the mathematical difficulty of computing inverse logarithms of large numbers. Today's computers are capable of raising a number to an extremely large power, of multiplying extremely large numbers, and of completing such operations within a reasonable time frame. The inverse operations, however—computing the inverse logarithm or factoring an extremely large number—cannot be accomplished within the requisite time frame necessary to exploit the keys unearthed in such a manner.

Once a Diffie-Hellman exchange has been completed, the two parties to the exchange possess a secret key known only to them. That key can be used as a symmetric key to encrypt communications between the peers. A more common technique for the derivation of the symmetric key is to use the shared secret as one of the building blocks but not the sole determinant of the key. The shared secret, along with other information, is plugged into a keyed hash algorithm, and the output of the hash is used as the secret key. If the required key is longer than the hash output, an iterative computation is used to "boost" the size of the available keying material. This is the technique used by IKE to compute the keys used for the AH and the ESP header. Chapter 5 examines the other pieces of data that are fed into the hash in addition to the Diffie-Hellman shared secret.

One advantage of this technique is that one Diffie-Hellman exchange, which involves a number of computationally expensive calculations, can be used to generate keys for multiple IPsec SAs. There is, however, a downside to that economy. If an attacker discovers the shared secret, sometimes referred to as the long-term key, all the traffic that was protected by symmetric keys generated from that long-term key can be in jeopardy. To avoid that, an additional Diffie-Hellman exchange may be performed each time a new symmetric key is required. If that is done, the discovery of the long-term key

will not jeopardize traffic that was protected by any of the subsequently calculated symmetric keys. This additional insurance is known as *perfect forward
secrecy*.

4.6 Conclusion

This chapter discussed the cryptographic algorithms used for authentication
and encryption in both the AH and the ESP header. It also introduced the
public key techniques used as building blocks in IKE. Now we are ready to
tackle the most complex and complicated part of IPsec: key negotiation, establishment, deletion, and reestablishment, all of which are handled by IKE.

4.7 Further Reading

For complete descriptions of the theoretical underpinnings, mechanics, and
computations of various cryptographic algorithms, techniques, and flaws,
see Schneier [2] or Menezes [1]. The hash algorithms MD5 and SHA-1 are
defined in [7] and in [8], respectively. HMAC is described and analyzed
in [9, 10]. The application of HMAC-MD5 to IPsec is defined in [11];
HMAC-SHA-1 for IPsec is described in [12]. The RIPEMD-160 hash algorithm is introduced in [13]; its use in IPsec is explicated in [44].

The encryption algorithm DES, its modes, and its implementation
are documented in [17–19]; its application to the ESP header is described
in [16], and its downfall in [20]. Triple DES is defined in [17], CAST-128
in [23], RC5 in [26], IDEA in [24, 25], and Blowfish in [21, 22]. Weak keys
for IDEA are discussed in [45] and those for DES in [2]. The application of
CBC Mode to the ESP header is found in [3], which explicitly applies to
Blowfish, DES, Triple DES, CAST-128, IDEA, and RC5, but by inference
it can apply to any encryption algorithm with a blocksize and IV length of
64 bytes. AES (Rijndael) is defined in [29].

With regard to the other AES finalists, MARS is described in [27],
RC6 in [28], Serpent in [30, 31], and Twofish in [32, 33]. The use of AES
and the other AES finalists in IPsec is explained in [34]. SHA-256,
SHA-384, and SHA-512 are defined in [35]. RSA digital signatures and
public key encryption are defined in [40]. The DSA is described in [41].
El-Gamal public key encryption is introduced in [42, 43]. Schneier [2]
explains numerous other public key techniques and applications. The
successful attack on MD5 is explained in [5], the DES-cracking industry is

described in [20], and other potential IPsec attacks and vulnerabilities are revealed in [38, 39, 46]. Recommended cipher key lengths, circa 1995, are prescribed in [47].

References

[1] Menezes, A., P. Van Oorschot, and S. Vanstone, *Handbook of Applied Cryptography*, CRC Press, Boca Raton, Florida, 1997.

[2] Schneier, B., *Applied Cryptography: Protocols, Algorithms and Source Code in C.* 2nd Ed., New York: Wiley, 1995.

[3] Pereira, R., and R. Adams, *The ESP CBC-Mode Cipher Algorithms*, RFC 2451, Nov. 1998.

[4] Atkinson, R., *The IP Authentication Header*, RFC 1826, Aug. 1995 (obsolete).

[5] Dobbertin, H., "The Status of MD5 After a Recent Attack," *RSA Laboratories' CryptoBytes*, Vol. 2, No. 2, Summer 1996, http://www.rsa.com/rsalabs/pubs/cryptobytes.html.

[6] Kent, S., and R. Atkinson, *The IP Authentication Header*, RFC 2402, Nov. 1998.

[7] Rivest, R., *MD5 Digest Algorithm*, RFC 1321, Apr. 1992.

[8] NIST, *Secure Hash Standard*, FIPS Pub. 180-1, Apr. 1995, http://csrc.nist.gov/fips/fip180-1.{txt,ps}.

[9] Bellare, M., R. Canetti, and H. Krawczyk, "Keyed Hash Functions and Message Authentication," *Proc. Crypto '96*, LNCS V. 1109, Springer-Verlag, Heidelberg, Germany, 1996, pp. 1–15, http://www.research.ibm.com/security/keyed-md5.html.

[10] Krawczyk, H., M. Bellare, and R. Canetti, *HMAC: Keyed-Hashing for Message Authentication*, RFC 2104, Feb. 1997.

[11] Madson, C., and R. Glenn, *The Use of HMAC-MD5-96 Within ESP and AH*, RFC 2403, Nov. 1998.

[12] Madson, C., and R. Glenn, *The Use of HMAC-SHA-1-96 Within ESP and AH*, RFC 2404, Nov. 1998.

[13] Dobbertin, H., A. Bosselaers, and B. Preneel, "RIPEMD-160: A Strengthened Version of RIPEMD," *Fast Software Encryption—Cambridge Workshop*, LNCS V. 1039, Springer-Verlag, Heidelberg, Germany, 1996, pp. 71–82, ftp://ftp.esat.kuleuven.ac.be/pub/COSIC/bosselae/ripemd/.

[14] Bellovin, S., and V. Gligor, "An iaPCBC Transform for IPsec," <draft-bellovin-iapcbc-00.txt>, Nov. 1999.

[15]   Gligor, V., and P. Donescu, "Integrity-Aware PCBC Encryption Schemes," *7th International Workshop on Security Protocols*, Cambridge, Eng., Apr. 1999, http://www.research.att.com/~smb/papers/iapcbc.ps.

[16]   Madson, C., and N. Doraswamy, *The ESP DES-CBC Cipher Algorithm With Explicit IV*, RFC 2405, Nov. 1998.

[17]   National Institute of Standards and Technology (NIST), *Data Encryption Standard (DES)*, FIPS Pub. 46-3, Jan. 1999.

[18]   National Institute of Standards and Technology (NIST), *DES Modes of Operation*, FIPS Pub. 81, Dec. 1980.

[19]   National Institute of Standards and Technology (NIST), *Guidelines for Implementing and Using the NBS Data Encryption Standard*, FIPS Pub. 74, Apr. 1981.

[20]   Electronic Frontier Foundation, *Cracking DES: Secrets of Encryption Research, Wiretap Politics & Chip Design*, O'Reilly, Cambridge, MA, July 1998, http://cryptome.org/cracking-des.htm.

[21]   Schneier, B., "The Blowfish Encryption Algorithm—One Year Later," *Dr. Dobb's Journal*, Sep. 1995, http://www.counterpane.com/bfdobsoyl.html.

[22]   Schneier, B., "Description of a New Variable-Length Key, 64-Bit Block Cipher (Blowfish)," *Fast Software Encryption, Cambridge Security Workshop Proc.*, Springer-Verlag, 1994, pp. 191–204, http://www.counterpane.com/bfsverlag.html.

[23]   Adams, C., *The CAST-128 Encryption Algorithm*, RFC 2144, 1997.

[24]   Lai, X., "On the Design and Security of Block Ciphers," *ETH Series in Information Processing*, Vol. 1, Hartung-Gorre Verlag, Kostanz, Switzerland, 1992.

[25]   Lai, X., and J. Massey, "A Proposal for a New Block Encryption Standard," *Advances in Cryptology—Eurocypt '90*, LNCS V. 473, Springer-Verlag, Heidelberg, Germany, 1991, pp. 389-404.

[26]   Baldwin, R., and R. Rivest, *The RC5, RC5-CBC, RC5-CBC-Pad, and RC5-CTS Algorithms*, RFC 2040, Oct. 1996.

[27]   Burwick, C., et al., "MARS—A Candidate Cipher for AES," *NIST AES Proposal*, June 1998, http://www.research.ibm.com/security/mars.{pdf,ps}.

[28]   Rivest, R., et al., "The RC6™ Block Cipher," *NIST AES Proposal*, June 1998, http://csrc.nist.gov/encryption/aes/round2/AESAlgs/RC6/cipher.pdf, http://www.rsasecurity.com/rsalabs/aes/.

[29]   Daemen, J., and V. Rijman, "AES Proposal: Rijndael," *NIST AES Proposal*, Jun 1998, http://csrc.nist.gov/encryption/aes/round2/AESAlgs/Rijndael/Rijndael.pdf, http://www.esat.kuleuven.ac.be/~rijmen/rijndael/.

[30]   Anderson, R., E. Biham, and L. Knudsen, "Serpent: A Proposal for the Advanced Encryption Standard," *NIST AES Proposal*, June 1998, http://csrc.nist.gov/encryption/aes/round2/AESAlgs/Serpent/Serpent.pdf, http://www.cl.cam.ac.uk/~rjal4/serpent.html.

[31]   Biham, E., R. Anderson, and L. Knudsen, "Serpent: A New Block Cipher Proposal," *Fast Software Encryption—FSE98*, Springer LNCS V. 1372, Springer-Verlag, Heidelberg, Germany, 1998, pp. 222–238.

[32]   Schneier, B., et al., "Twofish: A 128-Bit Block Cipher," *NIST AES Proposal*, June 1998, http://csrc.nist.gov/encryption/aes/round2/AESAlgs/Twofish/Twofish.pdf, http://www.counterpane.com/twofish.html.

[33]   Schneier, B., et al., *The Twofish Encryption Algorithm: A 128-Bit Block Cipher*, New York: Wiley, 1999.

[34]   Frankel, S., R. Glenn, and S. Kelly, "The AES Cipher Algorithm and Its Use With IPsec," <draft-ietf-ipsec-ciph-aes-cbc-01.txt>, Nov. 2000.

[35]   National Institute of Standards and Technology (NIST), "Descriptions of SHA-256, SHA-384, and SHA-512," http://csrc.nist.gov/cryptval/shs/sha256-384-512.{pdf,ps}, Oct. 12, 2000.

[36]   National Institute of Standards and Technology (NIST), "Secure Hash Standard (SHS)," http://www.nist.gov/sha, Oct. 12, 2000.

[37]   National Institute of Standards and Technology (NIST), "Symmetric Key Block Cipher Modes of Operation," http://www.nist.gov/modes, Oct., 2000.

[38]   Bellovin, S., "An Issue With DES-CBC When Used Without Strong Integrity," *Proc. 32nd IETF*, Danvers, MA, Apr. 1995.

[39]   Bellovin, S., "Problem Areas for the IP Security Protocols," *Proc. 6th Usenix UNIX Security Symposium*, San Jose, CA, July 1996, pp. 205–214, http://www.research.att.com/~smb/papers/badesp.{ps, pdf}.

[40]   Kaliski, B., *PKCS #1: RSA Encryption Version 1.5*, RFC 2313, Mar. 1998.

[41]   National Institute of Standards and Technology (NIST), *Digital Signature Standard*, FIPS Pub. 186-1, Dec. 1998.

[42]   El Gamal, T., "A Public-Key Cryptosystem and a Signature Scheme Based on Discrete Logarithms," *Advances in Cryptology: CRYPTO 84 Proc.*, LNCS V. 196, Springer-Verlag, Heidelberg, Germany, 1985, pp. 10–18.

[43]   El Gamal, T., "A Public-Key Cryptosystem and a Signature Scheme Based on Discrete Logarithms," *IEEE Trans. on Information Theory*, Vol. IT-31. No. 4, 1985, pp. 469–472.

[44]   Keromytis, A., and N. Provos, "The Use of HMAC-RIPEMD-160-96 Within ESP and AH," <draft-ietf-ipsec-auth-hmac-ripemd-160-96-04.txt>, Sep. 1999.

[45]   Daemen, J., R. Govaerts, and J. Vandewalle, "Weak Keys for IDEA," *Advances in Cryptology, CRYPTO '93 Proc.*, LNCS V. 77 Springer-Verlag, Heidelberg, Germany, 1994, pp. 224–230.

[46]   Bellovin, S., "Probable Plaintext Cryptanalysis of the IP Security Protocols," *Proc. Symposium on Network and Distributed System Security*, San Diego, CA, Feb. 1997, pp. 155–160. http://www.research.att.com/~smb/papers/probtxt.{ps, pdf}.

[47]   Blaze, M., et al., "Minimal Key Lengths for Symmetric Ciphers to Provide Adequate Commercial Security: A Report by an Ad Hoc Group of Cryptographers and Computer Scientists," Jan. 1996, http://www.bsa.org/policy/encryption/cryptographers_c.html.

5

The Fourth Puzzle Piece: The Internet Key Exchange (IKE)

> No one can truly be called an entomologist, sir; the subject is too vast for any single human intelligence to grasp.
>
> *Oliver Wendell Holmes, The Poet at the Breakfast Table*

So far, we have not addressed the derivation of the symmetric keys used for IPsec encryption and authentication or the mechanism through which the communicating peers agree on the algorithms, key sizes, and other minutiae critical to the successful functioning of the IPsec SAs. Wizardry, extrasensory perception, and carrier pigeons have their limitations, hence the need for IKE.

5.1 The IKE Two-Step Dance

The goal of any IKE [1–4] implementation is to negotiate an IPsec SA with a peer. That is accomplished through a two-phase negotiation: Phase 1 establishes an Internet Security Association and Key Management Protocol (ISAKMP) SA [3], which is a secure channel through which the IPsec SA negotiation can take place. Phase 2 establishes the actual IPsec SA or, more precisely, a pair of one-way IPsec SAs: an inbound SA and an outbound SA.

The establishment of the ISAKMP SA can be accomplished through the completion of one of several different phase 1 exchanges, also referred to as modes: Main Mode, Aggressive Mode, or Base Mode. Each mode is defined as a series of messages, which consist of multiple payloads and headers. The only phase 2 exchange that has been defined is Quick Mode. In phase 1, each participant assumes a distinct role: The party that sends the first message is called the initiator, and the peer is called the responder. In phase 2 or subsequent negotiations, the roles can be reversed.

Several other exchanges have been defined that perform other IKE-related functions but that do not qualify as either phase 1 or phase 2 exchanges: New Groups Mode, Unacknowledged Notification exchanges, and Acknowledged Notification exchanges. We first describe the basic building blocks and concepts underlying IKE and then describe the function of each building block within the compound objects that make up IKE.

5.2 Payloads and Exchanges

Each IKE negotiation is made up of a predefined set of messages that must be exchanged by the peers; the building blocks that make up each message are called payloads. For each message, IKE specifies the mandatory payloads; in general, the ordering of the payloads within the message is not significant, with a few exceptions. In addition to the mandatory payloads, there are a number of optional payloads. In most of the messages, the mandatory payloads sent by the initiator, containing initiator-specific information, will be returned by the responder, containing responder-specific information.

Every IKE message is preceded by a standard header; each payload within the message begins with a generic payload header. The contents of those headers are discussed later in this chapter. First, let us address a number of issues and problems that need to be handled by any key negotiation application, IKE's approach to such matters, and the payloads that carry that information.

5.3 Authentication Methods

In an IKE negotiation, it is essential that each party prove its identity to its peer; this process is called peer authentication. If the peer's identity is in doubt or conceivably could be falsified, then the whole SA negotiation process is worthless. Even if it results in an SA through which secure,

IPsec-protected traffic is exchanged, the entity receiving the protected traffic could be the very attacker from whom the traffic needs to be protected! Three authentication methods are used in IKE: preshared secret key, digital signatures, and public key encryption. Each method hinges on the peer's knowledge and use of some form of specialized information; the methods differ in the nature of the information, the way in which that information is obtained, and its use within the IKE negotiation.

Preshared secret key authentication relies on information—the pre-shared secret key—that is known only to the parties to the negotiation. The method through which the information is exchanged is unspecified but lies outside the realm of the IKE negotiation itself. The exchange method must be secure, however, because knowledge of the preshared secret key is the sole proof of identity. The peers use that information to generate symmetric keys, which are used to encrypt and authenticate the IKE messages. The information is also used to generate additional keying material that, ultimately, will be used in conjunction with the IPsec SA. The successful encryption and decryption of the IKE messages serve as proof of possession of the preshared secret key. The term *preshared secret key* can be somewhat confusing, but it is a different entity entirely from the symmetric secret keys connected to the eventual IPsec SA.

The biggest drawback to preshared secret key authentication is the lack of a secure and scalable method of exchanging preshared secret keys. It is usable in a small-scale environment with a moderate number of systems in which the set of peers is known in advance. However, if a preshared secret key is compromised, there is no universal method of notifying the peer and establishing a replacement.

The other two authentication methods, digital signatures and public key encryption (introduced in Chapter 4), can potentially remedy that draw-back. These methods require each peer to possess a public-private key pair. Each party uses its private key to sign or decrypt information; the other party uses the corresponding public key to verify or encrypt the information, thus authenticating the peer's identity. If the public keys are retrievable from a secure repository (more on that in Chapter 10), keys can be readily accessed and updated. In addition, any peers whose keys reside on the same repository or who trust each other's repositories (that, too, will be discussed in Chapter 10) can freely initiate IKE exchanges using these authentication methods with no prior special arrangement.

IKE peer authentication via public key encryption, as originally defined, requires each peer to perform two separate public key encryptions and decryptions. A revised mode of public key authentication was proposed that replaces two of the public key operations performed by each party (one encryption and one decryption) with symmetric key operations, which are computationally less demanding. Why are both methods still part of IKE? The answer lies in ancient IPsec history. Because the original public key authentication method was already in use in operational IPsec implementations, it was retained but the revised method was also adopted.

The two public key–based authentication methods, digital signature and public key encryption, use different public key operations to assert and verify the peer's identity. The first employs digital signature (with the peer's private key) and verification (with the peer's public key). The second uses public key encryption (with the peer's public key) and decryption (with the peer's private key). The content, order, and usage of the IKE payloads also dictate another difference. For digital signature authentication, the certificates containing the peers' public keys can be exchanged as part of the IKE negotiation. For public key authentication, the certificates must be obtained prior to the IKE exchange. That can be accomplished via retrieval from a public key infrastructure (PKI), as part of another IKE exchange, or by some other method. Until Chapter 10, a PKI will remain a murky creature that lurks somewhere on the Internet. For our purposes here, this chapter considers a PKI to be an entity that can generate certificates, store them in a secure manner, and vouch for their authenticity and timeliness.

5.4   Proposals and Counterproposals

The concept of proposing and selecting the protection suites that constitute an SA is straightforward, but the IKE terminology is full of terms that are used in multiple contexts, some of which are counterintuitive. In both phase 1 and phase 2, the SA's potential characteristics are described in an SA payload. The SA payload is a multilayered payload that contains one or more proposal payloads, each of which contains one or more transform payloads. Each transform payload defines the specific algorithms, negotiation mechanisms, and policy that characterize the SA; each entity contained within the transform payload is called an *attribute*. The totality of the SA payload sent by the initiator is a series of alternative combinations of the attributes to be negotiated. Each series of attributes collectively characterizes the operation and longevity of a particular proposed SA.

In phase 1, the initiator proposes one or more alternative collections of attributes. This takes the form of a single SA payload, containing a single proposal payload, which in turn contains one or more transform payloads.

Here is where the terminology confusion sets in. The proposal payload contains one or more proposals that define the different forms of ISAKMP SA that the initiator is willing to negotiate. However, each proposal is contained within a single transform payload. Figure 5.1 shows the attributes that might appear in a sample initiator proposal. Each row of the table constitutes a proposal. The responder selects one of the rows and sends that proposal back to the initiator. The responder's SA payload will contain an SA payload, containing a single proposal payload, which contains a single transform payload, a copy of one of the transform payloads that was sent by the initiator. This is the method used by the responder to indicate which of the initiator's proposals is preferable; the chosen one then becomes the basis for the ISAKMP SA negotiated in phase 1. The phase 1 attributes that are open to negotiation are as follows.

- *Encryption algorithm* (and *key length*). The algorithm to be used to encrypt all IKE messages once the secret key is established. The mandatory-to-implement algorithm is DES_CBC. If an encryption algorithm with a variable length key (e.g., BLOWFISH) is selected, then the key length must also be negotiated.

- *Hash algorithm*. The keyed hash algorithm to be used in some of the IKE calculations; if no pseudo-random function (PRF) is negotiated, the HMAC form of the hash algorithm is also used to generate the key material and to authenticate all IKE messages once the secret key is established. The mandatory-to-implement hash algorithms are MD5 and SHA-1.

- *Authentication method*. The method through which the peers mutually authenticate each other's identity (preshared key, digital signatures, public key original mode, or public key revised mode). The mandatory-to-implement authentication method is preshared key.

Proposal #	Transform #	Enc Alg	Hash Alg	Auth Method	DH Group #	Lifetime in Sec	Lifetime in KB
1	1	Triple DES	SHA-1	Digital signature	5	3,600	—
1	2	DES	MD5	Public key (original)	1	1,800	1,000

Figure 5.1 Sample phase 1 initiator proposal.

- *Group description, type, prime, generator(s), curve(s), order, field size.*
  The values that define the specifics of the Diffie-Hellman exchange
  that will establish the shared secret used in the generation of the key
  material. The mandatory-to-implement group (group 1) is a modular exponentiation (MODP) group with a generator of 2 and the
  following prime:

$$2^{768} - 2^{704} - 1 + 2^{64} * [(2^{638} \pi) + 149686]$$

  There are three other predefined groups: another MODP group
  (group 2) with a different prime and two elliptic curve groups
  (groups 3 and 4). The group-description attribute is used to specify
  which of the four groups will be used. It is recommended that
  implementations support group 2. In practice, that is the default
  group for most implementations.
      It also is possible to negotiate groups with different defining
  characteristics. In that case, the group-type attribute is used to specify whether the group is an MODP group or an elliptic curve
  group. The group-prime and group-generator attributes are used to
  define a new MODP group; the group-prime, group-generator,
  group-curve, group-order, and field-size attributes are used to
  define a new elliptic curve group.

- *Life type, life duration.* Attributes that specify whether the duration
  of the phase 1 SA will be measured in seconds or kilobytes and that
  give the numeric value of the SA's duration in the specified measure
  (seconds or kilobytes). There are no default values for life type and
  life duration. Life type can be specified as both seconds and kilobytes for a single SA, in which case the SA expires when either one
  of the lifetimes is reached. An SA that is authenticated through the
  use of a certificate should not last beyond the certificate's expiration
  date or, possibly, beyond the time the next certificate revocation list
  (CRL) is issued.

- *PRF.* Keyed pseudo-random function used to generate the key
  material and to authenticate all IKE messages once the secret key is
  established. There is no mandatory-to-implement PRF and no predefined values for this attribute; unless the peers agree to a privately
  defined PRF, the default PRF is the HMAC version of the negotiated hash function.

In phase 2, the SA proposals can be more complex, because the initiator needs to be able to propose an SA bundle in situations where more than one SA (e.g., an AH SA and an ESP SA) is required to protect the same traffic. An initiator's phase 2 SA payload can contain one or more proposal payloads, each of which contains one or more transform payloads. When multiple proposal payloads are identified by the same proposal number, they represent a single SA bundle, which results in the negotiation of multiple IPsec SA pairs. When multiple proposal payloads are identified by different proposal numbers, they represent a series of alternative proposals for a single SA, which results in the negotiation of a single IPsec SA pair. If any proposal contains more than one transform payload, these always represent alternatives. The responder then selects one proposal (to negotiate a single pair of IPsec SAs) or one proposal group (to negotiate an SA bundle). Within each proposal, the responder selects the single transform payload that contains its preferred combination of attributes. The following phase 2 attributes are open to negotiation.

- *Life type, life duration:* Attributes that specify whether the duration of the phase 2 SA will be measured in seconds or kilobytes and the SA's duration in the specified measure (seconds or kilobytes). There are no default values for these attributes. Life type can be specified as both seconds and kilobytes for a single SA, in which case the SA expires when either one of the lifetimes is reached.

- *Group description:* A value that defines the specifics of the optional phase 2 Diffie-Hellman exchange that will establish the shared secret(s) used in the generation of the key material if perfect forward secrecy (PFS) of keys is desired. PFS is a guarantee that only one key has been generated from a single Diffie-Hellman exchange and that that key has no relationship to any other keys used between the peers. The predefined groups are the same as those used for phase 1. It also is possible to negotiate groups with different defining characteristics. If a New Group Mode exchange previously has occurred between the peers, that newly defined group may be used.

- *Encapsulation Mode.* Describes whether the SA will be a Transport Mode SA or a Tunnel Mode SA.

- *Authentication algorithm.* The keyed hash algorithm to be used if the SA is to provide authentication. This is mandatory for an AH SA or an ESP SA whose encryption algorithm is ESP_NULL but optional for an ESP SA whose encryption algorithm is not ESP_NULL. The mandatory-to-implement authentication algorithms are HMAC-MD5 and HMAC-SHA.

- *Key length.* An attribute that must be negotiated for an ESP SA whose encryption algorithm takes a variable length key (e.g., Blowfish).

- *Key rounds.* For an ESP SA whose encryption algorithm key can be calculated with a variable number of rounds, the number of key rounds must be negotiated.

- *Compress dictionary size.* If the SA is to provide traffic compression, the maximum dictionary size must be negotiated.

- *Compress private algorithm.* If the SA is to provide traffic compression, the compression algorithm must be negotiated.

Proposals are always sent as part of an SA payload. The SA payload generally is required to be the first message payload. Phase 2 messages always begin with an authenticating hash payload; in this case, the SA payload is the first payload following the hash payload.

5.5 Cookies

During the course of a phase 1 negotiation, the peers conduct a Diffie-Hellman exchange, resulting in the calculation of a shared secret (a totally different kind of beast from the similarly named preshared secret key), which is used to calculate shared symmetric keys. It is prudent to verify, prior to performing the Diffie-Hellman calculations, that the peer actually exists and is interested in conducting an IKE exchange. In some of the IKE exchanges, verification is accomplished through the exchange of cookies. Each peer generates a unique, possibly pseudo-random value and sends it to the other party. Once the cookie exchange has taken place, each party is assured that the other party exists and is willing to respond. The cookie pair (the initiator cookie and the responder cookie) incorporates part of the ISAKMP header attached to almost every message. The only exception is the first phase 1 message, which contains only the initiator cookie, since the responder cookie has not yet been received.

An effective denial-of-service attack is one in which the attacker spoofs a variety of source addresses and sends multiple IKE negotiation requests to the victim. If the victim were to begin churning away at Diffie-Hellman calculations in response to each such request, without any sort of verification of the attacker's existence and intentions, the victim's system would quickly be swamped with those expensive calculations and unable to perform other, more useful work. The cookie calculations require less computational energy than the Diffie-Hellman calculations, preventing this type of denial-of-service attack. Of course, the responder still needs to exercise care, since a large enough number of cookie calculations also could overwhelm a system.

If the cookies contain a time-dependent value, they can be used to prevent replay attacks, in which the attacker attempts to resend messages from previously negotiated SAs.

The chief virtue of a cookie exchange is also its downside: the necessity to exchange two full messages prior to the Diffie-Hellman exchange. In IKE, that is mitigated in two ways. The two cookies, the initiator's cookie and the responder's cookie, are used as the identifying index of the phase 1 SA (analogous to the SPI of an IPsec SA), both during the SA negotiation and once the SA has been established. In addition, the messages that constitute the cookie exchange are used to negotiate the particulars of the SA itself.

5.6 The Security Association Payload

The SA payload itself contains the following fields:

- *Domain of interpretation* (DOI). The content, format, and interpretation of several types of data (e.g., addresses) are dependent on the DOI for those data. Currently, the IPsec DOI is the only DOI other than the generic ISAKMP DOI that has been specified. A phase 1 SA whose DOI is generic ISAKMP can be used to negotiate phase 2 SAs for any other DOI; a phase 1 SA whose DOI is IPsec can be used only to negotiate phase 2 IPsec SAs. A phase 2 IPsec SA always has a DOI of IPsec.

- *Situation.* For the IPsec DOI, the situation indicates whether standard IPsec ID payloads are sufficient to identify the peers to each other or some type of compartment secrecy or integrity labels are required.

5.7 The Proposal Payload

Each Proposal payload has two fields that define the general nature and access index of the proposed SA.

- *Protocol ID*. In phase 1, the protocol ID is ISAKMP, because an ISAKMP SA is being negotiated; in phase 2, it can be IPsec AH (for an AH SA), IPsec ESP (for an ESP SA), or IPCOMP (for a compression header).
- *SPI.* The SPI is the unique key used to access or identify the SA.

The phase 1 ISAKMP SA's SPI consists of the initiator's cookie followed by the responder's cookie. It is used by all messages subsequent to phase 1 (e.g., phase 2 messages, new group messages, and informational messages) that will use the phase 1 ISAKMP SA for protection.

The phase 2 IPsec SA's SPI is generated by each peer and, together with the protocol ID and the destination address, uniquely identifies the IPsec SA. This identification tuple (SPI, protocol, destination) appears in all traffic covered by the IPsec SA. (The responder's SPI is used in conjunction with the initiator's outbound SA for traffic from initiator to responder; the initiator's SPI is used in conjunction with the responder's outbound SA for traffic from responder to initiator.)

5.8   The Message ID

A single ISAKMP SA can be used as the umbrella under which multiple IPsec SAs are negotiated. A mechanism is needed to distinguish the messages related to one such phase 2 SA from another. That is the function of the message ID, which is part of the ISAKMP header. In phase 1, the message ID is always zero; in phase 2, it is a random number unique to its particular SA. In that way, a single ISAKMP SA can be used to negotiate several IPsec SAs between two peers; the IPsec SAs can operate either simultaneously or consecutively. Multiple simultaneous SAs can be used to protect several different types of traffic, each requiring a different level of cryptographic protection, between the peers. If the ISAKMP SA has a longer lifetime than the IPsec SA, a single ISAKMP SA can be used to negotiate consecutively a successor to an IPsec SA that is about to expire.

5.9   Nonces

A nonce is a randomly generated value that is used in IKE to provide proof of either "liveness" [3] or "liveliness" [1, 2]. Whether it is used to demonstrate bare existence or more creative activity, its intent is to prevent an attacker from replaying a previous IKE negotiation, either phase 1 or phase 2. Much of the content of an SA negotiation does not vary from one negotiation to the next. The proposed protection suite most likely will remain constant, as will the identities of the peers. If it were possible simply to replay a previous negotiation, the peer could be fooled into reestablishing an expired SA, providing additional exposure for the secret keys. To prevent that, in every negotiation each peer generates a new random nonce; both peers then compute a cryptographic hash of both nonces. Because a replay of a previous negotiation will not include the peer's newly generated nonce, it will fail.

The actual usage of the nonce is different in phase 1 and phase 2. In phase 1, the hashed nonces are used with other information to generate the value used as the basis of the phase 1 keys. In phase 2, the nonces are hashed, along with the remainder of each message, to create a keyed hash that authenticates the content of the message. Each nonce is sent in its own nonce (NONCE) payload.

5.10   Identities and Identity Protection

Several IKE exchanges involve the exchange of identities in an ID payload. That exchange is essential when the IP address of the entity negotiating the IPsec SA (e.g., a gateway) is different from the identity of the recipient of traffic protected by the SA (e.g., a subnet behind the gateway). Even if the negotiating entity is also the SA's intended user, identities can be useful. A system may want to limit an SA's application to particular types of traffic. That can be done by specifying not only an identity's address but also the applicable port or protocol.

Some IKE exchanges, most notably Main Mode, provide identity protection. That means the ID payload is never sent unencrypted or in the clear. When the identity of the SA's owner differs from the negotiator's IP address, that identity is hidden from eavesdroppers on the Internet. Identity protection is useful even when a system is negotiating its own host-to-host SA, because an attacker cannot be sure whether the encrypted identity is the sender's IP address.

Each peer can negotiate an SA on its own behalf or on the behalf of one or more other entities. The ID payload defines the nature of the entity for which the SA is being negotiated, which can be one of the following:

- A single IP address (IPv4 or IPv6). A phase 2 ID payload also contains port and protocol data. In phase 1, the port must be either 0 or

500 and the protocol must be 0 or UDP; that is the default port/protocol combination for IKE.

- A fully qualified domain name string (e.g., statecollege.edu).

- A fully qualified username string (e.g., joestudent@statecollege.edu).

- A subnet, defined by an IP address and an IP network mask (both IPv4 or IPv6).

- A range of IP addresses, represented by two IP addresses (both IPv4 or IPv6).

- An ASN.1 X.500 distinguished name or GeneralName (more on these in Chapter 10).

- A value agreed on in advance that identifies which preshared key should be used to authenticate Aggressive Mode negotiations.

The ID payload contains the actual identity in the proper format for the selected type. In phase 1, the identity is authenticated through one of the four peer authentication methods. Thus, its format is related to the data used for authentication. If a public key certificate is used, the identity should be that of the certificate's owner or user. For a preshared secret key, there is a slight chicken-and-egg problem. To hide the identity, we need to generate a secret symmetric key. Before we generate that key, we need to select the peer's preshared secret key. But before the identity has been revealed, the only identifying data we have for the peer is the source address of the IKE message. Thus, preshared secret keys must be tied to a single type of identity, that of the peer's IP address.

Identities are communicated within an ID payload. If one of the peers involved in the ISAKMP SA negotiation intends to negotiate an IPsec SA on behalf of another entity, that information is conveyed in ID payloads during the phase 2 negotiation. The most common example is a gateway that is negotiating an IPsec SA for a single host or a subnet. Another example is a host negotiating an IPsec SA for a specific type of traffic. The phase 2 IDs, referred to as client IDs, always come in pairs: The initiator's client ID payload is first, followed by the responder's client ID payload.

5.11   Certificates and Certificate Requests

For those authentication modes that depend on public key certificates, a host generally needs to obtain the peer's certificate to extract the public key. In some cases (notably for the initiator in public key authentication), the key must be available before the first phase 1 message is sent. In other cases, the certificate can be requested and sent as part of an IKE phase 1 exchange. That is accomplished through the use of two optional payloads that can be added to almost any phase 1 message: the certificate request (CR) payload and the certificate (CERT) payload.

The function of the CR payload is to request the peer's public key certificate and to specify the types of certificates that are acceptable to the requester. The certificate that is requested can be relevant to the current exchange, or it could be requested with the intention of caching it for future use. Since IKE exchanges consist of a specific number of messages, the exchange cannot be extended in order to send back the requested certificate. Thus, the only message that cannot include this payload is the last message of an exchange.

The CERT payload is used to convey a host's certificate to the peer. A CERT payload can be sent in response to the CR payload or, at the initiative of either peer, in anticipation of its need. However, if the exchange is an identity protection exchange, the certificate should not be sent in the clear.

When a certificate must be obtained before the phase 1 exchange, the host must get the peer's certificate in some non-IKE exchange before the IKE negotiation can begin. Alternatively, if the peers are able and willing to use an alternative authentication mode (e.g., preshared secret keys), certificates can be exchanged and saved for a future, certificate-based IKE negotiation.

5.12   Keys and Diffie-Hellman Exchanges

The phase 1 symmetric keys provide both authentication and encryption for the ISAKMP SA. The phase 1 key calculation formula differs slightly, depending on which method of peer authentication is used. In every case, the keys are derived from one or more pieces of information known only to the communicating peers. One type of information, used by all four peer authentication methods, is a shared secret, the result of a Diffie-Hellman exchange conducted in phase 1. Each host sends its Diffie-Hellman public value to its peer in a key exchange (KEY) payload. In Main Mode and Base Mode, the specific Diffie-Hellman parameters are agreed on as part of the exchange of proposal payloads. In Aggressive Mode, the proposal payload and the KE payload are included in a single message, so the responder must be willing to accept the Diffie-Hellman parameters selected by the initiator.

The phase 2 symmetric keys provide authentication and/or encryption for the IPsec SA. They are calculated in part from a value derived from the shared secret established by the phase 1 Diffie-Hellman exchange. Because multiple phase 2 negotiations can result from a single phase 1 negotiation, multiple symmetric keys are based on this single shared secret. If PFS is desired for the phase 2 keys, an additional Diffie-Hellman exchange is conducted as part of the phase 2 exchange. However, both the proposal payload and the KE payload are part of the first Quick Mode message, so the responder must accept the initiator's preference, whether for or against PFS.

In the course of each IKE exchange, various keys need to be calculated. Those values are generated as the output of a keyed HMAC. At times, the HMAC in use may not yield enough keying material for the intended use. For example, the output of HMAC-MD5 is 128 bits long. If HMAC-MD5 is used to generate an encryption key for Triple DES, which requires a 192-bit key, we wind up short of keying material for the intended purpose. In that case, IKE defines an iterative technique to expand the generated key to the desired length.

5.13 Notifications

The IKE informational exchange (discussed in Section 5.19) is designed to carry diagnostic messages [5]. There are times when it is desirable to attach an informative message to an ongoing exchange. That is the function of the notification payload; it is an optional payload that can be attached to any phase 1 or phase 2 message. For example, when an initiator starts a phase 1 negotiation with a peer, and the initiator has no existing SAs with that peer, the first phase 1 message can include a notification payload with an "initial contact" notification message. If the responder has any existing SAs with the initiator, the message informs the responder that the initiator no longer has any memory of those SAs, possibly as a result of a system crash or some other disaster. The responder can then delete any SAs that were previously established with the initiator. Similarly, if an initiator begins a phase 1 negotiation that does not include an "initial contact" message, and the responder has not previously negotiated SAs with the initiator, the responder can include a notification payload with an "initial contact" message in message 2 of the phase 1 exchange.

Another example is the "replay status" message, which can be sent in phase 2. The responder can use that message to inform the initiator whether replay protection will be enabled or disabled during IPsec-protected communications.

5.14   Lifetimes

In the world of Internet communications, even mutually beneficial items, such as SAs, do not last forever. To expose a secret key by using it to encrypt too much traffic or by allowing it to sit around begging to be compromised would be foolhardy. For that reason, all SAs have a negotiated lifetime, which is one of the attributes included in both the phase 1 and phase 2 proposals.

If the initiator's proposal is acceptable to the responder in every respect except the lifetime, it is not necessary to jettison the negotiation. If the lifetime is too short, that provides added security and should be accepted. If the lifetime is too long for the responder's comfort level, the proposal can be accepted; the responder's message will also include a notification payload with an "SA lifetime" message. Included in the notification payload will be the responder's selected lifetime length value.

5.15   Vendor IDs

In some cases, IKE implementations may want to add features, attributes, or other extensions that are not part of the standard IKE protocol. The vendor ID payload is used for that purpose and can be sent in any phase 1 message. Sending this payload is an announcement that the sender wants to use a proprietary extension. If the recipient recognizes the requested extension and can handle it, another vendor ID payload is sent in return. The extension can then be used, most often in phase 2.

5.16   The Phase 1 Negotiation

There are three possible types of phase 1 exchanges: Main Mode, Aggressive Mode, and Base Mode. A phase 1 exchange has three goals.

- *To negotiate security parameters.* The initiator and the responder must agree on the values and settings of a number of parameters that will govern the format of the last two (encrypted) messages of phase 1 and all the phase 2 messages. They also must negotiate which method the peers will use to authenticate each other; the maximum lifetime of the phase 1 SA, and how that lifetime will be measured; the method to be used to establish the shared secret that will be used to calculate the phase 1 keying material and the parameters used to generate the shared secret. Those values collectively make up the ISAKMP SA.

- *To establish a shared secret.* Once the peers have agreed on the method and the parameters to be used to generate the phase 1 shared secret, an exchange of messages is used to establish that shared secret, which will be used in the generation of secret keys.

- *To authenticate identities.* The peers authenticate each other's identity based on some additional out-of-band information.

Once the ISAKMP SA is established, it can be used to protect multiple phase 2 Quick Mode exchanges, New Group exchanges, and informational exchanges, until its lifetime expires or some other untoward event occurs (such as a rebooting of the machine, causing the current SAs to be lost).

5.16.1 Main Mode

A phase 1 Main Mode exchange consists of six messages: three messages from the initiator to the responder and three sent by the responder to the initiator.

The first two Main Mode messages (message 1 from the initiator to the responder and message 2 from the responder to the initiator) consist of an exchange of SA payloads. The initiator's SA payload contains a single proposal payload, which can have multiple, alternative transform payloads. Each transform payload defines the specific algorithms, negotiation mechanisms, and policy (collectively known as attributes) that will characterize the established SA. The responder must select one of the transform payloads offered by the initiator, which is then referred to as the selected "proposal" (the terminology definitely muddies the waters here). The responder's SA payload contains the single proposal (i.e., the transform payload) that the responder selected from all the proposals offered by the initiator.

After the first two messages have been exchanged, each peer is assured that the other peer exists and is ready to negotiate (as opposed to a denial of service attack, in which the initiator most likely would be unreachable by the responder). In addition, both peers have agreed to the security parameters that will govern the remaining message exchanges. In particular, the authentication method has been selected.

The nature and the order of the payloads that make up the next two Main Mode messages (message 3 from the initiator to the responder and message 4 from the responder to the initiator) vary, depending on the authentication method (preshared secret key, digital signature, public key original mode, or public key revised mode). Figure 5.2 shows the payloads contained in each Main Mode message with authentication through pre-shared secret keys; Figure 5.3 illustrates Main Mode with digital signature authentication; Figures 5.4 and 5.5 illustrate Main Mode with authentication through public key encryption and revised public key encryption, respectively. (In all the figures in this chapter and the following chapters, a

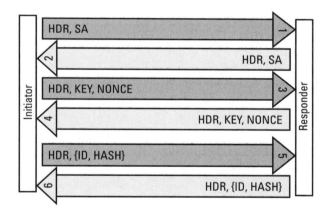

Figure 5.2 Main Mode exchange with authentication through preshared secret keys.

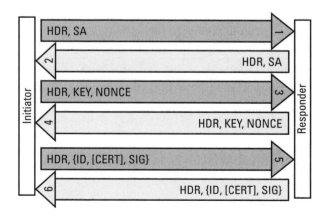

Figure 5.3 Main Mode exchange with authentication through digital signatures.

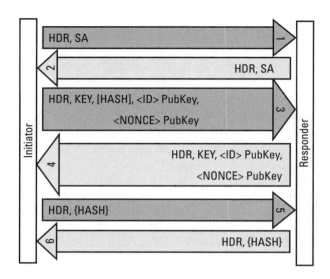

Figure 5.4 Main Mode exchange with authentication through original public key encryption.

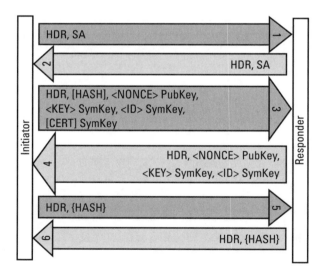

Figure 5.5 Main Mode exchange with authentication through revised public key encryption.

single payload or a series of payloads enclosed in braces, i.e., { }, is encrypted; payloads enclosed in brackets, i.e., [ ], are optional.)

For all the authentication methods, messages 3 and 4 contain a KEY payload and a nonce payload. The data portion of the KEY payload is used to conduct a Diffie-Hellman exchange. Each party sends its public value to the peer; the initiator sends the value g^x to the responder, and the responder sends the value g^y to the initiator. Each peer then combines its own private value with the public value that was received, resulting in the calculation of the shared secret, g^{xy}.

The nonces are random values generated by each peer that guarantee that the exchange is a current one rather than a replay of a previous exchange. They will be used in the phase 1 key material calculations.

If authentication is by either of the Public Key Modes, portions of messages 3 and 4 are encrypted through either direct or indirect use of the public keys. Because each payload's header has its own individual length field, which is essential for processing, only the data portions of the relevant payloads are encrypted, leaving the payload headers unencrypted. For the public key authentication modes, those messages contain an ID payload. For the original Public Key Mode, the data portions of the identification and nonce payloads are encrypted with the peer's public key. For the revised Public Key Mode, the data portion of the nonce payload is encrypted with the peer's public key, and the data portions of the KEY and ID payloads are encrypted with a symmetric private key derived from the host's nonce and cookie. Because symmetric encryption and decryption operations are less processor intensive than the corresponding public key operations but no less secure, the revised Public Key Mode is an improvement over the original Public Key Mode.

If the authentication method is one of the Public Key Modes and the responder has multiple public key certificates, the initiator must inform the responder which public key was used for payload encryption. That is accomplished by sending a hash payload, which contains a hash of the appropriate responder's public key certificate. The certificate is hashed using the hash function negotiated in the first two Main Mode messages. Similarly, if the authentication method is the revised Public Key Mode and the initiator has multiple public key certificates, the initiator must inform the responder which of the initiator's public keys the responder should use for payload encryption. That is accomplished by sending a CERT payload, which contains a copy of the appropriate initiator's public key certificate. The certificate is encrypted with the symmetric private key derived from the nonce. The initiator must possess the responder's public key before sending the message, since it is used to encrypt the nonce.

The secret phase 1 keys can now be calculated by each peer. A value called SKEYID is first calculated. The exact calculation, shown in Figure 5.6,

Pre-shared secret key:
    SKEYID = Keyed HMAC of Initiator's Nonce, Responder's Nonce
              With Key = pre-shared secret key

Signatures:
    SKEYID = Keyed HMAC of Diffie-Hellman shared secret
              With Key = Initiator's Nonce, Responder's Nonce

Public key encryption:
    SKEYID = Keyed HMAC of Initiator's Cookie, Responder's Cookie
              With Key = Hash of Initiator's Nonce, Responder's Nonce

Figure 5.6 SKEYID calculations.

depends on the authentication method. In each case, two types of information provide input to the calculation: information known only to the peers and information specific to this IKE negotiation. The secret information is the preshared key, the encrypted nonces, or the Diffie-Hellman shared secret. The exchange-specific information is either the cookies or the unencrypted nonces. Three secret keys are then calculated from SKEYID: SKEYID_e, the phase 1 encryption key; SKEYID_a, the phase 1 authentication key; and SKEYID_d, a value that will be used in the derivation of the phase 2 keys. The formulas for each of those values are shown in Figure 5.7.

After the first four messages have been exchanged and the secret phase 1 keys calculated, further traffic can be encrypted and authenticated. If the

Basis for calculation of Phase 2 keys:
SKEYID_d = Keyed HMAC of Diffie-Hellman shared secret,
          Initiator's Cookie, Responder's Cookie, 0
          With Key = SKEYID

Phase 1 authentication key:
SKEYID_a = Keyed HMAC of SKEYID_d, Diffie-Hellman shared secret,
          Initiator's Cookie, Responder's Cookie, 1
          With Key = SKEYID

Phase 1 encryption key:
SKEYID_e = Keyed HMAC of SKEYID_a, Diffie-Hellman shared secret,
          Initiator's Cookie, Responder's Cookie, 2
          With Key = SKEYID

Figure 5.7 Keys derived from SKEYID.

authentication method is either original Public Key Mode or revised Public Key Mode, an exchange of the peers' identities already has taken place; through the use of the public keys used for mutual authentication, it was possible to encrypt the identities and accomplish the exchange without publicly revealing either identity. If the authentication method is either through signatures or through preshared secret key, the exchange of identities has not yet taken place; it will occur in this exchange, under the protection of the negotiated keys. In either case, because the identities are encrypted, a phase 1 Main Mode provides identity protection for the participants. Besides that, all that remains to be accomplished in phase 1 is to authenticate the negotiation via the exchange and verification of keyed hashes.

The last two Main Mode messages (message 5 from the initiator to the responder and message 6 from the responder to the initiator) contain an ID payload (only if the authentication method is digital signature or preshared secret key) and a hash payload (if the authentication mode is not digital signature). If the authentication method is through digital signatures, the hash payload is replaced by a signature payload, in which the calculated hash is digitally signed. Optionally, the initiator or the responder can send a CERT payload containing the public key certificate whose associated private key was used to generate the digital signature. Figure 5.8 contains the formula for those hashes.

A number of ramifications and side effects stem from the interplay between message contents and authentication method in the Main Mode exchanges. Because the preshared secret key is used to generate the encryption key, and that key must be used to encrypt the ID payload, the preshared secret key must be selected based only on the peer's address. That means that, although phase 1 SAs of varying granularity can be negotiated with a single

Phase 1 Initiator's Hash = Keyed HMAC of Initiator's Public Diffie-Hellman value,
      Responder's Public Diffie-Hellman value,
      Initiator's Cookie, Responder's Cookie,
      Initiator's SA Payload, Initiator's ID
      With Key = SKEYID

Phase 1 Responder's Hash = Keyed HMAC of Responder's Public Diffie-Hellman value,
      Initiator's Public Diffie-Hellman value,
      Responder's Cookie, Initiator's Cookie,
      Initiator's SA Payload, Responder's ID
      With Key = SKEYID

Figure 5.8 Phase 1 hashes.

host once the ID payload is received, they all must be based on a single pre-shared secret key. It also means that the road warrior (a dial-up or mobile user who does not have a fixed address) cannot use preshared secret keys for authentication. In the absence of wide deployment of certificate-based solutions, that is a serious drawback. A number of solutions that have been suggested are enumerated in Chapter 6.

Identity protection adds another complication. Because the SA payloads are exchanged before the peer's identity is revealed, the responder must select the protection suite based only on the initiator's IP address. Once the actual identity is revealed, the responder may decide that the accepted proposal is not applicable to the peer. For example, in scenario 1 (see Chapter 1), H2 might select a proposal based on H1's IP address, assuming that H1 is a known quantity. But perhaps the identity sent in message 5 is an unfamiliar email address. In that case, H2 might require additional protection; at this point in the negotiation, the protection suite for the IKE SA cannot be changed. H2's only recourse is to terminate the negotiation, and subsequently to initiate another negotiation that includes the alternative proposal.

5.16.2 Aggressive Mode

The first Aggressive Mode message from the initiator contains the same fields normally contained in the initiator's first two Main Mode messages plus the ID payload. (In Main Mode, the ID payload is part of message 1 for both public key authentication methods but part of message 2 for the digital signature and preshared secret key authentication methods.) The first (and only) Aggressive Mode message from the responder contains all the fields spread across that peer's three Main Mode messages. Thus, a phase 1 Aggressive Mode exchange consists of three messages (two messages sent from the initiator to the responder and one sent from the responder to the initiator). Figure 5.9 shows the payloads contained in each Aggressive Mode message with authentication through preshared secret keys; Figure 5.10 illustrates

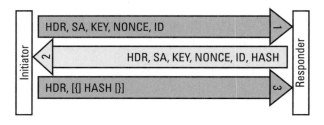

Figure 5.9 Aggressive Mode exchange with authentication through preshared secret keys.

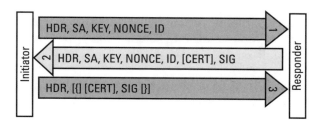

Figure 5.10 Aggressive Mode exchange with authentication through digital signatures.

Aggressive Mode with digital signature authentication; Figures 5.11 and 5.12 illustrate Aggressive Mode with authentication through public key encryption and revised public key encryption, respectively. The payloads of message 3 can be sent either encrypted or unencrypted.

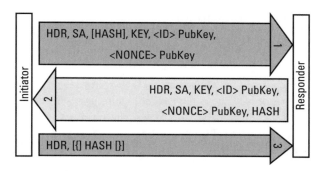

Figure 5.11 Aggressive Mode exchange with authentication through original public key encryption.

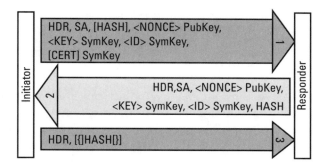

Figure 5.12 Aggressive Mode exchange with authentication tthrough revised public key encryption.

Unlike Main Mode, in Aggressive Mode the ID payload is received before the symmetric keys are calculated. Thus, preshared keys can be attached to the full range of identity types, not just to the peer's IP address.

Because the ID payload is sent before any sort of mutual key has been established, it is not encrypted if either preshared secret key authentication or digital signature authentication is used; in those cases, an Aggressive Mode exchange does not provide identity protection for the participants. However, if identify protection is not required, an Aggressive Mode exchange requires half the number of messages needed for a Main Mode exchange. Aggressive Mode with one of the public key authentication methods does provide identity protection, because the identity is encrypted with the peer's public key.

Aggressive Mode has two additional drawbacks. First, the peers must have agreed on the Diffie-Hellman group beforehand, because the Diffie-Hellman public values are exchanged in the same messages as the proposals. Second, Aggressive Mode cannot take full advantage of the cookie exchange's main purpose: to prevent denial-of-service attacks. Although SKEYID and the other secret keys do not have to be computed until after the third message has been received, ensuring that both initiator and responder are full participants, the responder does have to compute its own public value. That calculation is processor intensive and leaves the responder open to one type of denial-of-service attack. The initiator could flood the responder with requests to perform Aggressive Mode. If the initiator spoofs other hosts' addresses, the responder has no way of knowing that those requests all originate from the same host. The responder, to respond with real KE payloads, must perform the actual calculations; the initiator, knowing that the Diffie-Hellman exchange will not be completed, can just generate fake Diffie-Hellman public values rather than perform the actual calculations that result in a public-private value pair.

5.16.3 Base Mode

Base Mode [6] is an attempt to preserve the advantages of Aggressive Mode while at the same time eliminating its major disadvantages. Figures 5.13 through 5.16 illustrate its four variants. Base Mode consists of four messages, one more than Aggressive Mode. But that defers the KEY payload and its expensive Diffie-Hellman calculations, enabling the cookie exchange to mitigate the effects of a flooding attack. It also separates the KEY payload from

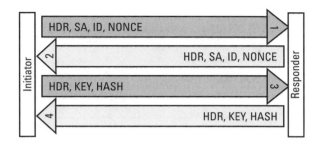

Figure 5.13 Base Mode exchange with authentication through preshared secret keys.

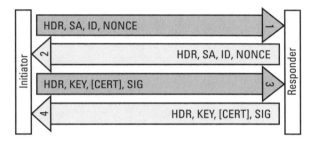

Figure 5.14 Base Mode exchange with authentication through digital signatures.

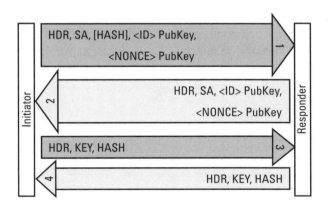

Figure 5.15 Base Mode exchange with authentication through original public key encryption.

the SA payload, allowing the peers to negotiate the Diffie-Hellman group's parameters. Because the identity payload precedes the key calculations,

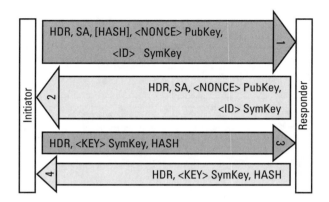

Figure 5.16 Base Mode exchange with authentication through revised public key encryption.

preshared secret keys can be used with the full range of identities. In addition, the peer is fully authenticated before the Diffie-Hellman shared secret is calculated. In authentication modes other than the public key encryption ones, those advantages come at the expense of identity protection.

Base Mode was an add-on to the original IKE definition, and was proposed after the initial IKE feature set had been somewhat frozen. For that reason, it has not been widely implemented. In addition, the consensus seems to be that identity protection is an important priority in a security-related protocol.

5.17   The Phase 2 Negotiation

Once the phase 1 negotiation is complete, an ISAKMP SA, which is a protected channel, has been established between the peers. The SA consists of agreed-on policy and parameters for further negotiations, along with symmetric secret keys that can be used to authenticate and encrypt those negotiations. The index, or SPI, used to reference the ISAKMP SA is the quantity formed by concatenating the initiator cookie and the responder cookie. Either peer can initiate subsequent negotiations, in which the ISAKMP SA is used to protect negotiations for a non-ISAKMP SA. The most common example of a non-ISAKMP SA is an IPsec SA that can then be used to protect IP communications in general between the peers. The only phase 2 IKE exchange that has been defined so far is Quick Mode.

5.17.1 Quick Mode

A phase 2 Quick Mode exchange has three goals.

- *To negotiate security parameters.* The initiator and the responder must agree on the values and settings of a number of parameters that will govern the operation of the negotiated IPsec SA. They also must negotiate the maximum lifetime of the SA and how that lifetime will be measured. If PFS is desired, they also must communicate the parameters used to generate the shared secret that will be used to calculate the phase 2 keying material and establish the shared secret itself.

- *To prevent replay.* Authenticating hashes, which include freshly generated nonces, are exchanged and verified to ensure that the negotiation is not merely a replay of a previous phase 2 negotiation.

- *To generate keying material.* Using the shared secret from phase 1 (or a newly generated shared secret if PFS is required), the keying material for the IPsec SA is produced. The phase 2 nonces also are used in the process, to ensure the freshness of the keying material.

In addition, two additional goals may be satisfied.

- *To provide PFS of keys and/or identities.* PFS is a guarantee that only one key has been generated from a single Diffie-Hellman exchange and that the key has no relationship to any other keys used between the peers. That ensures that discovery of the key by a third party will jeopardize only traffic protected with the single discovered key but not traffic protected by another key negotiated by the peers. PFS of keys is provided by performing a second Diffie-Hellman exchange during phase 2 and generating the IPsec SA's key from the new shared secret rather than using the same shared secret used to generate the phase 1 authentication key (SKEYID_a) and encryption key (SKEYID_e). PFS of identities is provided by deleting the phase 1 ISAKMP SA after it has been used for a single phase 2 Quick Mode exchange.

- *To exchange identities.* If the address of the negotiating peer is not sufficient to characterize the IPsec SA, the endpoint identities must be exchanged. This is necessary in the following cases:

- The peer is negotiating an SA on behalf of another entity (e.g., a gateway negotiating a tunnel-mode SA for one or more clients);

- Multiple SAs exist between the peers, each of which is character-ized by different port and/or protocol numbers, different identi-ties, or other combinations of selectors.

A phase 2 Quick Mode exchange consists of three messages (two messages from the initiator to the responder and one message from the responder to the initiator). Figure 5.17 shows the payloads contained in each Quick Mode message. The first two Quick Mode messages (message 1 from the initiator to the responder and message 2 from the responder to the initiator) always contain a hash payload, an SA payload, and a nonce payload. The hash con-tained in the hash payload serves to authenticate the message; it is a keyed hash, using SKEYID_a as the key, of the phase 2 message ID and all the other payloads in the message. The nonce is proof of the liveness of the exchange, protecting against a replay attack.

A phase 2 message can contain multiple SA payloads, which results in the negotiation of multiple IPsec SAs. Each SA payload can contain multiple proposal payloads, each of which characterizes a different protocol to be pro-vided by the SA, and each proposal payload can have multiple, alternative transform payloads. The responder's SA payload contains a single proposal (for each protocol for each proposed SA) that the responder selected from all the proposals offered by the initiator (for that SA). Figure 5.18 contains a sample Quick Mode initiator proposal. As a proposal, it allows the responder too many choices; as an example, it is instructive. The first two rows allow the responder to select an ESP SA with a choice of algorithms,

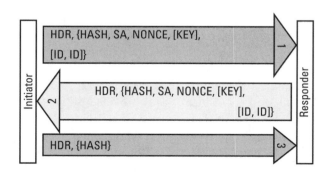

Figure 5.17 Quick Mode exchange.

Proposal #	Transform #	Protocol	Enc Alg	Auth Alg	Encapsulation Mode	DH Group #	Lifetime in Sec	Lifetime in KB
1	1	ESP	Triple DES	SHA-1	Tunnel	5	1800	—
1	2	ESP	DES	MD5	Tunnel	1	900	500
2	1	AH	—	SHA-1	Tunnel	—	900	500
2	1	ESP	Triple DES	—	Tunnel	—	900	500
2	2	ESP	DES	—	Tunnel	—	900	500

Figure 5.18 Sample Quick Mode initiator proposal.

Diffie-Hellman groups, and lifetimes. The inclusion of a Diffie-Hellman group in phase 2 indicates that the initiator wants PFS. The responder can send back a proposal corresponding to either of these "row" proposals. The last three rows are somewhat more complicated. Row 3 proposes an AH SA in conjunction with either the ESP SA in row 4 or the one in row 5. To select that combination, the responder would have to return a proposal corresponding to row 3 and another proposal corresponding to either row 4 or row 5. In that case, PFS is not selected. If it were, the Diffie-Hellman groups all would have to be the same.

If PFS of keys is required, the first two messages also include KEY payloads, and an additional Diffie-Hellman exchange occurs. If either of the negotiating peers is a gateway, negotiating an SA for some other host(s) or client, the messages also include two ID payloads, the first of which includes the identity of the initiator's client and the second of which includes the identity of the responder's client. Unlike Main Mode, in Quick Mode the identities are sent together with the proposal payload, so the responder is able to make an informed choice about which proposal to accept, including the initiator's client ID in the decision-making process if necessary.

After the first two messages have been exchanged, each peer possesses enough information to calculate the keying material that will be used for the IPsec SAs. Figure 5.19 shows the Quick Mode key calculations with and without PFS. Figure 5.20 illustrates the iterative expansion method used in Quick Mode to expand the keying material if the formula in Figure 5.19 does not yield a value of the required length. This keying material might be used for the authentication key of an AH SA, or it might be divided to provide the authentication key and the encryption key for an ESP SA.

Keying Material (without PFS) = Keyed HMAC of protocol (AH or ESP), SPI,
    Initiator's Nonce, Responder's Nonce
    with Key = SKEYID_d

Keying Material (with PFS) = Keyed HMAC of
    Quick Mode Diffie-Hellman shared secret,
    protocol (AH or ESP), SPI, Initiator's Nonce, Responder's Nonce
    with Key = SKEYID_d

Figure 5.19 Quick Mode key calculations.

Key1 = Keyed HMAC of [Quick Mode Diffie-Hellman shared secret,]
    protocol (AH or ESP), SPI, Initiator's Nonce, Responder's Nonce
    with Key = SKEYID_d
Key2 = Keyed HMAC of Key1, [Quick Mode Diffie-Hellman shared secret,]
    protocol (AH or ESP), SPI, Initiator's Nonce, Responder's Nonce
    with Key = SKEYID_d
Key3 = Keyed HMAC of Key2, [Quick Mode Diffie-Hellman shared secret,]
    protocol (AH or ESP), SPI, Initiator's Nonce, Responder's Nonce
    with Key = SKEYID_d

    $\vdots$

Expanded Keying Material = Key1, Key2, Key3, ...

Figure 5.20 Quick Mode key boost calculations.

The first exchange negotiates the IPsec SA's policy and parameters and generates the keying material in an authenticated manner that protects against a replay of a previous negotiation. The last message, from the initiator to the responder, concludes the exchange and reassures the responder that the responder's proposal was received. It consists of a hash payload, with a keyed hash computed over the message ID and the nonces from messages 1 and 2.

Once the IPsec SAs have been established, they can be used to protect all or some of the traffic between the endpoints, until their lifetimes expire or some other untoward event occurs (such as a rebooting of the machine that causes the SAs to be lost).

5.17.2 The Commit Bit

The commit bit shifts the onus of verifying and finalizing the IPsec SA's establishment from the initiator to the responder. Without the commit bit,

Quick Mode is a three-message protocol. After the first two messages have been exchanged, the peers have all the data necessary to compute the keying material and establish the IPsec SA. In the third message, the initiator computes an authenticated hash on both the initiator's Quick Mode nonce and the responder's Quick Mode nonce. Including the nonce that was just received from the responder serves to reassure the responder that this is a bona fide negotiation and not a replay of a previous one. But what if that message is lost? The initiator, assuming that it has arrived safely, will establish the IPsec SA; the responder, not having received the final Quick Mode message, will wait to establish the SA.

Either peer can convert Quick Mode into a four-message protocol by turning on the commit bit in the ISAKMP header. That way, if the initiator does not receive the fourth message, it will resend the third message. There is no ideal solution, because any lost message can create complications. But this solution avoids a situation in which an initiator preemptively sends the third message multiple times, because it has no good way to determine whether it has been received. The fourth Quick Mode message contains a hash payload and a notification payload with a "connected" notify message.

5.18 New Group Mode

New Group Mode, illustrated in Figure 5.21, is an exchange that uses an established phase 1 ISAKMP SA to protect the negotiation of a new Diffie-Hellman group that can then be used in subsequent exchanges. That allows the peers to negotiate a private group whose parameters are not known, except to the participants. In subsequent phase 1 exchanges, only the group description number is required; thus, the specific group parameters are not sent in an unencrypted message.

A New Group exchange consists of two messages (one message from the initiator to the responder and one from the responder to the initiator). Each message consists of an SA payload, used to negotiate the characteristics

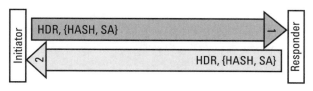

Figure 5.21 New Group Mode.

of the group, and a hash payload, which authenticates the message. Figure 5.22 shows the formula used to calculate the New Group hashes.

The New Group attributes open to negotiation are group description, type, prime, generator(s), curve(s), order, and field size. Those values define the specifics of the Diffie-Hellman exchange that will establish the shared secret used in the generation of the key material. The group description serves as the group's ID number. The group type attribute is used to specify whether the group is an MODP or elliptic curve group. The group prime and group generator attributes are used to define a new MODP group; the group prime, group generator, group curve, group order, and field size attributes are used to define a new elliptic curve group.

5.19 Informational Exchanges

There are two types of informational exchanges: an unacknowledged informational exchange and an acknowledged informational exchange. An unacknowledged informational exchange is a one-way single message used to send the peer status or diagnostic information. If an ISAKMP SA has been established between the peers, the ISAKMP SA is used to protect the exchange, and the exchange is authenticated with a hash payload. Either the initiator or the responder of the phase 1 or phase 2 exchange can act as the initiator of an informational exchange. Each informational exchange has a unique message ID distinct from the phase 2 message ID (if any). The message contains either a "notify payload" or a "delete payload." A "notify payload" contains the identifying number of a predefined status (e.g., "initial contact received") or diagnostic (e.g., "invalid payload type") message. A "delete payload" is used to notify the peer that an SA has been deleted and contains data identifying the deleted SA.

There are circumstances in which the sender requires confirmation that the informational message was received. For example, if the message is a

Initiator's Hash = Keyed HMAC of Message ID,
Initiator's SA Payload,
With Key = SKEYID_a

Responder's Hash = Keyed HMAC of Message ID,
Responder's SA Payload,
With Key = SKEYID_a

Figure 5.22 New Group hash calculations.

delete message, the initiator should not delete its SA until the responder has been notified about the deletion. That goal can be accomplished through the use of an acknowledged informational exchange, which consists of two messages, each containing a hash payload, a "notify payload" or a "delete payload," and a nonce payload for liveness.

If the ISAKMP SA has not been fully established, a situation can occur that calls for a diagnostic message. For example, if the initiator's phase 1 proposal sent in message 1 is not acceptable to the responder, the responder will not send message 2. But an informational "no proposal chosen" message is a more helpful reaction than no response at all. Alternatively, if one of the peer's messages is erroneous, a "bad proposal syntax" or "payload malformed" informational message is in order. An unprotected informational message does present a dilemma for the recipient. Because it is neither authenticated nor encrypted, it could come from an attacker, or its contents could have been altered in transit. In such a case, it makes sense for one peer to send an informational message and for the other peer to evaluate the security ramifications of acting on an unsecured message.

5.20   The ISAKMP Header

The ISAKMP header precedes every IKE message. Even when the body of the IKE message is encrypted, the ISAKMP header is not encrypted. It consists of the following fields:

- *Initiator Cookie.* The initiator's anticlogging device and part of the phase 1 SA's SPI, it is the unique key used to identify the phase 1 SA.

- *Responder Cookie.* The responder's counterpart to the initiator cookie, it is zero in phase 1 message 1, because the initiator has not yet received this value.

- *Next Payload.* Each message contains one or more payloads; this header field identifies the type of the first payload.

- *Major Version Number/Minor Version Number.* These numbers allow the peer's IKE implementation to determine whether it is compatible with the current IKE version; if not, it can reject this negotiation.

- *Exchange Type.* This field indicates the type of exchange to which this message belongs. If this is the first message of an exchange, the exchange type alerts the recipient to the format, content, and order of the payloads to be expected in this message and the subsequent messages for this exchange, as well as the total number of messages to expect. If this is not the first message of an exchange, the exchange type generally can be deduced from other header fields, but the exchange type still acts as a sanity check. The possible exchange types are phase 1: Main Mode, Aggressive Mode, or Base Mode; phase 2: Quick Mode; and Other: New Group Mode, informational, or acknowledged informational.

- *Flags.* The encryption flag indicates that the message following this header is encrypted; the commit flag is set by one of the negotiators to notify the peer that an SA in the process of being established should not be used until the sender sends an informational message that the SA has been completely established; the authentication-only flag indicates that the message following this header is an informational message that is authenticated but not encrypted

- *Message ID.* A random value generated by the initiator, which serves as the unique key used to identify the phase 2 SA during negotiation (zero in phase 1).

- *Length.* This field indicates the length of the entire message (header and payloads).

5.21 The Generic Payload Header

Every payload contained in an IKE message is prefaced by a generic payload header, which contains the following fields.

- *Next Payload.* This field, which indicates the type of payload that follows this payload (0 if none), can be somewhat confusing. To find the payload type of any payload, you need to look at the generic payload header of the previous payload; for the first payload in a message, its payload type is found in the next payload field of the ISAKMP header. It was suggested on the IPsec list that the payload type should be handled in a more intuitive manner and appear in the generic payload header immediately preceding the payload. Because the payload lengths are, for the most part, variable, and because each generic payload header includes the payload length, it is not necessary to encounter the payload type prior to reaching the payload itself.

Because the SA payload contains its proposal and transform payloads, they are not considered the SA payload's next payload; its next payload field points to the payload following the SA payload (or None). If an SA payload contains multiple proposal payloads, each proposal payload (except the last) within the SA payload has "proposal payload" as its next payload field. Similarly, if a proposal payload contains multiple transform payloads, each transform payload (except the last) has "transform payload" as its next payload field.

- *Reserved.* This field is unused (set to 0).

- *Payload Length.* This field indicates the length of the payload, including the generic payload header. The length of an SA payload includes the lengths of all its proposal and transform payloads; the length of a proposal payload includes the lengths of all its transform payloads; and the length of a transform payload includes all its associated data attributes.

5.22   The IKE State Machine

IKE is a stateful protocol. In a stateless protocol, each message is an independent entity and must contain within it all the information necessary for its processing and interpretation. In a stateful protocol such as IKE, each message of an ongoing exchange is tied to the exchange's previous messages and is evaluated within that context. After a responder receives the first IKE message, it possesses three pieces of information: the initiator's IP address, the initiator cookie, and the phase 1 proposal. That information must be saved in IKE's SAD, but until another message is received from the initiator, proving that the IP address was not spoofed and that the initiator intends to proceed with the negotiation, the responder will not expend resources on any further processing.

As each message is received and the IKE SAD entry is found, a sanity check must be performed to ensure that the message ordering has been preserved. If the expected response to a message has not been received in a reasonable amount of time, IKE retransmits the message a specific number of times before giving up. If a message that is received is not the expected message but is instead a retransmission of the previous message, IKE assumes that its previous message was not received by the peer and retransmits it.

5.23   The Origins of IKE

In the beginning, there was ISAKMP. There were also Simple Key Management for Internet Protocol (SKIP) [7] and Photuris [8, 9]. Each was a candidate to be selected as the "official" IPsec key management protocol. SKIP is an inline keying protocol that carries the encryption key for each packet, encrypted by a long-term key, within the packet itself. Photuris is a mature and complex protocol for key negotiation and exchange. ISAKMP is a key negotiation framework that enables but does not fully specify the key exchange. Each contender had its advocates in the IPsec group, with no clear majority distinguishable. The IETF security area director, Jeff Schiller, selected ISAKMP. SKIP's packet formats did not conform to IPsec; it carried extra data in every packet; it was felt to be too inflexible to meet the totality of IPsec's future requirements; and it did not allow for PFS. Photuris was judged to be too fully specified, not allowing modular changes to the protocol if the necessity arose in the future. ISAKMP was adjudged to be modular, flexible, and adaptable to the key negotiation requirements of a wide variety of protocols.

5.24   An Example

We have now discussed a number of the major components of IPsec, but the question remains: How do we progress from the creative gleam in a user's eye to safely entrusting the resulting creation to the vagaries of the Internet? Using Scenario 1, the steps would be as follows.

1. Host H1 needs to have an IPsec implementation and an IKE implementation, with both in a state of readiness.

2. Local policy governing IPsec protection of communications must be configured by a user or system administrator (more on this in Chapter 9). Let us assume that H1's policy requires all communications, inbound and outbound, to be both encrypted with Triple DES and authenticated with HMAC-SHA-1 through the use of an ESP header.

3. When a user or a process on H1 attempts to send an outbound communication to host H2, a policy check is made before it is sent for network processing. The IPsec requirement is found, and the SAD is interrogated. If there is already an existing outbound IPsec SA (ESP/Triple DES/HMAC-SHA-1) with H2, the

IPsec-processing routines use it to apply IPsec protection, and the message continues on its way.

4. If no applicable IPsec SA is found, IKE is brought in for consultation. IKE checks its own internal SAD. If there is a current ISAKMP SA between H1 and H2, IKE initiates a Quick Mode negotiation under the protection of the existing ISAKMP SA. Once the negotiation successfully concludes, the message can be expeditiously sent.

5. If an ISAKMP SA is lacking between H1 and H2, H1's IKE initiates a phase 1 negotiation with H2, followed by a Quick Mode negotiation. The message then can be sent on its way.

6. If a problem occurs during the IKE negotiation, the message is stonewalled and lost to posterity.

What about inbound messages from H2 to H1? The processing would be as follows.

1. If the message is protected by the appropriate IPsec SA, it is forwarded for normal inbound processing.

2. If the message is protected by an inappropriate IPsec SA, perhaps one that has expired or one whose selectors do not match the local policy requirements, it is abandoned on the spot.

3. If the message arrives without any IPsec protection, H1 drops the message. But because H1 requires IPsec protection for all inbound traffic, and clearly H2 is not similarly enlightened, H1 has the option of requesting its IKE to negotiate an SA with H2. That prevents the receipt of further unprotected traffic from H2.

This is a sample of IKE and IPsec processing in the simplest, most straightforward case.

5.25 Criticisms and Counterclaims

Ferguson and Schneier [10] reserve their harshest criticisms for ISAKMP and IKE, which they evaluate separately. They correctly point out that the separate documents for ISAKMP, IKE, and the DOI would lead one to believe that these are independent modules. Were that the case, a security analysis could focus separately on each module. Feature interaction among the modules increases the analysis requirements exponentially. These modules originally were viewed as independent: ISAKMP would provide the framework, IKE would add the key negotiation, and DOI would include specifics for application to the Internet. However, as the protocol developed, numerous interdependencies and inconsistencies crept in. The next version of the IKE documentation is expected to consist of a unified, consistent document.

Some of Ferguson and Schneier's comments relate to vagueness or underspecification in the documents, a number of which have been discovered in the course of operational experience; solutions have been agreed on but not yet documented. The order of payloads and which payloads can appear in which message have been a constant problem; it has been somewhat clarified in the course of numerous bake-offs but not completely. They also criticize the terminology and layering of the SA payload, a known source of confusion. Another source of severe displeasure is the use of the word *hash* (a noncryptographic entity) when what is actually being referred to is a Message Authentication Code (MAC), a keyed, cryptographic hash. (That failing may well be shared by this author, immersed as she has been in the IPsec documents. However, the phrases *authenticated hash*, *authenticating hash*, and *keyed hash* generally are considered to be equivalent to the term *MAC*.)

A number of criticisms and attacks should be prevented by any well-designed implementation. One attack requires the attacker to assume the peer's identity. Routine ID sanity-checking should discover that and dodge the bullet on the attack by halting the negotiation. Another attack assumes that IKE will respond to a replayed message, even after the negotiation successfully has progressed past that stage of the negotiation. The IKE state machine should prevent that from happening. For example, once an initiator receives Main Mode message 2 from the responder and sends out message 3, it will ignore a subsequent replay of message 2. If it recognizes this message 2 as belonging to a current negotiation, by virtue of the peer's source address and the cookies, it will ignore it because it already has been processed. And if the message is not recognized as part of a current negotiation (e.g., if the ISAKMP SA has expired), it still will be ignored, because the state machine will realize that no corresponding message 1 had been sent out. A third attack could result in identical keying material for the inbound and outbound SAs, if both peers select identical SPIs. That is easy to avoid, because the responder sees the initiator's SPI and can avoid duplicating it.

Several of their criticisms are on target, and will undoubtedly be included in the next version of IKE, referred to as son-of-IKE, which has been long anticipated. They criticize the IKE payload-chaining and pointers, a valid criticism, which will hopefully be addressed in the updated version. They also suggest that every message element should be authenticated by a

MAC. This is already done in any of the new IKE protocol extensions, and will undoubtedly be part of a new, revised IKE.

They point out that the initiator's SA payload is authenticated by a MAC, but the responder's SA payload is not. This problem was already known, and a solution has been proposed [11]. However, the effects of a possible attack are limited: An attacker could modify the proposed lifetime, which should be mitigated by the initiator's own lifetime constraints; or the attacker could select the weakest proposal among the initiator's alternatives. Because the initiator should not propose anything it is not prepared to accept, this also should not be a serious drawback.

The critics also insist that the properties of all cryptographic primitives, including hashes and pseudo-random functions, should be spelled out. This is to avoid adding new algorithms to IKE that may be secure in some contexts but might not fulfill IKE's requirements. Up to now, most implementations have limited themselves to well-known, tried-and-true algorithms, but more explicit specification would be a reasonable hedge against future problems.

Any future revisions to IKE undoubtedly will take these criticisms and suggestions seriously.

5.26 Threat Mitigation

What real-life threats are prevented through the use of IKE? This elaborate and complicated protocol is designed to thwart several types of classic attacks. The cookie mechanism ensures that the responder will invest only in cookie processing and in sending a single message in response to an attempted denial-of-service attack. The more expensive Diffie-Hellman calculations will not be attempted if the initiator's first message turns out to be bogus.

The integral connection between peer authentication and the key calculations prevents several types of attackers from successfully completing a phase 1 exchange. It thwarts an attacker that hijacks the connection or spoofs the peer's address, as well as an attacker that attempts a man-in-the-middle attack. The use of authenticated time-dependent nonces also is helpful in preventing replay attacks.

5.27 Summary

IKE is a complex protocol, with a rocky and somewhat contentious history. It needs to be extended to handle the common road warrior scenario. If each peer does not have some foreknowledge of the other's policy requirements and capabilities (see Chapter 9), negotiations may break down. If you ask an opinion of anyone who is involved with IKE, you'll get this response, "IKE is too complex and cumbersome; furthermore, it's missing features X and Y." However, warts and all, it is an essential element of IPsec, and its advocates are committed to eliminating inconsistencies and shortcomings.

5.28   Further Reading

Aside from its scope and complexity, a major obstacle to understanding IKE is the fact that its definition is scattered among no less than four documents. Because some of them contradict each other, there is a pecking order: In case of an inconsistency, IKE rules. Actually, each document has a unique purpose. ISAKMP [3] defines the payload types and the general framework but does not tie that framework to a specific key exchange mechanism. Oakley [4] fleshes out the key exchange and provides some theoretical background. IKE [1, 2], originally titled "The Resolution of ISAKMP and Oakley," specifies the actual phase 1 and 2 exchanges and the payloads that make up each. DOI [12] further defines a number of payload types, formats, and identifying constants that were not detailed in the other documents, since they are specifically tied to IPsec.

Further confusion surrounds the IKE document itself. [1] is the definitive description of IKE. [2] was a welcome update, which clarified a number of ambiguities and resolved several problems. Its expiration date was November 1999; because an updated draft was not issued, officially it does not exist. But most implementations have added features defined in [2]. The son-of-IKE, which has been promised for some time, will, we hope, resolve that dilemma. ISAKMP defines a series of exchanges that generally correspond with IKE's phase 1 modes. ISAKMP's identity protection exchange is IKE's Main Mode; both have Aggressive Modes. ISAKMP also has a Base exchange, which had no corresponding mode in IKE as originally defined. [6] added an IKE Base Mode. [5] elaborates on the content and applicability of IKE notification messages. SKIP is described in [7] and Photuris in [8, 9].

References

[1]   Harkins, D., and D. Carrel, *The Internet Key Exchange (IKE)*, RFC 2409, Nov. 1998.

[2]   Harkins, D., and D. Carrel, "The Internet Key Exchange (IKE)," <draft-ietf-ipsec-ike-01.txt>, May 1999.

[3]   Maughan, D., et al, *Internet Security Association and Key Management Protocol (ISAKMP)*, RFC 2408, Nov. 1998.

[4]   Orman, H., *The OAKLEY Key Determination Protocol*, RFC 2412, Nov. 1998.

[5]   Kelly, S., and T. Kivinen, "Content Requirements for ISAKMP Notify Messages," <draft-ietf-ipsec-notifymsg-03.txt>, July 2000.

[6]   Dayan, Y., and S. Bitan, "IKE Base Mode," <draft-ietf-ipsec-ike-base-mode-02.txt>, Jan. 2000.

[7]   Aziz, A., T. Markson, and H. Prafullchandra, "Simple Key-Management for Internet Protocols (SKIP)," http://www.skip-vpn.org/spec/SKIP.html, Oct. 1996.

[8]   Karn, P., and W. Simpson, *Photuris: Extended Schemes and Attributes*, RFC 2523, Mar. 1999.

[9]   Karn, P., and W. Simpson, *Photuris: Session Key-Management Protocol*, RFC 2522, Mar. 1999.

[10] Ferguson, N., and B. Schneier, "A Cryptographic Evaluation of IPsec," http://www.counterpane.com/ipsec.{pdf,ps.zip}, Feb. 1999.

[11] Kivinen, T., "Fixing IKE Phase 1 and 2 Authentication HASHs," <draft-ietf-ipsec-ike-hash-revised-01.txt>, Mar. 2000.

[12] Piper, D., *The Internet IP Security Domain of Interpretation for ISAKMP*, RFC 2407, Nov. 1998.

6

The Fifth Puzzle Piece: IKE and the Road Warrior

> And when you're alone, there's a very good chance you'll meet things that scare you right out of your pants. There are some, down the road between hither and yon that can scare you so much you won't want to go on.
>
> *Dr. Seuss, Oh the Places You'll Go*

The initial IKE standards work well for peers with fixed IP addresses. For example, a business with several branch offices, suppliers, and trading partners can use IKE to establish a variety of SAs for the different classes of secure communications, classifying the traffic into different categories according to IP address, subnet, and application type. IKE also can handle peers with address-independent credentials verified through the use of certificates. For those that have neither a fixed address nor a certificate infrastructure, it is a different situation. In particular, it is necessary to consider the road warrior, a business employee who would like to access a network protected by a security gateway but whose IP address is either not known or not trusted by the gateway. A catch-22 situation then ensues. If identity protection is desired and the road warrior lacks certificate-based credentials, the only remaining authentication method is preshared secret keys. At the point in the IKE negotiation in which the preshared secret key needs to be used, the IP address is the only known data item that can be used as an index into the database of preshared secret keys. But the gateway cannot trust the road warrior's IP address.

This situation occurs in a number of different scenarios [1–3]. The case of the unknown IP address occurs when the road warrior dials into an ISP and then connects to the gateway over the Internet. Because the ISP-assigned address is variable, it cannot be known in advance by the gateway. An untrusted IP address can arise when the road warrior uses someone else's host, either an Internet kiosk in an airport, shopping mall, or library or a host in a location that can be accessed both by trusted company employees and by outsiders. In that case, the IP address suffices only to authenticate the host machine. Some active user input is required to ensure that the host is being used by an authorized user.

One possible solution to the problem is the use of a shared road warrior secret. That could work for a small number of trusted road warriors, but as the number of road warriors increases, the likelihood that a "group secret" will remain secret decreases. In the absence of a deployed PKI, how can the road warrior tap into the company's IPsec-secured network?

The early approaches to the problem all required modifications to IKE. Some proposed an alternative phase 1 mode, and some added what became known as "phase 1 1/2," an additional exchange of messages inserted between phase 1 and phase 2. Because the fixed-address gateway is able to authenticate itself to the road warrior during phase 1, the intermediate exchange would complete the authentication process by using some non-IKE authentication method through which the road warrior would authenticate its identity to the gateway.

Although each of those solutions has been implemented by one or more vendors in VPN-enabling products, none has advanced to RFC status. Once it became clear that each of those approaches had detractors in the IPsec group, and a long-range solution to the problem was not yet in sight, a spinoff group, the IP Secure Remote Access (IPsra) group, was formed within the IETF to handle the road warrior problem and other, related issues involved in secure remote access.

In the IPsra group, a number of new approaches, all of which are based on short-term credentials or certificates, have been proposed and are still undergoing debate. The approaches have a number of distinct advantages. First and foremost, they do not require any alterations to the IKE protocol. Second, they do not encourage the long-term use of authentication technologies that some consider outdated or, in some cases, insecure. Third, the companies that use the approach are free to dictate the details related to credential issuance procedures, proof of identity, authentication method, and certificate longevity.

Figure 6.1 shows the components of a typical road warrior scenario.

- A host with an IP address that cannot be authenticated by the security gateway, either because it is a temporary address assigned by an ISP to a dial-up connection or because it is a host that is not known to be contained within a secured area.

- *Security gateway.* A gateway that negotiates IPsec SAs on behalf of clients on a protected network, to which the road warrior is requesting access.

- *Legacy authentication server.* Server that contains an authentication database and an application that uses the database to verify the identities of road warriors. It can be located on the same host as the security gateway. If it is separate from the gateway and lies outside the protected network, denial-of-service attacks on the authentication server can prevent new authentications from taking place but will not prevent the gateway from working its wonders on IPsec traffic. In some scenarios, the authentication server might lie behind the gateway.

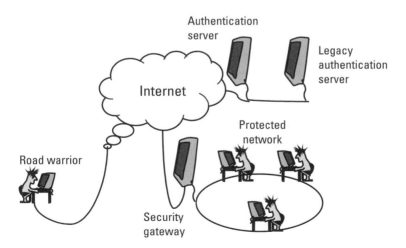

Figure 6.1 Road warrior scenario.

The credential-generating approaches require an additional component:

- *Authentication server.* A server that generates the short-term credential (generally a certificate or a preshared secret key) once the user has been authenticated by the legacy authentication server. It can be on the same host as the legacy authentication server and/or the security gateway.

6.1 Legacy Authentication Methods

What methods of user authentication are acceptable and feasible within the constraints of IPsec? There are a number of well-known authentication mechanisms that could be used.

- *Username/password.* A well-known mechanism by which the user enters an identifying username and its associated secret password. If the password leaves the user's host unencrypted, this method is totally unacceptable; even with an encrypted password, it is considered to be minimally secure. If the host does not belong to the user, a long-term secret password could be snatched, cached by the machine, and used to impersonate the user.
- *One-time password* (OTP) [4]. A method that combines the simplicity of the username/password approach with an extra measure of security: Each password is used only once. In that way, even if an eavesdropper sees the password, it is no longer useful.
- *Challenge-response mechanism.* A method in which the user's secret password, often called a passphrase in this context, is known to both the user and the legacy authentication server. However, the passphrase itself is not exchanged as part of the authentication negotiation; thus, it does not leave the user's host and is not exposed to eavesdroppers. The server sends a string—the challenge—to the user. The user's response, which is sent back to the server, is the result of a computation that involves the challenge, the user's passphrase, and possibly some other information.
- *Two-factor mechanism.* A method that combines two security mechanisms: something the user knows, such as a password, and something the user possesses, for example, a SmartCard or a biometric device. In some devices, the password may allow the user to access the device, at which point the device generates a one-time

password. In others, the user might have to enter the password and the server's challenge, after which the device generates a response. Some devices can be plugged directly into the user's host and conduct the authentication negotiation with the server once the user has entered the password or personal identification number (PIN). Other devices generate a one-time password or a response to a challenge but require the user to enter them manually. A single-factor authentication system can authenticate either the user or the host, depending on whether active input from the user is required or the negotiation is conducted by the host without user input. A two-factor system can authenticate both the user and the host, because it can require active user input along with host-generated input.

Many authentication systems of each type are deployed today. This chapter presents an example of each type, along with a sample authentication session.

S/Key [5] is a one-time password program that generally is implemented in software. Initially, the server and the user must agree on a secret passphrase and a nonsecret seed. The use of a seed allows the user to reuse the same passphrase on the same host or on multiple hosts and to generate a different series of one-time passwords each time. The server initially applies a one-way cryptographic hash to the user's passphrase and the seed a specified number of times and stores the result. Say that number is 1,000. The server keeps track of the number of times the user has logged on via S/Key and prompts the user with that number and the seed. The first time the user logs on, the one-time password is computed by hashing the secret key 999 times; the second time, 998 times; and so on. To verify the password, the server simply has to hash the one-time password once and compare it with the stored value. If they match, the authentication succeeds and the server replaces the stored value with the new one. If they do not match, the authentication fails.

SecurID [6] is a two-factor authentication token, a SmartCard that generates a one-time password. The user begins the authentication by entering a secret PIN. The SecurID token computes the one-time password, combining the user's PIN with the card's unique seed and the current time, and sends it to the server. The server, which knows the PIN and the seed of each deployed token, verifies whether the one-time password is correct. For SecurID to work properly, the token and the server must have the same value for the current time. SecurID is a popular, albeit proprietary, authenticator.

Remote access dial-in user service (RADIUS) [7] is not an authentication method by itself; rather, it is a framework for dial-up authentication that can accommodate a number of different authentication methods. In addition to authentication, RADIUS also handles policy configuration, but those functions are not relevant to this chapter. The RADIUS server has an associated database that contains all the information necessary to authenticate each user, including the authentication method to be used, the user ID, and (depending on the method) the user's passphrase, PIN, and so forth. Two authentication methods in particular are often used with RADIUS: Password Authentication Protocol (PAP) and Challenge Handshake Authentication Protocol (CHAP). PAP relies on a static password sent from client to server, is considered to be insecure, and is not recommended for use with IKE. CHAP [8] is a challenge-response method, in which the server sends a random challenge to the user. The user's response is a cryptographic hash of the challenge and the user's secret key. The server, which also knows the user's secret key, verifies the accuracy of the user's response.

If legacy authentication methods are to be used to authenticate road warriors, how best can they be sandwiched into IKE? There is a whole smorgasbord of possible approaches. A revised phase 1 negotiation? Try Challenge-Response for Authenticated Cryptographic Keys (CRACK). A revised phase 1 followed by user authentication in phase 1-1/2? Try either extended authentication (XAUTH) or hybrid authentication. A revised phase 2 negotiation? Try user-level authentication (ULA). A pre-IKE credential-generating negotiation? Try Pre-IKE Credential (PIC) Provisioning Protocol or one of the four IKE client certificate and key retrieval methods (no catchy acronyms suggested). Table 6.1 compares the features of each of those approaches, all of which are described in this chapter.

The methods that propose new IKE variations use either the phase 1 ISAKMP SA or the phase 2 IPsec SA to protect the legacy authentication negotiation. That ensures that the user authentication information sent to the authentication server, which includes user ID, passphrases, and the like, is protected from eavesdropping and replay attacks.

6.2 ISAKMP Configuration Method

Because the kind of data exchanged by the legacy authentication protocols are different from those normally used by IKE, additional payload types and message formats are needed. The different types of authentication protocols require varying numbers of messages, and some of the exchanges can include a variable number of messages. Thus, a mechanism also is needed to signal the end of the authentication exchange. Those requirements are fulfilled

Table 6.1
Authentication Negotiation Schemes

Scheme	XAUTH	Hybrid Authentication	CRACK	ULA	PIC
Phase 1 authentication method	Any IKE	Digital signature (gateway only)	Digital signature (gateway only)	Any IKE	Digital signature
Phase 1 authentication mutual/ one-way?	Mutual (gateway and client host)	One-way (gateway)	Mutual (gateway and user)	Mutual (gateway and client host)	Mutual (gateway and user)
Phase 1 authentication symmetric/ asymmetric?	Symmetric	Asymmetric	Asymmetric	Symmetric	Symmetric
User authentication	Phase 1-1/2	Phase 1-1/2	Phase 1	Post–phase 2	Pre–phase 1
Non-IKE dependencies	Configuration method	XAUTH configuration method	None	None	None

by the ISAKMP configuration method, which defines the requisite exchange mechanism and payloads.

To IKE's arsenal of payload types, the configuration method adds a new one: the attribute payload. The data carried by that payload are interpreted differently, based on the payload's message type. The configuration method defines four message types:

- *Request.* One of the peers requests information from the other.
- *Reply.* The recipient of the request message responds with the requested information.
- *Set.* One of the peers informs the other of the value of some data.
- *Acknowledge.* The recipient of the set message signals receipt of that message and acceptance or refusal of the data values.

Each of the messages contains a single attribute payload, which consists of zero or more IKE-type attributes. In a request message, those attributes for which the sender is requesting information have either an empty value or a suggested value. In the resulting reply message, the peer fills in the values of some or all of the requested attributes; if that is either not possible or not desirable, the peer sends an empty attribute payload. In a set message, the sender suggests values for the specified attributes. In the resulting acknowledge message, the peer returns those attributes whose values it has accepted but does not return the values themselves; those attributes whose suggested values were rejected are not returned by the peer.

What types of information can be exchanged using the configuration method? The authentication-related attributes [9], some or all of which might be used by a specific authentication mechanism, are the following:

- *Authentication type.* The authentication protocol or mechanism to be used. Currently, the only ones specifically identified are RADIUS-CHAP, OTP, and S/KEY. They demand a specific sequence of messages and attributes. To use one of these methods, the server must specifically propose one or more authentication types, and the client must agree to the method or methods to be used. Numerous other authentication methods, including Unix and NT Domain Logins, SecurID, and DIAMETER, are included in an umbrella generic authentication type. If no authentication type is proposed, it is assumed to be one of the generic types.

- *User name.* The unique identifier used by the user to sign on to the authentication server. It can be a user name log-on string, an email address, an X.500 distinguished name, or any other unique identifier that is acceptable to the server.

- *User password.* The user's password that serves to verify the user's identity to the server.

- *Passcode.* The single-use password generated by an authentication token (i.e., a SmartCard) or software program.

- *Textual message.* An informative message, prompt, or diagnostic message sent to the human user by the authentication server.

- *Challenge string.* An unpredictable value sent by the server to the user's authentication device or software, to be used in its calculations. Different authentication protocols use a challenge string in diverse ways. For example, RADIUS-CHAP uses it to hide the secret password by generating a cryptographic hash of the challenge string and the password.

- *Domain.* The authentication domain. This value is specific to the authentication type.

- *Status.* Indicates whether the authentication succeeded or failed. The server can send either value, but the client can indicate only failure.

The following configuration-related attributes [10] can be used by a server to assign values to a client.

- *IP address* (IPv4 or IPv6). An internal or private network address that the server assigns to the client.

- *Network mask* (IPv4 or IPv6). The network mask of the internal network.

- *Subnet* (IPv4 only). The subnet addresses of one or more internal subnets protected by the gateway.

- *Domain name system (DNS) server* (IPv4 or IPv6). The addresses of one or more DNS servers for the internal network.

- *Windows Internet Naming Service (WINS) server* (IPv4 or IPv6). The addresses of one or more WINS servers for the internal network.

- *Dynamic Host Configuration Protocol (DHCP) server* (IPv4 or IPv6). The addresses of one or more DHCP servers for the internal network.

- *Address expiration.* Number of seconds that the internal IP address that was assigned via the configuration method remains valid. The address actually expires when one of several events occurs: when the address expiration limit is reached, when the phase 1 SA used to protect the exchange expires, (optionally) when the phase 2 SA nego- tiated following the configuration method expires, or (if none of those applies) at an implementation-dependent time mandated by the client.

Several useful housekeeping-type attributes also have been defined [10].

- *Version.* Used by consenting implementations to communicate which software version or applications are supported.

- *Attributes supported.* Used if, prior to an exchange, one of the peers wants to query which attributes are supported by the other peer.

The paradigm of repeated request messages and interspersed reply messages is well suited for the types of authentication methods currently used in IKE. The set and acknowledge pair of messages is appropriate to end the exchange and ensure that the peers agree on the success or failure of the authentication.

When the configuration method is used for road warrior authentication, it needs to follow a phase 1 exchange; the configuration method messages are then encrypted and authenticated by the ISAKMP SA. That is why this type of exchange is called phase 1-1/2. It is not a phase 2 exchange, because it does not result in the negotiation of an IPsec SA, but it is dependent on the phase 1 SA. In such a case, each message consists of the ISAKMP header, a hash payload, and the characteristic attributes payload. The configuration method exchange is connected to the phase 1 exchange through the use of the identifying cookies but is distinguished from the phase 1 exchange through the use of a unique message ID. The phase 1 encryption key, SKEYID_e, is used to encrypt each message, and the phase 1 authentication key, SKEYID_a, is used to generate a keyed hash of the message ID and the attributes payload. The encryption IV for the first message of the exchange is computed using the same formula used to compute the initial IV in a phase 2 exchange; subsequent IVs are taken from the last block of the previous message.

The configuration method can be used to exchange other information as well. Prior to an authentication-related configuration method exchange, the server might want to ensure that a client can handle the requisite attributes or that the client's authentication application's version can communicate with the server. If that exchange takes place before the ISAKMP SA has been established, and if the information is not sensitive, those messages can be sent in the clear. Following a successful authentication-related exchange, the server can use the configuration method messages to assign configuration-related information to the client. For the road warrior to have full access to the network, it can be useful to assign it an internal network address. The address generally should be accompanied by other network-related information, such as server addresses and a network mask. Additional network parameters that may also be required (but which are not discussed in the context of the configuration method) are [3] PMTU, router-related information, static routes, additional servers (SMTP, POP, WWW), and other server-related options. The policy-related ramifications of those configuration choices are explored in Chapter 9.

The configuration method is not a stand-alone protocol. Rather, it is an enabler for exchanges that are more fully defined in other protocols, such as hybrid authentication and XAUTH. The original phase 1 negotiations consist of mutual, symmetric peer authentication; IKE negotiations based on the configuration method result in mutual authentication, but in an asymmetric manner.

6.3 Extended Authentication

Picture a scenario in which a gateway needs to authenticate both a communicating host and its user. When does that happen? Perhaps a company has a number of laptops preconfigured with a common road warrior preshared secret key or with certificates that can be used to authenticate the particular host. That does not ensure that the laptop's user has the proper credentials to access the company's network protected by the gateway. That is a job for Extended Authentication (XAUTH).

XAUTH begins with a mostly normal phase 1 exchange, with just two modifications: the peers exchange a vendor ID payload whose data consist of a keyed hash of the XAUTH document's Internet Draft name and version number, to ensure that both are operating under the same rules and assumptions. XAUTH also has its own special authentication method IDs, which distinguish this type of phase 1 SA from others, guaranteeing that the phase 1 SA will not be used to negotiate an IPsec SA without the intervening XAUTH exchange. The XAUTH authentication method ID conveys three pieces of information.

- The ISAKMP authentication method (preshared secret key, RSA digital signature, DSS digital signature, encryption, or revised encryption) to be used in phase 1.
- The role assumed by the road warrior (initiator or responder), that is, the entity that needs to be authenticated via XAUTH. The majority of these negotiations most likely will be initiated by the road warrior; however, if the gateway is the initiator, it must somehow know beforehand that the peer is a road warrior and that XAUTH is required.
- An XAUTH authentication will follow the phase 1 negotiation.

Once the phase 1 exchange is completed, the gateway has fully authenticated itself to the road warrior, and an ISAKMP SA has been established between the gateway and the road warrior's host. That is followed by a unidirectional authentication, which constitutes the XAUTH exchange, in which the road warrior assumes the role of a client and proves his or her identity to the gateway. That generally is accomplished through the use of an existing authentication server that lies behind the gateway. The gateway acts as a conduit between the authentication server and the client, but all communications between client and gateway are protected by the ISAKMP SA.

The XAUTH exchange takes the form of one or more request messages sent from the server (via the gateway) to the client and the same number of reply messages from client to server. If the authentication method is known in advance, or once the authentication method has been agreed on, the attributes payload contains those authentication-related attributes dictated by the particular authentication mechanism. A successful negotiation is followed by a set message from server to client that consists of a status attribute whose value is OK, followed by an acknowledge message with an empty status attribute from client to server. If the server is not satisfied with the negotiation, the status attribute's value will be FAIL. If at any point the client is unable to complete the negotiation, it sends a reply message with a status attribute set to FAIL. If the XAUTH exchange fails, the ISAKMP SA must be deleted, because a phase 2 negotiation cannot now follow.

For a paranoid (or prudent) gateway, the user can be periodically reauthenticated, without necessitating a new phase 1 negotiation, as long as the ISAKMP SA has not expired.

A number of criticisms have been leveled at XAUTH. It is a new, relatively untested but complex protocol that is layered on top of IKE, another complex protocol. The fact that it is an open-ended protocol, rather than one with a fixed number of messages, leaves it open to denial-of-service attacks. The use of preshared keys with XAUTH presents a choice of major drawbacks: XAUTH in Main Mode with preshared keys is vulnerable to a man-in-the-middle attack by another host that possesses the preshared key; Aggressive Mode eliminates that problem but does not provide identity protection. The XAUTH messages that enable a gateway to send a prompt string to a user contain a considerable amount of known plaintext. In addition, the use of XAUTH gives rise to an infrastructure that encourages continued support of legacy authentication mechanisms, rather than supporting a phased conversion to client certificates. Figure 6.2 illustrates a sample XAUTH RADIUS-CHAP negotiation.

6.4 Hybrid Authentication

Classical XAUTH cannot be used in some road warrior cases. If the host has no means of authenticating itself to the gateway, the phase 1 XAUTH

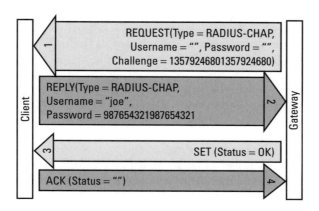

Figure 6.2 Sample XAUTH negotiation: RADIUS-CHAP.

exchange cannot take place. This can happen in a case where a road warrior is using someone else's host, for example, an Internet kiosk in an airport, shopping mall, or library, or where the road warrior's own host is not equipped with the appropriate host-based authentication credentials. Another configuration method variant, called Hybrid Authentication [11], can be used in such a case. It involves a special phase 1 negotiation, which is followed by an XAUTH authentication negotiation.

The phase 1 negotiation, which can be either Main Mode or Aggressive Mode, is based on a one-way peer authentication, in which the gateway authenticates itself to the remote user. Either of the digital signature authentication methods can be used to authenticate the gateway; in place of the signed hash that normally would be used to authenticate the road warrior, an unsigned keyed hash is sent. Because the client's identity cannot be proved through any phase 1 mechanism, it does not have any place in this phase 1 negotiation. The client ID payload generally contains an empty client ID; thus, ID protection for the road warrior is preserved in Aggressive Mode as well as in Main Mode. If the gateway sends a CR payload, the road warrior generally responds with an empty CERT payload.

Hybrid authentication also has its own special authentication method IDs, which convey three pieces of information.

- The ISAKMP authentication method (RSA digital signature or DSS digital signature) to be used in phase 1.

- The role assumed by the road warrior (initiator or responder), that is, the entity that needs to be authenticated via XAUTH. The majority of these negotiations most likely will be initiated by the road warrior; however, if the gateway is the initiator, it somehow must know beforehand that the peer is a road warrior and that XAUTH is required.

- This is a phase 1 hybrid authentication exchange, which will be followed by an XAUTH authentication.

The phase 1 negotiation is followed by an XAUTH exchange, which authenticates the road warrior using one of the challenge-response authentication methods appropriate for XAUTH. This negotiation is initiated by the gateway and protected by the ISAKMP SA. The ISAKMP SA cannot be used to protect any other type of exchange until the XAUTH exchange successfully terminates; if XAUTH fails, the ISAKMP SA must be deleted.

Hybrid authentication is layered on top of XAUTH, so it shares most of XAUTH's drawbacks while adding an additional layer of complexity. Because the gateway is authenticated through digital signatures and not through preshared secret keys, it is not vulnerable to a man-in-the-middle attack.

6.5   Challenge-Response for Authenticated Cryptographic Keys

Challenge-Response for Authenticated Cryptographic Keys (CRACK) [12] is a new phase 1 negotiation that includes the legacy authentication negotiation as part of phase 1. That ties the authentication more directly to phase 1. It most closely resembles the phase 1 digital signature negotiations and uses a digital signature to authenticate the gateway, so the authentication method must be one of the digital signature variants. A CRACK exchange is always initiated by the client. The first two messages of the exchange include all the payloads that normally are distributed over the first four IKE phase 1 messages. Because CRACK is not yet a standard, it is suggested that the peers exchange a vendor ID payload whose data consist of a keyed hash of the CRACK document's Internet Draft name and version number, to ensure that both are operating under the same rules and assumptions. Because the Diffie-Hellman exchange occurs in the first two messages, the cookie exchange does not fulfill one of its normal roles, the prevention of a denial-of-service attack. If the client does not already possess the gateway's public key, it can request it via a CR payload in message 1; the gateway then sends the certificate in a CERT payload in message 2. To ensure that the gateway's

Diffie-Hellman value originates from the gateway and to protect it from tampering, the gateway includes a signed hash of its Diffie-Hellman value in message 2. If the gateway has multiple public keys used for digital signatures, it can include a CERT payload containing the appropriate key, even if the client has not requested the certificate. Once the first two messages have been exchanged, the shared symmetric keys SKEYID and its derivatives SKEYID_a, SKEYID_e, and SKEYID_d are calculated, using the same calculations that are used for a standard IKE phase 1 digital signature exchange. The client trusts this secure channel because the gateway has signed its Diffie-Hellman value, and the gateway trusts it because the client is willing to entrust its authentication information to the channel. In addition, the gateway will not allow the client to access any part of the protected network until the authentication has succeeded, thus verifying the client's identity.

The first two messages are followed by the legacy authentication negotiation, which is protected by the secure channel established once the Diffie-Hellman exchange has taken place. This negotiation consists of one or more messages, depending on the demands of the particular legacy authentication method. It necessitates two additional IKE payload types:

- *Public key payload.* The client uses the public key payload to send its public key, which will be used for a signed hash following the authentication negotiation. Once the client has proved its identity via the authentication negotiation, the gateway can trust its public-private key pair.

- *Challenge-response payload.* This payload is used by both the client and the gateway to conduct the authentication negotiation. It contains the legacy authentication method's ID along with the relevant challenge-response information.

The first challenge-response payload is always sent by the client, along with the public key payload. If the authentication consists only of information supplied by the client and verified by the gateway (e.g., either a long-term password or a one-time password coupled with a user ID), then only one message with a challenge-response payload is required. For challenge-response or other more complex methods, multiple challenge-response payloads are exchanged. The gateway terminates the authentication in one of two ways: If the client has been successfully authenticated, the gateway sends a signature payload containing a digital signature of the cryptographic hash of all of the payloads, including headers, that preceded the message. The cryptographic hash uses SKEYID_a as its key. It hashes the payloads in their unencrypted form; messages that were retransmitted are hashed only once. If the authentication failed, the gateway sends an "authentication failed" notification message, also protected by the secure channel. A successful authentication ends with a signature payload, sent from the client to the gateway, that signs all the payloads of the previous messages, including the gateway's signature payload.

Figure 6.3 shows a CRACK exchange using a challenge-response authentication method. The challenge-response (ChResp) payload in message 3 is empty, the ChResp payload in message 4 contains the challenge, and the ChResp payload in message 5 contains the response. Figure 6.4 shows a CRACK exchange using a password-based legacy authentication method. In this case, only one ChResp payload is needed, containing the client's password and user ID.

An exchange of identity payloads is not necessary in this negotiation. The gateway's identity is known to the client and is authenticated with the digital signature. The client's identity is authenticated with the legacy authentication method. Thus, the exchange can qualify as an identity protection exchange, because identities are not directly exchanged and, thus, are not exchanged in the clear. However, if the gateway's certificate is sent to the client as a result of a CR payload, an eavesdropper can glean the gateway's identity from the certificate.

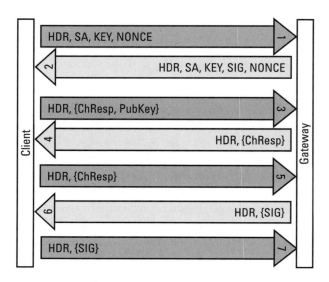

Figure 6.3   Sample CRACK negotiation: challenge-response.

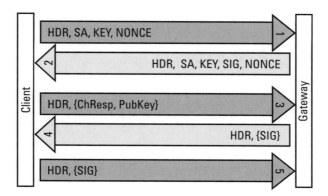

Figure 6.4 Sample CRACK negotiation: password/user ID.

6.6 User-Level Authentication

To round out the approaches, a post–phase 2 negotiation has been defined: user-level authentication (ULA) [13]. This approach necessitates a standard IKE negotiation, which requires either a preshared secret key or a client host that has been provided with its own certificate. It also adds an additional ingredient: a proxy application for the authentication protocol on the security gateway. The IPsec SA is established with the gateway, but its selectors allow access only to the authentication server via the authentication proxy application. That SA then is used to protect the legacy authentication negotiation. If the authentication succeeds, the IKE SA's selectors can be changed to allow the client access to the network through the gateway. Alternatively, the limited SA can remain, to be used repeatedly to reauthenticate the client, and an additional SA can be added for network access. If several authentication attempts fail, the limited SA should be deleted. This approach authenticates both the client host and the user.

6.7 Credential-Based Approaches

A number of criticisms have been leveled at the configuration method and CRACK approaches. One criticism is that they add complicated, open-ended modifications to an already complex protocol. Another is their reliance on outmoded and possibly insecure technology. A third criticism, which applies only to the phase 1-1/2 methods, is that an exchange that is only loosely tied to the phase 1 exchange is less secure than the tightly coupled IKE exchanges. A promising alternative is to tie the authentication methods, not to the phase 1 negotiation, but to the issuing of credentials. Those credentials could be either short-term certificates that attest to the user's identity or short-term preshared secret keys. IKE could remain intact, and the users of the credentials could make their own decisions about the security of credentials wedded to the various legacy authentication methods. Because the credentials would be issued prior to the IKE negotiation, IKE would not have to be modified.

That approach relies on the assumption that the gateway already has a certificate that the road warrior trusts. It only remains to leverage the legacy authentication method to issue a credential, possibly a short-lived one, that can serve to authenticate the road warrior to the gateway. The credential-based methods differ in several aspects: the underlying transport mechanisms and protocols used for the client authentication; which entity generates the client's public-private key pair; and where the certificates are stored. Because these methods are in the early stages of definition, a number of aspects have yet to be defined.

Because the user's credentials are generated before the IKE negotiation begins, a secure channel is needed for the authentication. Two possibilities have been proposed.

- *Transport layer security* (TLS). This IETF-blessed form of secure sockets layer (SSL), which is commonly used to protect Web-based transactions, seems a natural solution. It requires only a single certificate, that of the server. It uses a transport protocol (HTTP) and language (HTML) that are universally available. Although it generally is used to protect communications between a Web server and browser, other applications also can be retrofitted to use TLS mechanisms for the negotiation.

- *IKE.* A variant of an existing IKE phase 1 negotiation can be used prior to phase 1 to authenticate the authentication server to the user.

If the credential to be issued is a certificate, there are a number of additional variations among the approaches. One of those issues is who generates the user's public-private key pair. There are two possibilities: the user's host and the authentication server.

- *User's host.* If the user generates its own public-private key pair, the public key is transmitted to the authentication server via the preestablished secure channel. The server then issues and signs the certificate.

- *Authentication server.* Rather than burdening the client with key generation, that responsibility can be transferred to the server, which can use spare processing cycles to generate key pairs in advance. The server then issues and signs the certificate and sends the certificate and private key to the client. Under normal circumstances, it is unwise for a host to allow another entity to generate its private key, because that entity then would have all the information necessary to impersonate the host. In this case, however, the server can be assumed to be trustworthy, because its primary mission is the protection of the network through the establishment of secure communications.

Another issue is the location in which the private key will be stored. Once again, there are two possibilities: the user's host and the authentication server.

- *User's host.* If the client's host is a single-user host that can be trusted, the natural place for private key storage is on the client host.

- *Authentication server.* If the host is a shared host and the client cannot safely store the private key, it can be stored on the server. The key is encrypted before it is stored on the server, in case the server's security is ever compromised. To ensure against unauthorized encryption or decryption of the key, a cipher with a feedback mechanism (IV) is used each time the key is transmitted between client and server.

Five possible schemes have been proposed [14, 15], mixing and matching the various building blocks in different ways. Three of the schemes result in the issuance of certificates. Issuing a certificate and the ancillary public-private key-pair generation consume a lot of processing power. When that processing is used to generate short-lived certificates, and that is followed by an IKE negotiation, which also involves expensive public-key operations, the resources expended may exceed the capabilities of one of the hosts. The fourth scheme avoids those pitfalls. Instead of producing a temporary certificate, it generates a short-lived preshared secret key, enabling a less expensive IKE negotiation as well. The fifth scheme can result in either a certificate or a preshared secret key. Table 6.2 compares the features of the five different approaches, which are as follows.

- *Client-side certificate generation.* A TLS session is established between the authentication server and the client, and the server sends the client the appropriate prompt or challenge for the authentication method, along with a request that the client generate a public/private key pair. The client generates the keys, and sends the public key back to the server, along with the authentication method's response; both the key and the response are encrypted with the client's private key. The server signs the certificate and sends it back to the client

- *Server-side key-pair generation.* A TLS session is used to protect the authentication negotiation, and the server then sends the certificate and private key to the client.

- *Server-side key storage.* This scenario is similar to the previous one, in which the server generates the client's keys and certificate. In this case, the server functions as the private key's storage repository as well.

Table 6.2
Credential-Generating Authentication Schemes

Scheme	Client-Side Certificate Generation	Server-Side Key-Pair Generation	Server-Side Key Storage	Server-Generated Shared Secret	PIC
Credential authentication negotiation protected by	TLS	TLS	TLS	TLS	New IKE variant
Credential	Certificate	Certificate	Certificate	Shared secret	Certificate or shared secret
Credential generated by	Client	Server	Server	Server	Server
Keys generated by	Client	Server	Server	N/A	Server
Credential stored by	Client	Client	Server	Both	Client

- *Server-generated shared secrets.* This solution uses the TLS umbrella for authentication and then sends a short-lived preshared secret key to the client. The authentication server also must communicate the shared secret and the road warrior's current IP address to the IPsec gateway. That allows IKE to use preshared secret keys for authentication but avoids the pitfalls that result from allowing multiple road warriors to use the same preshared secret key.

- *PIC.* A revised Aggressive Mode exchange has been suggested [15] in which the server is authenticated via digital signatures. Figure 6.5 illustrates the exchange, which consists of a one-way authentication that results in a secure channel between the server, whose identity is authenticated by the exchange, and the user, whose identity will be authenticated in an exchange protected by this secure channel. For that reason, the user's identity and digital signature are not needed, which shortens the exchange by one message. SKEYID, SKEYID_a, and SKEYID_e are then calculated as they are for a standard Aggressive Mode exchange. That is followed by an Extensible Authentication Protocol (EAP) [16] exchange to authenticate the user. The user then requests the appropriate credentials from the server, which delivers them to the user.

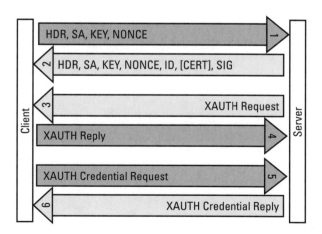

Figure 6.5 Sample PIC negotiation.

For all five methods, once the road warrior is in possession of its own certificate and private key or its short-lived preshared secret key, it must make this essential information available to IKE before the phase 1 negotiation can proceed.

There are concerns about full-scale IKE and IPsec deployment in the context of today's networks, especially on networks with limited bandwidth, such as wireless networks, and on today's less than state-of-the-art hosts. Preceding an expensive IKE negotiation with an even more expensive authentication negotiation thus is problematic. However, if the negotiation is seen as a short-term expedient that will facilitate the transition to full-fledged PKI, to be used for limited numbers of road warriors, trading partners, or extranet nodes, the cost can be considered to be bearable.

The details of each of the five approaches have not been nailed down, but that is not necessarily a drawback to their deployment. Remote authentication of road warriors is one area in which differing proprietary solutions can coexist and can successfully be part of a global IPsec infrastructure. That happens when a locally deployed proprietary solution produces a certificate that can be used to authenticate the road warrior to peers that do not necessarily espouse the same method of pre-IKE authentication. Of course, that presupposes acceptance of those certificates within the wider arena. It is also essential that the road warrior verify the authenticity of the server's certificate. If that is not done, a man-in-the-middle attack can take place.

A straw poll was conducted on the IPsra mailing list to select one of the first four scenarios on which to focus. The first scenario, client-side certificate generation, was selected, so it appears that that approach, along with PIC, will be the approach of choice as a bridge to full PKI deployment.

6.8 Complications

Other than the drawbacks and vulnerabilities of each of the individual approaches, an underlying problem is inherent to all the legacy authentication systems. An attacker can repeatedly attempt to impersonate a user and initiate a legacy authentication. Each of the authentication systems will lock out a user, not allowing further authentication attempts, after a specified number of failed negotiations. That constitutes a denial of service, because the road warrior is denied network access either for a specific length of time or until the user's account is reinitialized. Such vulnerability is inherent to the legacy authentication methods and is inherited by any system that uses them as building blocks.

6.9   Threat Mitigation

What real-life threats are prevented through the use of the IKE remote authentication scenarios? The remote user's authentication information, including the password and the user ID, is hidden from eavesdroppers. In addition, should an eavesdropper save the packets that constitute an authentication negotiation and replay them in an attempt to sign on to the network protected by the security gateway, that, too, should fail.

6.10   Summary

With the increasing popularity of telecommuting and the general mobility of business users, the magnitude of the road warrior problem promises to increase. Although today's solutions require mostly IKE modifications and legacy authentication methods, it seems reasonable that the near future will see an increase in the use of legacy authentication methods to issue short-term credentials. That will enable the gradual migration to a full-blown PKI infrastructure, with long-term user-specific and function-specific credentials.

6.11   Further Reading

The legacy authentication methods described in this chapter are all defined in IETF documents: S/Key [5], SecurID [6], the latest version of RADIUS [7], RADIUS-CHAP [8], and EAP [16]. A generic one-time password protocol is discussed in [4]. Each of the IKE remote access approaches has its own document as well: ISAKMP configuration method [10], XAUTH [9], hybrid authentication [11], CRACK [12], ULA [13], and PIC [15]. [14] describes the four other pre-IKE credential-generating authentication methods. The authors have made quite clear their hope that full-scale PKI deployment will overtake those methods and negate their necessity well before this document achieves RFC status. A number of drafts [1–3] contain more general discussions of criteria and requirements of secure remote access in the context of IKE and IPsec. The IPsra email list archive can be found at http://www.vpnc.org/ietf-ipsra.

References

[1]   Aboba, B., "IPSEC Remote Access Protocol Evaluation Criteria," <draft-aboba-ipsra-req-00.txt>, Dec. 1999.

[2]   Gupta, V., "Secure Remote Access Over the Internet Using IPSec," <draft-gupta-ipsec-remote-access-03.txt>, Oct. 1999.

[3]   Kelly, S., and S. Ramamoorthi, "Requirements for IPsec Remote Access Scenarios," <draft-ipsra-reqmts-00.txt>, Mar. 2000.

[4]   Haller, N., et al., *A One-Time Password System*, RFC 2289, Feb. 1998.

[5]   Haller, N., *The S/KEY One-Time Password System*, RFC 1760, Feb. 1995.

[6]   Nystrom, M., *The SecurID(r) SASL Mechanism*, RFC 2808, Apr. 2000.

[7]   Rigney, C., et al., "Remote Authentication Dial In User Service (RADIUS)," <draft-ietf-radius-radius-v2-06.txt>, Feb. 2000.

[8]   Simpson, W., *PPP Challenge Handshake Authentication Protocol (CHAP)*, RFC 1994, Aug. 1996.

[9]   Beaulieu, S., and R. Pereira, "Extended Authentication Within IKE (XAUTH)," <draft-beaulieu-ike-xauth-00.txt>, Oct. 2000.

[10]   Dukes, D., and R. Pereira, "The ISAKMP Configuration Method," <draft-dukes-ike-mode-cgf-00.txt>, Oct. 2000.

[11]   Litvin, M., R. Shamir, and T. Zegman, "A Hybrid Authentication Mode for IKE," <draft-ietf-ipsec-hybrid-auth-05.txt>, Aug. 2000.

[12]   Harkins, D., and D. Piper, "IKE Challenge/Response for Authenticated Cryptographic Keys," <draft-harkins-ipsra-crack-00.txt>, Aug. 2000.

[13]   Kelly, S., J. Knowles, and B. Aboba, "User-Level Authentication Mechanisms for IPsec," <draft-kelly-ipsra-userauth-00.txt>, Oct. 1999.

[14]   Bellovin, S., and R. Moskowitz, "Client Certificate and Key Retrieval for IKE," <draft-bellovin-ipsra-getcert-00.txt>, Feb. 2000.

[15]   Sheffer, Y., and H. Krawczyk, "PIC, a Pre-IKE Credential Provisioning Protocol," <dratf-ietf-ipsra-pic-oo.txt>, Mar. 2000.

[16]   Blunk, L., and J. Vollbrecht, *PPP Extensible Authentication Protocol (EAP)*, RFC 2284, Mar. 1998.

7

The Sixth Puzzle Piece: IKE Frills and Add-Ons

> Software is like entropy. It is difficult to grasp, weighs nothing, and obeys the Second Law of Thermodynamics, i.e., it always increases.
>
> *Norman R. Augustine, Augustine's Laws, Law Number XVII*

The IPsec standards generally specify packet formats and other observable details that affect Internet traffic. Numerous other details are often labeled implementation-specific and left to the discretion of the individual implementers. Sometimes, suggested behavior, or "best common practice," is defined in an informational RFC. Many times, implementation details are not discussed at all, even though they can decidedly affect interoperability of multiple implementations. A number of such details either were omitted from the original IKE documents or were underspecified. Day-to-day operational experience with IKE highlighted the need for standardization or clarification of such features, including SA renegotiation, ISAKMP heartbeats, and dangling SAs. These features are all somewhat controversial, and it is not clear which will remain for the long haul and which will be consigned to the dustbin of digital history.

7.1　Renegotiation

The timing of IKE renegotiations is an operational detail that can seriously degrade network communications between two implementations that implement it in different ways, even if both conform to the IKE specifications [1].

Most implementations do not wait for an IPsec SA to expire; it is common practice to initiate renegotiation at some interval, either time based or traffic based, prior to expiration. The interval is generally a random one, because predictable behavior is the Achilles' heel of security.

One question remains: When should an initiating peer begin using the newly negotiated outbound SA, and when should the receiving peer stop accepting traffic on the about-to-expire inbound SA? There are two schools of thought. The first school advocates "using up" the old SA and not using the new SA until the old one has actually expired; the second suggests switching over to the new SA as soon as it is in place, without worrying that the old SA has not been totally exploited. The cautious approach, which enables interoperability with both schools, leaves three of the four SAs (the old and new inbound SAs and the new outbound SA) in place as long as possible. Outbound traffic, which is under the control of the sender, is sent on the new SA, just in case the peer has deleted the old one. Inbound traffic, over which the recipient does not have control, is accepted on the old SA, which is not deleted until inbound traffic has been received that uses the new SA; it also is accepted on the new inbound SA.

In any IKE exchange, one peer assumes the role of initiator and the other the role of responder. However, in any subsequent IKE exchange, the roles can be reversed. That applies to a phase 2 negotiation that follows a phase 1, or to a phase 1 exchange that renegotiates an about-to-expire phase 1 SA or any other IKE negotiation.

The *renegotiation* or *rekeying* of an IPsec SA is triggered by the end of the SA's lifetime as measured in elapsed time or number of kilobytes of data protected by the SA. Although a new SA must be negotiated, including the complete set of SA parameters, the process is often referred to as *rekeying*, because it is the exposure of the secret keys that motivates the SA renegotiation. Too much elapsed time since the SA negotiation or too much data encrypted by the encryption key can provide enough time and ammunition for a variety of attacks aimed at discovering the secret key. If the ISAKMP SA through which the IPsec SA was negotiated is still alive, it can again be used to negotiate the IPsec SA's successor, and only a phase 2 negotiation takes place. If the ISAKMP SA has also expired, a full-blown two-phase negotiation must again occur.

One of the problems that bedevils IKE in a number of different contexts is its reliance on an unreliable transport protocol, UDP. That means reliance on the delivery of different messages in a prespecified order can and will result in problems. Thus, the specifications must always anticipate these *race conditions* and dictate IKE's behavior under alternative conditions. One race condition that pertains to rekeying is the timing of the responder's reception of the final phase 2 message relative to receiving the first incoming message protected by the new SA. Figure 7.1 demonstrates this problem. Assume that host H1 is the initiator of the phase 2 negotiation. If H1 is a high-powered machine and can encrypt that first message rapidly, and if the two messages traverse different paths to reach the responder, H2, then the encrypted message can arrive at H2 before the final phase 2 message.

Because that final message does not contribute any new information to the SA, and because H2 can calculate the key before it sends the second phase 2 message, this scenario can have a happy ending, with protected communications exchanged in either case. But that does involve some flexibility on the part of the responder, which has to be prepared to accept and process the packet that relies on the new SA before the SA negotiation has formally concluded. It also leaves the responder open to a replay attack, because the third message, in which the initiator computes an authenticated hash that includes the responder's nonce, constitutes proof that this is not a replayed negotiation. In the event that this is a replay attack, it could disrupt communications between H1 and H2. H2 would be convinced that a new pair of SAs had been established with H1; the keying material would be calculated from the replayed initiator's nonce and H2's newly generated responder's nonce. When H2 would send outbound traffic on the bogus outbound SA,

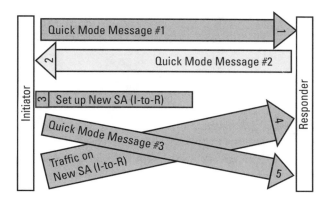

Figure 7.1 Rekeying race condition.

that traffic would be rejected by H1, because H1 had not negotiated the new SA. Obviously, H2 would not receive inbound messages from H1 using this SA. Any inbound messages would have to be sent by the attacker, which would replay genuine messages that had been sent to H2 by H1. Those messages would be protected with the keying material from the old SA, so they would be rejected by H2. The result would be a disruption of communications from H2 to H1 and wasted processing performed by H2.

Figure 7.2 shows a suggested sequence of Quick Mode negotiation, illustrating the order of SA activation and deletion relative to the launch or arrival of each Quick Mode message. The order was selected to maximize interoperability and security and to minimize dropped packets. The responder has the option of activating the new inbound SA either before or after the third Quick Mode message has been received. Each approach has its pluses and minuses. The earlier SA activation allows a smooth transition to the new inbound SA, even if the third Quick Mode message is lost or delayed. If the first Quick Mode message is a replayed message, or if there is a problem with the second Quick Mode message (e.g., an incorrect authenticating hash), the new inbound SA is invalid; if the responder then deletes the old inbound SA, inbound packets are dropped. The initiator will still be

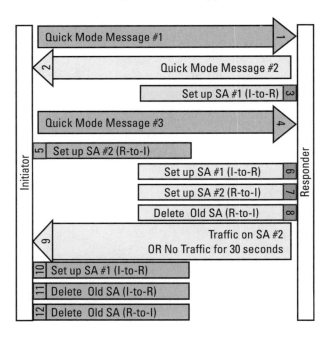

Figure 7.2 Quick Mode rekeying order of operations.

using the old SA, which was deleted by the responder; the responder will be expecting packets to use the new, invalid SA. The later SA activation avoids those pitfalls, but it opens up the possibility that the responder would receive traffic protected by the new SA before receiving the third Quick Mode message and, therefore, before activating the new inbound SA. That causes a (temporary, we hope) black hole, resulting in a cessation of inbound traffic until the third Quick Mode message is received.

7.2   Heartbeats

What happens when a busy gateway or a host that sends most or all of its traffic under the IPsec umbrella negotiates a large number of IPsec SAs? Some of them will be used regularly, but some will be used once or twice to fulfill a specific transaction and then sit idle until they expire. In the event that an SA was foolishly negotiated to expire only on traffic volume and not on elapsed time, it may never expire. Unused SAs can cause clutter, at best, or, in the case of a malicious peer, they can contribute to a denial-of-service attack. For those reasons, some implementations delete SAs that are unused for a specific time, even if they have not yet expired.

Another possible cause for the termination of an unexpired SA is the unexpected shutdown of a host system, either as the result of a system crash or, for a road warrior, a phone hangup. When the system reappears, it can send an initial contact message, so that the peer deletes all previously negotiated SAs. Until that happens (if it happens), the peer that neither crashed nor deleted dormant SAs assumes that those SAs are still operative and blithely sends outgoing traffic that relies on them. That can result in considerable wasted processing and lost communications.

To handle that problem, a new mechanism, originally called a *keep-alive* but now referred to as a *heartbeat* [2], has been defined. A heartbeat is a one-way message sent at periodic intervals that notifies the recipient that its peer is still alive. The message can optionally include the SPIs of some or all of the existing outbound SAs between the sender and the recipient, as a sanity check for the recipient.

The negotiation to set up a heartbeat is a configuration method exchange that takes place under the protection of an existing ISAKMP SA. It is always initiated by the intended recipient of the heartbeats. That allows the recipient to dictate the behavior and timing of the heartbeat messages, subject to the agreement of the sender. If both peers require this type of assurance, two separate heartbeat negotiations can take place. Because the heartbeat is used to prove the continued health of the system as a whole, even if multiple SAs exist between two peers, the maximum number of heartbeat negotiations that would be required is two, one in each direction. Five attributes can be negotiated.

- *Heartbeat type.* Only a single, standard type is currently defined. This attribute can be used to extend the protocol in the future or to agree privately on a different mechanism.

- *Heartbeat options.* The options are used to negotiate the support of optional behavior. Generally, heartbeat messages are encrypted and authenticated, but the "authentication only" option can be used to negotiate a heartbeat message that will be authenticated but not encrypted. If the recipient does not propose this option, the sender should not downgrade security by suggesting its use. The "SPI list supported" option allows the sender to include an optional SPI list, detailing some or all of the SPIs in effect between the peers, in some or all of the heartbeat messages. If the recipient does not propose the use of this option, it would be wasteful for the sender to suggest it, knowing that the recipient most likely will just discard the information.

- *Heartbeat interval.* The interval is the number of seconds between heartbeat messages. The suggested default value is 20 seconds. If the heartbeats' recipient proposes a heartbeat interval, the sender is allowed to increase the interval to send fewer heartbeats and thus consume less processing power.

- *Heartbeat message accepted.* This attribute is used by the heartbeat negotiation responder (who will be the sender of the heartbeat messages themselves) to either agree or refuse to initiate the heartbeat message mechanism.

- *Initial sequence number.* This attribute is the sequence number to be sent in the first heartbeat message.

Figures 7.3 and 7.4 show two sample heartbeat negotiations, one in which the responder sets the parameters that will govern the heartbeat message and one in which the values are proposed by the initiator.

Once the heartbeat message has been negotiated, the sender can start sending heartbeats, which consist of regular ISAKMP messages with a new exchange type: Heartbeat Exchange Mode. Figure 7.5 shows the payloads

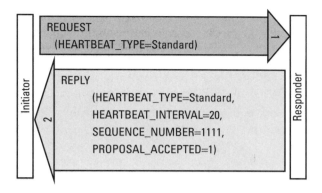

Figure 7.3 Heartbeat negotiation with parameters set by the responder.

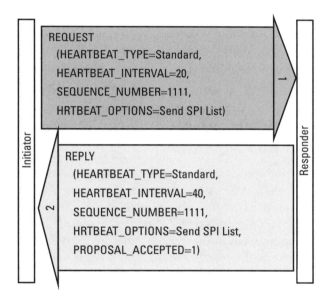

Figure 7.4 Heartbeat negotiation with parameters proposed by the initiator.

Figure 7.5 Heartbeat payloads.

sent in a typical heartbeat message. Two new payloads were defined for the heartbeat message.

- *Sequence number payload* contains the heartbeats' sequence number, used for replay protection.
- *SPI list payload* contains a full or partial list of the SPIs of the outbound SAs that currently are in place between the sender and the recipient.

The notify payload contains a special informational message, "notify still connected." The hash payload contains the authenticating hash, a keyed hash of the complete message with SKEYID_a as the key. To authenticate the complete message, the hash input consists of three parts.

- The ISAKMP header and the message payloads that precede the hash payload;
- A hash payload, consisting of the generic payload header with a zero hash value;
- The message payloads that follow the hash payload.

Figure 7.6 shows the authenticating hash for the message shown in Figure 7.5.

When the recipient gets a heartbeat message, it first verifies the authenticating hash to ensure that the message is legitimate. It then examines the sequence number and performs replay checking by comparing it with the last sequence number received, in the same manner that is done by IPsec. If the replay check succeeds, the current sequence number is updated; if the packet's sequence number lies outside the current replay window and the replay check fails, the heartbeat packet is ignored. Generally, the ISAKMP SA

Hash = Keyed HMAC of HDR,

SEQ_NO,

HASH_0,

NOTIFY,

SPI_LIST

With Key = SKEYID_a

Figure 7.6 Heartbeats message hash calculation.

is renegotiated before the sequence number reaches the maximum possible value. If it does reach that value, however, the heartbeat messages must cease, because there is no way to distinguish a heartbeat with a restarted low value from the replay of a previous heartbeat message.

Once the predetermined interval passes without receiving a heartbeat, the recipient can assume that the sender is now incommunicado and can delete the ISAKMP SA, along with its subsidiary IPsec SAs. If the sender decides to delete the ISAKMP SA, thus halting the heartbeats as well, the recipient should be notified of the deletion in a reliable manner, either through the use of an acknowledged informational message or by repeatedly sending the delete message to maximize the possibility that it will be received.

Other relevant metrics are determined or recorded by the heartbeats' recipient.

- *Lost packet tolerance.* The number of lost heartbeats that can be tolerated before the peer is considered to be dead. The suggested default value is 3.

- *Packet transmission window.* The maximum number of seconds required from heartbeat message origination by the sender until acceptance by the recipient, including travel time. The suggested default value is 5 seconds.

- *Timeout interval.* The number of seconds since the last heartbeat message considered to signify the peer's death. The suggested default value, based on a heartbeat interval of 20 seconds, is 65 seconds, using the formula

$$\text{Timeout interval} =$$
$$(\text{heartbeat interval} * \text{lost packet tolerance}) +$$
$$\text{packet transmission window}$$

- *Last good sequence number.* Last sequence number received in a valid heartbeat message.

- *Sequence number window.* The size of the replay window, that is, the maximum allowable deviation in sequence number for two consecutive heartbeat packets.

If the SPI list option is supported, it can be sent in each heartbeat message or periodically every few messages. In addition to the SPIs themselves, the SPI list payload contains two special values: the minimum SPI contained in the list and the maximum SPI. That serves two purposes: It helps the recipient to process the SPIs more efficiently, and it enables the SPIs to be distributed among multiple SPI payloads or multiple heartbeat messages. Thus, if the peers share a large number of SAs, each heartbeat message does not have to carry that heavy baggage. The recipient of the SA payload should examine all inbound SAs established with the peer and delete any SAs from the SAD whose SPIs fall within the minimum-maximum bound but do not appear in the payload's list of SPIs.

Because the heartbeats are sent under the protection of the ISAKMP SA, a new heartbeat negotiation must take place each time the ISAKMP SA is renegotiated.

What types of attacks are the heartbeat packets designed to avoid? The sequence number protects the recipient from replay attacks, and the authenticated hash protects against spoofed packets. That prevents replayed and spoofed packets from presenting false proofs of liveness once a machine has gone down. In addition, unauthenticated notify messages (e.g., deletes) that contradict the SPI list in a current heartbeat message can be ignored and assumed to be bogus. Some types of attacks cannot be avoided. If heartbeat packets are prevented from reaching the recipient, and the recipient mistakenly deletes still-current SAs, that constitutes at least a temporary denial of service. If the heartbeat packets are authenticated but not encrypted, and the SPI list option is selected, the SPIs are sent in the clear, exposing that sensitive information to eavesdroppers.

7.3 Initial Contact

Then there is the opposite problem. What happens when one peer disappears for a while? That can happen as the result of an unplanned reboot or, for a road warrior, an unplanned disconnect. When the unfortunate system resurfaces, it may have lost all its SAs and have to start negotiating new ones. Its communicating peers, however, still think the old SAs are valid. When the newly reborn peer begins a phase 1 negotiation, it should include an initial contact [3] notification message in its first ISAKMP message. That notifies the peer that this is not a renegotiation of an existing SA but rather a new start, and any SAs with this peer that are still intact should be deleted.

7.4   Dangling SAs

What happens when a phase 1 SA expires or is deleted as a result of a delete notification? In particular, should the phase 2 SAs that were negotiated under its protection be deleted? In general, a phase 2 SA will not outlast its phase 1 SA, but there are exceptions. In implementations that expire a phase 1 SA on traffic volume, a phase 1 SA that is used to negotiate multiple phase 2 SAs can expire before some of its phase 2 SAs. Alternatively, a phase 1 SA can be deleted unilaterally due to reasons that might invalidate its phase 2 SAs (certificate revocation, for instance) or due to reasons that would not affect its phase 2 SAs (such as housekeeping that results in the deletion of inactive SAs). As often happens, two philosophies govern the relationship between phase 1 and phase 2 SAs: the continuous channel and the dangling SA.

The *continuous-channel* advocates believe that there is an intrinsic dependency between a phase 1 SA and the phase 2 SAs established under its umbrella. If the phase 1 SA is deleted, because of a security breach, the expiration of an authentication credential, or time-based or traffic-based expiration, then the phase 2 SAs also must be summarily deleted, because phase 2 SAs owe their legitimacy to the phase 1 SA that authenticated the peer.

Advocates of the *dangling SA* take a more cavalier view of the relationship. They counter that once a phase 1 SA has completed the tasks of peer authentication and the provision of a secure negotiating channel, the resulting phase 2 SAs possess their own independent validity, even after the phase 1 SA is deleted. That outlook allows the continued existence of dangling or orphaned phase 2 SAs. Those phase 2 SAs, once negotiated, have an independent life and should continue to function until they expire on their own. For a while, this dispute was the source of a religious war. Finally, the two camps agreed to disagree. In a spirit of tolerance, implementations on either side of this great divide should be able to interoperate. However, implementations that dangle SAs cannot make use of the heartbeats protocol, because nonarrival of a heartbeat might just indicate the current lack of an ISAKMP SA between the peers rather than the failure of the sender's host. Another problem introduced by this approach is the disappearance of a secure channel through which informational messages can be sent. The ISAKMP SA, normally used for diagnostic messages and delete notifications, is no longer available for that purpose.

7.5 Summary

Clearly, IKE implementation details can ensure or impede the interoperability of two implementations. Unfortunately, in some cases an all-seeing oracle (or a proprietary solution) is needed, because some of the details cannot be specified or negotiated in the course of an IKE negotiation. Future versions of IKE undoubtedly will address those issues, facilitating more widespread and interoperable IKE deployment.

7.6 Further Reading

[1] contains an extensive analysis of rekeying, along with suggestions for future versions of IKE. [2] defines the heartbeats protocol. The "initial contact" message is described in [3].

References

[1]   Jenkins, T., "IPsec Re-keying Issues," <draft-jenkins-ipsec-rekeying-06.txt>, May 2000.

[2]   Krywaniuk, A., and T. Kivinen, "Using Isakmp Heartbeats for Dead Peer Detection," <draft-ietf-ipsec-heartbeats-01.txt>, July 2000.

[3]   Piper, D., *The Internet IP Security Domain of Interpretation for ISAKMP*, RFC 2407, Nov. 1998.

8

The Glue: PF_KEY

That must be wonderful. I have no idea what it means.

Molière

The two general IPsec mechanisms that have been discussed so far, the IPsec headers (AH and ESP) and the key negotiation (IKE), are implemented in different parts of the host system. The header processing can be implemented as part of the operating system, as a software add-on to the networking stack, or as a hardware processor external to the host. IKE is a special application-level process. In operating systems capable of assigning different levels of privileges to various classes of users, IKE can be run only by users who have root privileges. How do the IPsec header-processing routines notify IKE that a negotiation is required, and how does IKE in turn give the header-processing routines the secret keys and other parameters that have been negotiated? Generally, some sort of process-to-process communication mechanism, such as sockets, is used for this task.

Interoperability of different IKE and IPsec implementations is critical to widespread deployment of IPsec. That means that vendor A's IPsec and IKE running on host H1 should be able to perform IKE negotiations and exchange IPsec-protected communications with vendor B's IPsec and IKE running on host H2. Is it also possible to run vendor A's IPsec implementation with vendor B's IKE on host H1? That depends on the format, contents, and sequence of the messages exchanged between each vendor's IPsec and

IKE implementations. PF_KEY is an attempt to standardize intrahost communications, to promote an increased level of IPsec-IKE interoperability.

8.1 The PF_KEY Messages

In its most general form, PF_KEY is an application programming interface (API) between an SA negotiation application, such as IKE, and the system-level or kernel routines that create and access the SA database. In fact, the IPsec header-processing routines perform two disparate functions: (1) the creation and maintenance of the SAD and (2) the application of a particular SA to inbound and outbound traffic. SAD creation and maintenance consist of adding IPsec SAs to the SAD, retrieving SAs from the SAD for header processing, and deleting expired SAs from the SAD. The PF_KEY RFC uses the term *key engine* to describe the IPsec routines that create and maintain the SAD. To enhance clarity, this chapter refers to the IPsec SAD creation and maintenance routines simply as IPsec. Although IKE should in truth be called an SA negotiation program or application, it is more commonly referred to as a key negotiation program or application; we use that term here as well.

The PF_KEY API consists of the following 10 messages.

- *SADB_REGISTER.* If a new SA is required to provide IPsec protection for outgoing traffic, IPsec needs to know whether a key negotiation application, such as IKE, is available; if not, the traffic will not be sent. When IKE starts up, it sends two SADB_REGISTER messages to IPsec that inform IPsec that IKE is available to negotiate both types of IPsec SAs (AH and ESP). Each time a new key negotiation program registers an SA type with IPsec, IPsec echoes the SADB_REGISTER message and sends it to all key negotiation programs that have registered to handle that type of SA. The echoed message also contains a list of the cryptographic algorithms supported by IPsec. Subsequently, if new algorithms are dynamically added to IPsec, an updated SADB_REGISTER message is sent to all registered programs.

  Application programs other than key negotiation programs also can use PF_KEY to communicate with IPsec. They generally are not user application programs but privileged system application programs. An example of such a program is an application used by a system administrator to interrogate and maintain the SAD. That

program would use the SADB_REGISTER message for two purposes: (1) to make itself known to IPsec so it can send other
PF_KEY messages to IPsec and (2) to ensure that it receives IPsec-
related PF_KEY messages sent by IPsec to all its registered application programs.

- *SADB_ACQUIRE.* When an application attempts to send outbound
traffic that requires IPsec protection (more on this in Chapter 9)
but the SAD has no SA that is appropriate, IPsec sends an
SADB_ACQUIRE message to all registered application programs,
including IKE. The message includes all the information that IKE
needs to negotiate the SA, including the peer address and the security gateway address (if any). It also informs IKE which security
headers and cryptographic algorithms should be proposed to the
peer. If the SA is to apply only to the application that requested the
SA, the application's port number is also included. The operative
assumption is that the appropriate key negotiation program will act
on this message and the others will ignore it. IPsec then waits for
IKE (or another key negotiation program) to negotiate an SA and
report back to IPsec. If IKE successfully negotiates a new SA, it
informs IPsec via other PF_KEY messages (SADB_GETSPI,
SADB_UPDATE, SADB_ADD). If the SA negotiation fails, IKE
notifies IPsec by responding with another SADB_ACQUIRE
message.

  At any given time, IPsec can be waiting for the responses to multiple SADB_ACQUIRE messages. How does it associate a response
with the appropriate SADB_ACQUIRE request? IPsec generates
a unique sequence number for each SADB_ACQUIRE message;
all PF_KEY messages issued in response to that SADB_ACQUIRE,
whether they are sent by IPsec or by IKE, carry that sequence
number. In that way, multiple simultaneous SA negotiations can be
handled using PF_KEY.

- *SADB_GETSPI.* To negotiate an IPsec SA, IKE first must generate
the inbound SPI, which is sent in the first or second Quick Mode
message together with the IPsec SA proposal. To ensure that the SPI
is unique and consistent with any local constraints, it is best to allow
IPsec to generate all SPIs. That is the function of the PF_KEY
SADB_GETSPI message to IPsec. If multiple key management programs are operating, it makes sense to divide all the valid potential
SPI values among the various key management applications. Valid

IPsec SPIs must be greater than 255; IKE sends the applicable boundary values to IPsec in the SADB_GETSPI message, ensuring that a valid IPsec SPI will be returned.

In response, IPsec generates the SPI and enters a partial IPsec SA, also called a *larval SA*, into the SAD. Because the IKE negotiation has not yet taken place, IPsec does not know most of the SA's parameters; it knows neither the IPsec header to be applied nor the details of its cryptographic algorithms and secret keys. The only information that can be inserted into the SAD at this point is the peer's address and the SPI. If a security gateway will conduct the IKE negotiation, its address also may be known at this point (more on this in Chapter 9). Thus, the larval SA is the initialization of a one-way inbound SA from the peer to IKE's host. It is not yet a functional SA; it is a placeholder that saves all the currently known SA parameters in the SAD. It also guarantees that the SPI about to be proposed by IKE will not be reused while the SA is being negotiated.

IPsec echoes the SADB_GETSPI message, containing the newly generated SPI, back to all the registered application programs, including the one that sent the original SADB_GETSPI message.

In general, only one key management application should respond to a particular SADB_ACQUIRE message, and IPsec should receive only a single SADB_GETSPI request for each negotiation. If, somehow, multiple key management applications claim the privilege of responding to the same SADB_ACQUIRE, there is a mechanism that enables IPsec to distinguish among messages belonging to the separate exchanges. Each time a key management application sends a PF_KEY message to IPsec, it attaches its unique process ID (PID) to the message, and IPsec uses the same PID in its response. In that way, IPsec knows which key management application has sent each message, and each key management application can distinguish the responses to its own messages.

- *SADB_UPDATE.* Once IKE is satisfied that the IPsec SA negotiation is complete, the larval inbound IPsec SA must be transformed into a completed SAD entry. IKE sends an SADB_UPDATE message to IPsec, which includes all the IPsec SA parameters that were negotiated with the peer. The SADB_UPDATE message instructs IPsec to add the missing information to the partial inbound SA and convert its status from larval to mature. When IPsec echoes the

SADB_UPDATE message to the registered application programs, it includes most of the negotiated IPsec SA parameters, but omits the SA's secret keys. There are several situations in which IPsec is not able to update the larval SA into a fully mature SA. If the SA information furnished by IKE is unsatisfactory or erroneous, perhaps containing a secret key that is known to be weak, the update is not performed. If IPsec does not receive an SADB_UPDATE message within a reasonable time following the creation of the larval SA, it deletes the larval SA, freeing its SPI for reuse by another SA. An SADB_UPDATE message that is subsequently sent will fail, because the larval SA no longer exists.

If a mature IPsec SA needs to be renegotiated, either because it has expired or because the requesting application's security requirements have changed, a new SA with a different SPI needs to be established. In such a case, an SADB_UPDATE cannot be used simply to change the SA's parameters. However, the lifetime of an existing mature SA can be modified through the use of an SADB_UPDATE message.

- *SADB_ADD.* An IKE negotiation results in the establishment of two one-way SAs between the peers. The inbound SA is inserted into the SAD through the use of the SADB_GETSPI PF_KEY message, followed by the SADB_UPDATE message. The SPI of the outbound SA is selected by the peer, so no SADB_GETSPI message is required. That SA is added to the SAD, in its completed form, through the use of an SADB_ADD PF_KEY message. An SADB_ADD message also can be used to add manually keyed SAs, both inbound and outbound, to the SAD. The SADB_ADD message, minus secret keys, is then echoed by IPsec to the registered application programs.

- *SADB_GET.* Most applications are not aware of SA negotiations conducted to protect their traffic and have no need to display or access those SAs. For example, an outbound HTTP packet may trigger an IKE negotiation, but it is IPsec that issues the SADB_ACQUIRE message rather than the Web server or browser. Some privileged applications might want to display or retrieve SAs from the SAD. For example, a network administrator may periodically want to examine the SAD as a whole or specific SAs within the SAD. To accomplish that, an SADB_GET message can be sent from a privileged application program to IPsec to request information about a particular SA. IPsec then finds the requested SA in the SAD through a match on source address, destination address, SA type, and SPI and echoes the SADB_GET message only to the application program that issued the initial SADB_GET. The echoed message contains all the specifics related to the requested SA, including the secret keys. As for all PF_KEY messages, the privileged application program must send an SADB_REGISTER message to the kernel prior to issuing the SADB_GET message.

- *SADB_DUMP.* Although this chapter focuses on the application of PF_KEY to IPsec and IPsec SAs, the SAD can contain non-IPsec SAs as well. In a manner analogous to the use of the SADB_GET message, SADB_DUMP is used to display either all the SAs in the SAD or all the SAs of a particular type. A privileged application sends an SADB_DUMP message to IPsec; IPsec then sends a series of SADB_DUMP messages, each containing the information for a single SA, back to the application program that issued the initial SADB_DUMP message. Because this message can cause the exchange of huge amounts of data, it should be used with caution.

- *SADB_EXPIRE.* In the PF_KEY paradigm, every IPsec SA has three types of lifetimes: hard, soft, and current. The hard lifetime is the one negotiated by IKE; when it is reached, IPsec deletes the SA. The soft lifetime is unilaterally determined by the host system; it should be less than the hard lifetime and is the point at which the SA generally is renegotiated, to ensure that the new SA is in place before the old one expires. The current lifetime is a snapshot of the state of the SA at any given time; it is used to calculate how much time or traffic remains until the SA reaches either its soft or hard lifetime. When the soft lifetime is reached, IPsec generally sends an SADB_EXPIRE message to IKE to suggest that IKE initiate an SA renegotiation. The SADB_EXPIRE message also contains the current lifetime of the SA (elapsed time, packets sent, etc.). If, for some reason, the renegotiation does not take place before the hard lifetime expires, IPsec can send IKE an SADB_EXPIRE when it deletes the SA. At that point, however, there will be a period during which IPsec-protected communications will be disrupted while the new SA is negotiated. Other than possibly conducting an IKE negotiation, the registered application programs do not send IPsec any response to the SADB_EXPIRE message.

- *SADB_DELETE.* When an IPsec SA expires or needs to be deleted as the result of a system crash or security breach, IKE sends an SADB_DELETE message to IPsec. The corresponding SA is located in the SAD by matching the source and destination addresses and the SPI. IPsec deletes the SA and echoes the SADB_DELETE message to the registered application programs.

- *SADB_FLUSH.* Just as SADB_DUMP is a generalization of SADB_GET, SADB_FLUSH is a broader form of the SADB_DELETE message. At times, it may be necessary to restart the SAD by deleting all the SAs of a particular type, such as all IPsec SAs, or all the SAs in the SAD, regardless of type. A privileged application program or a key negotiation program can use the SADB_FLUSH message to accomplish this function. Once IPsec has deleted all the relevant SAs, it echoes the SADB_FLUSH message to all registered application programs.

8.2 A Sample PF_KEY Exchange

The PF_KEY RFC [1] describes a number of messages that can be exchanged between IKE and IPsec. It does not dictate a specific sequence of messages, so there is some leeway in their use. Following is one possible exchange of messages that would result in the addition of an IPsec SA to the SAD.

1. IKE registers with IPsec.

2. IPsec requests an IKE negotiation. When an application attempts to send outbound traffic that requires IPsec protection, IPsec sends an SADB_ACQUIRE message with a unique sequence number to IKE and all other registered programs.

3. IKE requests an inbound SPI from IPsec. Once the ISAKMP SA has been established, IKE is ready to negotiate the IPsec SA. Before sending the first Quick Mode message, which contains the inbound SPI, IKE sends an SADB_GETSPI message to IPsec. In response, IPsec generates the SPI and adds the larval SA to the SAD. IPsec sends an SADB_GETSPI message containing the newly generated SPI and IKE's unique process ID to IKE and all the other registered programs. IKE then sends the first Quick Mode message.

4. IKE notifies IPsec that an IPsec SA has been successfully negotiated. Once IKE is satisfied that the IPsec SA negotiation is complete, IKE sends an SADB_UPDATE message to IPsec, which instructs IPsec

to add the missing information to the partial inbound SA and convert its status from larval to mature. IKE also sends an SADB_ADD message to IPsec, causing IPsec to add the new outbound IPsec SA, including an outbound SPI that was selected by the peer, to the SAD. IPsec echoes both the SADB_UPDATE message and the SADB_ADD message to all registered programs.

Figure 8.1 shows the sequence of PF_KEY messages exchanged between the initiator host's IPsec and IKE routines, interspersed with the IKE messages exchanged by the host and its peer. The IKE responder will exchange the same PF_key messages (except the SADB_ACQUIRE) with its IPsec routines. Its IKE negotiation will be triggered when it receives Main Mode Message #1.

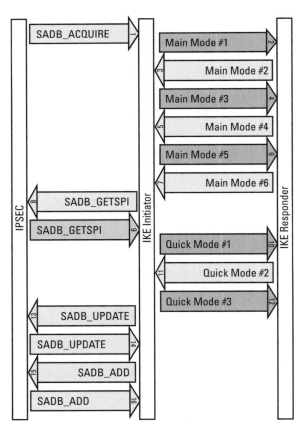

Figure 8.1 A sample PF_KEY exchange.

8.3 Composition of PF_KEY Messages

What sort of information is conveyed in a PF_KEY message? Each PF_KEY message contains an invariant portion, the base message header, which includes the following information.

- *PF_KEY message type.* SADB_REGISTER, SADB_GETSPI, and so forth.

- *PF_KEY sequence number.* This value is initialized by IPsec in the SADB_ACQUIRE message that begins a particular series of PF_KEY messages and is included in each subsequent message of the resulting negotiation and SA creation.

- *Key management program process ID.* This is zero if the message exchange is initiated by IPsec. If the message exchange (e.g., an SADB_GETSPI) is initiated by the key management program and echoed by IPsec, it contains the PID of the initiating key management program.

To supplement the base message header, most PF_KEY messages contain one or more extension headers. Table 8.1 shows, for each PF_KEY message type, which extension headers are required and which are optional. The extension headers are as follows.

- *Security association.* Those PF_KEY messages that access specific SAs (SADB_GET) or update the SAD (SADB_UPDATE, SADB_ADD, SADB_DELETE) use the SAD to exchange or specify SA-related information. To access (SADB_GET) or delete (SADB_DELETE) a mature SA, the only SA-specific information needed is the SPI, because the source and destination addresses are found in the address extension. The security association extension is also used by IPsec to send a requested SPI to IKE via the SADB_GETSPI message. When a new SA is added to the SAD (SADB_ADD) or a larval SA is transformed into a mature SA (SADB_UPDATE), additional SA parameters are sent to IPsec and echoed to the registered programs. Those parameters include the SA's encryption or authentication algorithms, the size of the replay window, and whether PFS applies to the SA's negotiation and renegotiation.

Table 8.1
PF_KEY Message Extensions: Required and Optional

Extension	Security Association	Lifetime	Address	Key	Identity	Proposal	Algorithms Supported	SPI Range
PF_KEY Message								
REGISTER								
IKE	—	—	—	—	—	—	—	—
IPsec	—	—	—	—	—	—	Req	—
ACQUIRE								
IPsec	—	—	Req (SD) Opt(P)	—	Opt(SD)	Req	—	—
IKE	—	—	—	—	—	—	—	—
GETSPI								
IKE	—	—	Req	—	—	—	—	Req
IPsec	Req(SPI)	—	Req(SD)	—	—	—	—	—
UPDATE								
IKE	Req	Opt(CHS)	Req(SD) Opt(P)	Req(AE)	Opt(SD)	—	—	—
IPsec	Req	Opt(CHS)	Req(SD) Opt(P)	—	Opt(SD)	—	—	—
ADD								
IKE	Req	Opt(HS)	Req(SD) Opt(P)	Req(AE)	Opt(SD)	—	—	—
IPsec	Req	Opt(HS)	Req(SD) Opt(P)	—	Opt(SD)	—	—	—
GET								
IKE	Req(SPI)	—	Req(SD)	—	—	—	—	—
IPsec	Req	Opt(CHS)	Req(SD) Opt(P)	Req(AE)	Opt(SD)	—	—	—
EXPIRE								
IPsec	Req	Req(CH/S)	Req(SD)	—	—	—	—	—

Table 8.1 (continued)

Extension	Security Association	Lifetime	Address	Key	Identity	Proposal	Algorithms Supported	SPI Range
DELETE								
IKE	Req(SPI)	—	Req(SD)	—	—	—	—	—
IPsec	Req(SPI)	—	Req(SD)	—	—	—	—	—
FLUSH								
IKE	—	—	—	—	—	—	—	—
IPsec	—	—	—	—	—	—	—	—
DUMP								
IKE	—	—	—	—	—	—	—	—
IPsec	Req	Opt(CHS)	Req(SD) Opt(P)	Req(AE)	Opt(SD)	—	—	—

Key

Req = required	SPI = SPI only
Opt = optional	AE = authentication and/or encryption
— = not applicable	C = current
SD = source and destination	HS = hard and soft
P = proxy	H/S = hard or soft

- *Lifetime.* When an SA is added (SADB_ADD) or updated (SADB_UPDATE), the hard and soft lifetime extensions are used to specify the SA's hard and soft lifetimes in bytes, seconds, or both. They are also used by IPsec in the SADB_GET message to inform IKE of the SA's hard and soft lifetimes. In addition, the current lifetime extension is used to let IKE know the SA's current lifetime, which is either the number of bytes of data that have been protected by the SA or the number of seconds that have elapsed since the SA was established.

- *Address.* There are three types of address extensions: source, destination, and proxy. PF_KEY messages that access or update a specific SA use the source and destination address extensions to specify the SA's source and destination addresses. Together with the SPI from the security association extension, that suffices to pinpoint the SA in the SAD. If a gateway is negotiating an SA for a host that lies behind the gateway, the proxy address extension is used to specify the host's address.

- *Key.* When a new SA is added to the SAD (SADB_ADD) or a larval SA is transformed into a mature SA (SADB_UPDATE), IKE uses the key extension to send the SA's secret keys to IPsec. For an ESP SA, an ESP key extension is used to convey the encryption and authentication keys; for an AH SA, an AH key extension transmits just the authentication key. When a new SA is added to the SAD, IPsec does not echo that sensitive information to the registered programs. However, when a registered program uses the SADB_GET message to retrieve an SA from the SAD, the key extension is included in the echoed message. That is necessary, because the requesting program may be an application program that will apply the SA to traffic. The inclusion of the secret keys is the reason an SADB_GET message is echoed only to the application program that actually issued this message.

- *Identity.* If the source and destination addresses are not sufficient to identify the SA's endpoints, the source and destination identity extensions are used. Those identities can take one of several forms: a network prefix, a fully qualified domain name, or an email address.

- *Proposal.* When IPsec sends an SADB_ACQUIRE message to IKE, the proposal extension is used to convey the details of the SA protection parameters that IKE, as initiator, should propose to the peer. Because IKE will translate those into a valid IKE IPsec proposal, they are arranged in order of precedence, highest to lowest. The proposal extension specifies whether the SA will include replay protection. In addition, each proposal includes the encryption and authentication algorithms, minimum and maximum allowable key lengths, and hard and soft lifetimes in bytes, seconds, or both.

- *Supported algorithms.* The supported authentication algorithms extension and the supported encryption algorithms extension are used in the SADB_REGISTER message sent by IPsec to the registered programs each time a new program registers with IPsec and each time a new algorithm is added to IPsec. For each algorithm, the following information is included: the IV length and the minimum and maximum permissible key sizes.

- *SPI range.* IKE uses the SPI range extension to limit the value of the SPI generated by IPsec as a result of an SADB_GETSPI message.

8.4 Complications

As IPsec and IKE continue to develop, the nature of the information exchanged also needs to change. New scenarios, additional IKE modes, and policy extensions can require modified IPsec-IKE communications. PF_KEY Version 2 dates from July 1998, so it has not kept pace with the latest IKE and IPsec developments. That means implementations that use PF_KEY most likely will find it necessary to add extensions not defined in the PF_KEY document, eliminating the possibility of plugging one vendor's unmodified IPsec implementation into another vendor's IKE. However, the use of a common underlying mechanism still makes such a merge infinitely more manageable than it would be without PF_KEY.

8.5 Summary

Ideally, if PF_KEY were usable without proprietary extensions, it would facilitate mix-and-match deployment of multiple vendors' IKE and IPsec implementations, even without source code accessibility. Because that is not yet the case, PF_KEY is widely deployed in public-domain IPsec and IKE implementations, where the source code can be tweaked to accommodate the exchange of information not defined as part of the standard PF_KEY messages. However, an attempt to standardize the messages and data exchanged by IPsec and IKE serves to clarify and refine the relationship between system security services and privileged key management applications.

8.6 Further Reading

[1] is the complete description of PF_KEY. Because it describes only inter-process communications but not "bits on the wire," it is an informational RFC rather than a standards track RFC. This chapter concentrated on PF_KEY exchanges between IPsec and IKE, resulting in IPsec SAs; the RFC also describes the use of PF_KEY to negotiate non-IPsec SAs with key management applications other than IKE.

Reference

[1]   McDonald, D., C. Metz, and B. Phan, *PF_KEY Key Management API, Version 2*, RFC 2367, July 1998.

9

The Missing Puzzle Piece: Policy Setting and Enforcement

> To get something done, a committee should consist of three men, two of whom are absent.
>
> *Anonymous*

In the very beginning, there was IPsec network-layer packet protection, with its governing databases, the SPD and the SAD. Then along came IKE, which negotiates the SAs that populate the SAD. Those SAs, singly or in groups, are also called *protection suites*. On the local level, they govern IPsec communications policy, both inbound and outbound, for a single host relative to its potential peers. But other questions arise: How does a host decide, or configure, its IPsec security policies? How can two peers minimize the prospect that their IPsec policies are totally different, thus maximizing the possibility that an IKE negotiation between the peers will be productive, resulting in the establishment of one or more SAs? There also are issues related to the use of security gateways. How can peers that require IPsec protection but cannot provide it themselves locate security gateways to accomplish that task? How can a host determine whether to negotiate policy directly with its peer or with a security gateway? If the peer is protected by a gateway, how does the host securely ascertain the gateway's location?

A separate IETF group, the IPsec Policy (IPSP) Working Group, was established to address those issues [1–4]. Its tricky mandate is to solve the problems in a manner consistent with existing policy-related terminology [5], theory, and solutions, requiring no changes to the classic IPsec protocols or IKE but filling in the blanks with approaches that are both generally applicable and secure.

9.1 The Security Policy Database

To address those issues and their solutions, we first need to understand the place of the SPD within IPsec. In particular, we need to know how the SPD functions in the context of IPsec communications and how it interacts with the SAD. We already have determined the functions of the SAD in relation to IPsec-protected communications and IKE. We know that the SAD dictates which IPsec headers, if any, are applied to outbound traffic and controls the interpretation and unbundling of inbound IPsec-protected traffic. We also know that IKE is responsible for negotiating the SAs that populate the SAD. Now let us take one step back and look at the broader picture, to determine the placement of the SPD in this partially assembled puzzle. A succinct generalization of the roles of these two powerful entities would be that the SAD is the enabler of protected communications and the SPD is the enforcer.

The SPD fulfills somewhat different roles for outbound and inbound communications. For outbound packets, it sets down either broad or finer-grained rules related to each packet's disposition and possible IPsec processing. For inbound packets, the SPD dictates the circumstances under which the packet can be accepted by the host. Each rule consists of one or more selectors, which distinguish among the packets, and an action to be applied to those packets that match the rule's selectors. The selectors used by the SPD are the same ones used by the SAD (see Chapter 2). Three possible actions can result from the application of an SPD rule.

- *Drop the packet.* Certain types of traffic may be viewed as inherently insecure and prohibited from being sent or received in any situation.

- *Send out the packet without IPsec protection.* A host or security gateway may allow some types of communications to be sent or received in the clear.

- *Apply IPsec protection to the packet.* If IPsec protection is required for a packet, the SPD specifies the details of that protection: The IPsec header(s) to be applied, the cryptographic algorithms to be used, the encapsulation mode, and so forth. Each outbound SPD rule can contain pointers to all SAs in the SAD that have been negotiated to satisfy the rule. Inbound SPD rules also can contain SA pointers, but, as we will see, those pointers do not necessarily apply to all inbound traffic selected by the rule; even if they do apply, more than one SPD rule may have to be applied to a single inbound packet.

For scenario 2 (see Chapter 1), Figure 9.1 demonstrates the SPD rules that might govern communications between the hosts on networks N1 and N2 and between the security gateways (i.e., SG1 and SG2) themselves. This sample SPD could be either SG1's outbound SPD or SG2's inbound SPD. The selectors shown are the source and destination addresses, the source and destination ports, and the protocol. If IPsec protection is to be applied, each rule specifies the IPsec header, algorithms, and Transport Mode. Rule 1 allows IKE packets, which customarily are sent on port 500, to be sent or received without any IPsec protection. Rule 2 requires all other gateway-to-gateway packets to be authenticated with AH HMAC-SHA-1 in Tunnel Mode. For supersecure host H1-1, rule 3 ensures that all its communications must be encrypted with AES and authenticated with HMAC-SHA-1. Rule 4 specifies that the other hosts on networks N1 and N2 require only an ESP header with Triple DES and HMAC-SHA-1.

The relationship between SPD rules and SAs is not necessarily a one-to-one relationship. A single SPD rule can spawn multiple SAs. If each of the rule's selectors has a single value, then only one SA is negotiated for that rule. However, if any of the rule's selectors is a wildcard or a range, multiple SAs can result from that single rule. For example, in scenario 2, security gateways SG1 and SG2 each negotiate SAs on behalf of multiple machines. Rule 3 in Figure 9.1 covers all communications between host H1-1 on network N1 and any host on network N2. The gateways can satisfy that rule by

Rule #	Src Addr	Dest Addr	Src Port	Dest Port	Prot	Action	IPsec Hdr	Enc Alg	Auth Alg	Mode
1	SG1	SG2	500	500	Any	Accept	—	—	—	—
2	SG1	SG2	Any	Any	Any	IPsec	AH	—	HMAC-SHA-1	Tunnel
3	H1-1	Any	Any	Any	Any	IPsec	ESP	AES	HMAC-SHA-1	Tunnel
4	N1	N2	Any	Any	Any	IPsec	ESP	3DES	HMAC-SHA-1	Tunnel

Figure 9.1 Sample SPD rules for a security gateway.

negotiating a single SA to protect all traffic between H1-1 and network N1. Alternatively, they can negotiate one SA for each pair of protected hosts. The latter approach will result in multiple SAs attached to a single SPD rule. Which approach should be taken is specified as part of each such SPD rule. Each approach has its benefits and its drawbacks. The one-SA-fits-all approach consumes fewer resources, requiring only a single IKE negotiation and a single SAD slot. The one-SA-per-host-pair approach provides less fodder for an attacker, because each SA has its own secret key(s) and the volume of traffic per unit time will be less. However, that approach increases the IKE traffic load and the size of the SAD. Figure 9.2(a) shows the single SA resulting from the one-SA-fits all approach; Figure 9.2(b) shows the SAs resulting from the one-SA-per-host-pair approach; Figure 9.2(c) shows an alternative approach, one SA per protocol.

SA #	Src Addr	Dest Addr	Src Port	Dest Port	Prot	IPsec Hdr	Enc Alg	Auth Alg	Mode
1	H1-1	Any	Any	Any	Any	ESP	AES	HMAC-SHA-1	Tunnel

Figure 9.2(a) SAs generated from an SPD rule: one SA per rule.

SA #	Src Addr	Dest Addr	Src Port	Dest Port	Prot	IPsec Hdr	Enc Alg	Auth Alg	Mode
1	H1-1	H2-1	Any	Any	Any	ESP	AES	HMAC-SHA-1	Tunnel
2	H1-1	H2-2	Any	Any	Any	ESP	AES	HMAC-SHA-1	Tunnel
3	H1-1	H2-3	Any	Any	Any	ESP	AES	HMAC-SHA-1	Tunnel
4	H1-1	H2-4	Any	Any	Any	ESP	AES	HMAC-SHA-1	Tunnel

Figure 9.2(b) SAs generated from an SPD rule: one SA per host pair.

SA #	Src Addr	Dest Addr	Src Port	Dest Port	Prot	IPsec Hdr	Enc Alg	Auth Alg	Mode
1	H1-1	Any	Any	Any	TCP	ESP	AES	HMAC-SHA-1	Tunnel
2	H1-1	Any	Any	Any	UDP	ESP	AES	HMAC-SHA-1	Tunnel

Figure 9.2(c) SAs generated from an SPD rule: one SA per protocol type.

Outbound SPD processing consists of the following steps.

1. Find the first rule in the SPD whose selectors match the packet. The SPD consists of a set of ordered rules. With the use of wildcards as selectors, it is quite possible that multiple rules could apply to a single packet. Thus, it is essential to put the most restrictive or strictest rules first.

2. If the rule's action is to drop the packet or if no applicable rule can be found, the packet is dropped.

3. If the rule's action is to send the packet without IPsec protection, the packet is sent on its way.

4. If the rule specifies IPsec protection, existing SAs that cover that rule are examined. In the case in which the SA's selectors match the packet, the packet is sent to the IPsec-processing routines.

5. If no existing SA can be used for the packet, IKE must negotiate an SA. If no IKE implementation is available or if the IKE negotiation fails, the packet is dropped.

6. If a new SA is successfully negotiated, the packet is sent to the IPsec-processing routines.

As stated in step 2, the RFC on IPsec architecture [6] requires that any packet for which no applicable SPD rule can be found should be dropped. In practice, some implementations adhere to that requirement; others allow such packets to be sent without IPsec protection.

SPD processing for inbound packets differs from outbound SPD processing; multiple SPD rules and multiple SAs can be called into play for a single inbound packet. The IPsec-processing routines first must authenticate or decrypt packets with IPsec headers whose destination addresses match the current host's address. Any IPsec tunnel headers are removed. For each such header, the applicable SA is found in the SAD using the requisite three indices: SPI, destination address, and protocol. The packet's selector values also are verified through comparison to the SA's selector values. A record of the SAs that were used and the order in which they were applied is kept and passed to the SPD-processing routines. Inbound SPD processing then proceeds as follows.

1. If each SA in the SAD contains a pointer to its parent SPD rule, select that rule to be tested first. Otherwise, using the packet's selector values, find the first applicable policy rule in the SPD. If the

packet was tunneled, the selector values are taken from the inner header.

2. Make sure each SA or SA bundle that protected the packet is attached to this SPD rule and applied in the required order.

3. If the SPD rule does not apply, try the next applicable rule in the SPD. Once the appropriate SPD rule has been found, apply the rule's action to the packet.

4. If the packet does not satisfy any SPD rule, discard it.

Why might iterative processing be necessary? A single SA can be shared by multiple SPD rules; if it points to a single rule of the SPD, the pointer might not point to the correct rule. Figure 9.3(a) illustrates that case. SPD rule 1 requires both encryption with ESP and authentication with AH for TCP packets; SPD rule 2 requires only authentication with AH for UDP packets. To conserve on SA negotiation, a single AH SA is negotiated to cover both SPD rules, as shown in Figure 9.3(b). The ESP SA has a back pointer to SPD rule 1, and the AH SA has a back pointer to SPD rule 2. When a TCP packet comes in, protected by both an ESP header and an AH header, the AH header is processed last, and its SPD pointer is used. The packet's selectors do not match those of SPD rule 2. SPD rule 1 is then tested, and the TCP packet is a perfect match.

Rule #	Src Addr	Dest Addr	Src Port	Dest Port	Prot	Action	IPsec Prot	Enc Alg	Auth Alg	Mode
1	H1-1	H2-1	Any	Any	TCP	IPsec	ESP AH	3DES —	— HMAC-SHA-1	Tunnel Tunnel
2	H1-1	H2-1	Any	Any	UDP	IPsec	AH	—	HMAC-SHA-1	Tunnel

Figure 9.3(a) SPD rules: complications and pitfalls.

SA #	Src Addr	Dest Addr	Src Port	Dest Port	Prot	IPsec Hdr	Enc Alg	Auth Alg	Mode	SPD Ptr
1	H1-1	H2-1	Any	Any	TCP	ESP	3DES	—	Tunnel	Rule #1
2	H1-1	H2-1	Any	Any	Any	AH	—	HMAC-SHA-1	Tunnel	Rule #2

Figure 9.3(b) SAs pointing to SPD.

How can a packet pass the SAD checks but fail at the SPD level? That can happen in the case of an SA bundle. In Figure 9.3(b), a TCP packet that arrives with only an AH header would satisfy the SAD selectors for SA 1. However, it would fail both SPD rules shown in Figure 9.3(a): The action portion of rule 1 would fail because no ESP header was found, and the selector portion of rule 2 would fail because it was not a UDP packet.

Following the SPD inbound processing rules as they are presented in the RFC on IPsec architecture can lead to unwanted results. Figure 9.4(a) shows a relatively straightforward SPD: Encryption and authentication are required for all communications to H2-1, with a more stringent encryption algorithm (AES) for those originating from H1-1 and a less stringent encryption algorithm (Triple DES) from all other hosts. That gives rise to two SAs, shown in Figure 9.4(b), one for each rule. If pointers are used from the SAD to the SPD, a message arriving from H1-1 that erroneously uses Triple DES is directed to SPD rule 2 and accepted. Similarly, if pointers are not used, but iterative processing is used, the result is the same. SPD rule 1 will be examined but will fail, because the encryption algorithm is not AES. Then SPD rule 2 will be examined, and it will pass, again accepting the erroneous packet. It appears that, although a prioritized outbound SPD successfully enforces the most stringent rule, a prioritized inbound SPD with iterative processing allows the least stringent rule to be followed. To avoid that, the rules need to be altered. If pointers are not used, the prioritized SPD should be searched and the search should halt at the first SPD rule whose selectors match those of the packet. If pointers from the SAD to the SPD are used, the

Rule #	Src Addr	Dest Addr	Src Port	Dest Port	Prot	Action	IPsec Prot	Enc Alg	Auth Alg	Mode
1	H1-1	H2-1	Any	Any	Any	IPsec	ESP	AES	HMAC-SHA-1	Tunnel
2	H1-*	H2-1	Any	Any	Any	IPsec	ESP	3DES	HMAC-SHA-1	Tunnel

Figure 9.4(a) Inbound SPD.

SA #	Src Addr	Dest Addr	Src Port	Dest Port	Prot	IPsec Hdr	Enc Alg	Auth Alg	Mode	SPD Ptr
1	H1-1	H2-1	Any	Any	Any	ESP	AES	HMAC-SHA-1	Tunnel	Rule #1
2	H1-*	H2-1	Any	Any	Any	ESP	3DES	HMAC-SHA-1	Tunnel	Rule #2

Figure 9.4(b) Inbound SA rules with pointers to SPD.

SPD should not be allowed to have multiple entries whose selectors can select the same packet (more on this later).

These cases illustrate a sad fact of life in the policy arena: Even seemingly simple cases, studied independently, rapidly become complicated.

The most general way to characterize the SAD and SPD is as a series of databases, one of each type for outbound communications and one of each type for inbound communications. For a host or gateway that has multiple external IPsec-enabled interfaces, a separate set of databases would be required for each such interface. In actuality, the SAD and SPD do not have to be separate entities within an implementation; they can be implemented separately, merged into a single entity, or combined with other networking constructs, such as routing tables or socket definitions. Thus, they do not necessarily have to take the form of databases. As long as the outward functionality conforms to our description, the organization or placement of the constructs is irrelevant.

At what point in the communications process is the SPD consulted? If the IPsec implementation is a sockets-based one that is tightly integrated with the operating system, it may be necessary only to interrogate the SPD each time a new socket, inbound or outbound, is created. The action portion of the relevant SPD rule will be a tightly integrated part of the new socket's properties. In other types of implementations, the SPD might be consulted for each inbound and outbound packet; caching recently applied SPD rules can expedite the process. For outbound packets, the proper SPD rule must be found so an SA can be negotiated or applied. If IPsec protection is required, the packet is then delivered to the IPsec routines; otherwise, it is dropped or sent on its way. For inbound packets, IPsec processing must occur first; after those IPsec headers that apply to the current host have been verified and removed, the SPD must be consulted to ensure that the packet was properly protected. Only then can the packet be transmitted to its intended application or forwarded to another destination.

Now that we understand the function of the SPD for a single host, we can explore the more global policy issues. We have seen how the SPD's rules, in conjunction with the SAD's SAs, are used to control communications, whether those communications are IPsec-protected or not. The SPD and SAD are sufficient to handle a single host's policies and to allow it to use IPsec to communicate with like-minded hosts. A more global solution requires several additional elements not handled by this database duo. Obviously, the next question is this: Where do those rules come from and how are they enforced?

9.2 The Policy Problem

To understand the broader policy problem and solution, we need to examine its possible components, the underlying issues, and some new terms relevant to this area.

9.2.1 Policy Configuration

A single stand-alone host theoretically can set its own policy rules without affecting or jeopardizing other hosts. But that is not the normal case. Most hosts belong to networks, whether corporate or private; security gateways also are often one piece of an extensive and complex whole. In this interdependent model, a host's security policies can affect other hosts. Insecure traffic allowed onto a network can jeopardize the whole network, not just the initial recipient of the traffic. With this scenario in mind, it is critical to define, distribute, and enforce uniform policy rules across multiple hosts and domains. How can that be accomplished in a secure and efficient manner?

One issue that IPSP has sidestepped is the method in which a host receives its own policy configuration information. That information is not necessarily limited to IPsec policy variables. It can also include other configuration information, such as IP address and DNS servers. A number of mechanisms already are in place to perform that function, and the IPSP group has declined to add another one to the list. Included in the list of potential policy configuration delivery mechanisms are: COPS-PR [7] and SNMPCONF [8, 9]; LDAP [10, 11] for security gateways; DHCP [12, 13] for hosts; and IPSRA (see Chapter 7) or SACRED [14] for mobile hosts.

The security policies that govern multiple hosts or gateways may originate from a single source. For example, a single security gateway can be used to protect multiple network domains within a single site. Each domain can have its own individual IPsec security policies, all of which will then reside in the security gateway's SPD.

An ancillary issue related to policy configuration is the level of independence accorded to an individual host relative to its policy configuration. Whether a host receives its policy-related rules from another host, is preconfigured by a network administrator, or has a user-friendly policy configuration mechanism, the question remains: Can a user override or change the configured rules or add new ones? One possible scenario is to assign a priority to each policy rule. An individual host cannot change high-priority rules; lesser priority rules cannot be overridden, but they can be strengthened. For example, if the network's global policy requires email to be integrity protected but not encrypted, individual hosts can require encryption as well. Of course, adding more stringent policy requirements can result in preventing communications with entities not equipped to meet those demands. On the other hand, some companies might want to dictate policy and not allow clients to change it; they might require that all traffic be IPsec-protected and all traffic be routed through a security gateway.

9.2.2 Policy Servers

If IPsec policy is to be centrally distributed and administered, a new entity can be injected into the equation: a policy server. This entity is either a security gateway that also assumes those functions or a separate host dedicated to its policy functions. The policy server knows which hosts it is responsible for. Its policy-related information is configured by a network administrator. That information is then distributed to the network hosts for which the policy server is responsible, to the hosts' potential peers, or to both. All policy-related information affecting a local host can be distributed to that host at boot time, when policy changes occur, or as the result of a query. More limited information can be sent to a nonlocal host that wishes to communicate with a local host; that action will always result from a query.

If the policy server resides within a protected network, communications with local hosts that also reside within the same network can be unprotected. But communications with road warriors that are physically located outside the network and receive their policy instructions from the policy server must be protected. Communications with potential peers must be authenticated and, possibly, encrypted as well. In addition, the gateway's SPD must contain rules that allow policy-related queries to reach the policy server and allow policy-related responses to exit the gateway.

There currently is no clear consensus regarding protection of policy-related communications. On the one hand, potential peers need to know the policy server's location and need to be able to query the policy server. On the other hand, revealing too much network-related and policy-related information can increase the network's vulnerability to attacks.

9.2.3 Gateway Discovery

When a host sets off on the journey toward IPsec-protected communications, a number of factors not under the host's control can facilitate or impede that journey. Before an IKE negotiation can proceed, a host needs to know whether its peer is empowered to conduct its own IKE negotiations and provide its own IPsec protections, or whether those protections will be provided by one or more security gateways. In the latter case, it must be able to determine the location and identity of the gateways.

A host may be ignorant of the location of its own security gateways. That can happen in a complex, multilayered network or because of changes to network topology. In such cases, gateway discovery necessitates the identification of all security gateways that lie between a host and its peer, whether those gateways provide IPsec protection for the initiating host or for the peer.

There are a number of facets to security gateway discovery.

- *Locating the security gateway.* This can be done either directly or indirectly. A query can be directed to a policy server or a secure DNS repository, which then responds with the security gateway's address. Alternatively, some sort of gateway probe message can be sent to the peer and intercepted by the gateway. The gateway can then respond with its address. There is a dichotomy inherent in this type of exchange. On the one hand, allowing bona fide peers to discover the identity of a network's security gateway is an essential enabler for secure communications. On the other hand, handing out that information unnecessarily can allow attackers to map out network topology that is not publicly available.

- *Authenticating the gateway.* Not only does the peer have to prove its identity to the host, but its security gateway must also authenticate itself.

- *Proving that the gateway is authorized to act on behalf of the host.* This issue is separate from gateway authentication. A host has to have irrefutable proof that the peer's IPsec protection is actually provided by the gateway.

- *Locating a backup gateway.* If a gateway fails, communications with the peer will come to a standstill, even though the peer is still available. A backup gateway can pick up where the original gateway halted and renegotiate SAs to account for the revised gateway location and identification.

9.2.4 Policy Discovery

It also can be beneficial to know in advance whether an IKE negotiation has a chance of succeeding. When the SPD's rules are somewhat complex, involving selectors other than IP addresses, it is doubtful that an IKE negotiation can succeed without some foreknowledge of the peer's security requirements. If a host can discover, prior to IKE initiation, whether any of its approved security policies also will be acceptable to its peer, that eliminates a major obstacle. If multiple security gateways are involved, policy discovery may have to be performed recursively, to accommodate multiple SAs with differing endpoints.

There are two models of peer policy discovery. In the centralized model, there are multiple security policy domains, each consisting of a collection of hosts and security gateways. Each domain also has one or more policy servers, which are responsible for distributing IPsec policies to subsidiary hosts and gateways. Hosts external to the domain would also be able to obtain policy information from the server prior to initiating an IKE negotiation with one of the domain's hosts. In the distributed model, each host is an island of IPsec independence. It can obtain its policy from another source, but responsibility for communicating those policies to potential peers rests solely on the individual host.

The question of whether gateway discovery information should be protected from eavesdroppers also applies to policy discovery. In both cases, the information clearly needs to be authenticated and integrity protected. But it is not as clear-cut whether it should be encrypted. If not, it can be exchanged before an IKE phase 1 exchange; if it requires encryption, it can be exchanged under the protection of an IKE SA.

Another issue is whether policy discovery should be combined with either gateway discovery or policy server discovery. An obvious benefit is minimizing the amount of traffic necessary to conduct the pre-IKE policy processing. However, separating the processes can result in greater security. Once the gateway or policy server has been authenticated, the policy information will be delivered only to a known and trusted entity. In addition, policy discovery can take place in a more secure manner, with encryption if that is viewed as desirable.

9.2.5   Policy Exchange

To ensure a productive IKE negotiation and subsequent IPsec communications, it may not be sufficient to engage in unilateral policy discovery. The peers may have to conduct a pre-IKE policy exchange, so that each peer knows exactly what types of SAs are required by the peer and its security gateways. A series of prioritized policy alternatives may have to be offered. Each alternative may require multiple SAs, some with the same endpoints and some with different endpoints. The IKE payloads do not lend themselves to this type of complex, multilayered exchange. Thus, in addition to a protocol that will be used to conduct the policy exchange, a new language or message format is required that will facilitate the pre-IKE policy discovery.

9.2.6 Policy Resolution

Once the peers have exchanged prioritized policy discovery information, one of the peers must attempt to resolve the peers' disparate policies and find out whether any common ground can be found. Thus, the language used for pre-IKE policy exchange should lend itself to the resolution process as well. Alternatively, it should be in a format that can be easily translated into a resolution-applicable format. The policy exchange language must be well defined, vendor neutral, and capable of interoperability. It should be easy for humans to understand, so that security snafus and black holes can be avoided. It also should be amenable to automated processing and verification. If the policy resolution language is distinct from the policy exchange language, it can be proprietary.

Policy resolution does not necessarily have to be performed by the end hosts. If a policy server is involved, it can handle the policy discovery and resolution for the end hosts and gateways. An added benefit is that the policy server can cache other hosts' policy requirements, making the process more efficient in the long run. The policy server can also sign and authenticate the policy information, removing those burdens from the end hosts as well.

Adding pre-IKE policy discovery, exchange, and resolution increases the processing burden and could leave hosts open to a massive denial-of-service attack. That possibility is mitigated by the fact that the most expensive operations are borne by the initiator.

9.2.7 Policy Decorrelation

As we have seen, the SPD contains an ordered set of policy rules. The use of wildcards in one or more selector fields can result in overlapping policy entries. For SPD processing, as it is defined in the document on IPsec architecture, careful ordering of the rules generally prevents the unintended application of a general rule to traffic that necessitates a more specific one. When we attempt to connect the SPD's policy rules with other aspects of policy processing, overlapping selectors can be extremely problematic.

If a host receives its policy configuration rules from more than one source, or if a local network administrator is allowed to override the default policy configuration rules imposed by a central policy server, it may be necessary to merge two sets of ordered policy rules, which can be a complex undertaking and may result in unintended consequences. In the areas of policy exchange and policy resolution, two peers are exchanging and resolving sets of alternative and possibly complex policy rules. Evaluating each rule or bundle of rules as an independent entity is enough of a task; adding the aspect of interplay between the alternatives would make it an impossible undertaking. Thus was born the notion of policy rule *decorrelation*, which is a requirement that, within a set of policy-related rules, the selectors of any two rules cannot apply to the same packet. Figure 9.5(a) shows a sample set of SPD rules for scenario 2, and Figure 9.5(b) shows the decorrelated version of the same set of rules. In general, the only difference is the transformation of wildcard

Rule #	Src Addr	Dest Addr	Src Port	Dest Port	Prot	Action	IPsec Hdr	Enc Alg	Auth Alg	Mode
1	SG1	SG2	500	500	Any	Accept	—	—	—	—
2	SG1	SG2	Any	Any	Any	IPsec	AH		HMAC-SHA-1	Tunnel
3	H1-1	Any	Any	Any	Any	IPsec	ESP	AES	HMAC-SHA-1	Tunnel
4	Any	H2-1	Any	Any	Any	IPsec	ESP	AES	HMAC-SHA-1	Tunnel
5	N1	N2	Any	Any	Any	IPsec	ESP	3DES	HMAC-SHA-1	Tunnel

Figure 9.5(a) Sample SPD rules before decorrelation.

Rule #	Src Addr	Dest Addr	Src Port	Dest Port	Prot	Action	IPsec Hdr	Enc Alg	Auth Alg	Mode
1	SG1	SG2	500	500	Any	Accept	—	—	—	—
2	SG1	SG2	Not 500	Not 500	Any	IPsec	AH	—	HMAC-SHA-1	Tunnel
3	H1-1	Not H2-1	Any	Any	Any	IPsec	ESP	AES	HMAC-SHA-1	Tunnel
4	Not H1-1	H2-1	Any	Any	Any	IPsec	ESP	AES	HMAC-SHA-1	Tunnel
5	Not H1-1	Not H2-1	Any	Any	Any	IPsec	ESP	3DES	HMAC-SHA-1	Tunnel

Figure 9.5(b) Sample SPD rules after decorrelation.

selectors to a list of values to which the rule does not apply. The values are the ones for which other rules have already been defined.

9.2.8   Policy Compliance Checking

Even after a host has configured its policy, decorrelated the rules, and exchanged and resolved policy information with every possible communicating peer for every possible type of traffic, eternal vigilance is still necessary. Inbound and outbound traffic must be inspected to ensure that no packets contrary to policy sneak through. Although the preliminary steps may be more complicated and processor intensive, without constant policy compliance checking the whole edifice will crumble. The SPD processing incorporates such checks; implementing them would require each implementation to code and debug this critical and complex methodology. The SPD rules and their relationship to the SAD have given rise to much confused and befuddled debate. Another, quite possibly safer approach is to define a universal policy language for which an automated compliance checker can be developed. This language's use could be restricted to compliance checking, or it could also be used for some of the other policy-related exchanges as well.

9.3   Revisiting the Road Warrior

Chapter 6 discussed the ways in which a road warrior can establish or prove its identity-related credentials to conduct an IKE negotiation. A number of policy ramifications also affect the road warrior.

An important issue is the placement, both actual and virtual, of the road warrior within the corporate network. If a remote client is assigned an internal network address, but it physically resides outside the network, the client could conduct two distinct types of communications: direct Internet communications from its actual physical address and indirect communications from its virtual address via the security gateway. Figure 9.6 shows both types of traffic. Solid lines 1 and 2 constitute an IPsec-protected tunnel from the remote host to the security gateway. If the client was assigned an internal network address, it can then send unprotected traffic inside the network, represented by dotted line 5, or protected traffic outside the network covered by SG2's policy, represented by solid line 3. From its external address, it can send traffic, represented by broken line 4, that is controlled by its own local policy. Alternatively, SG2's security policy might prohibit that type of traffic

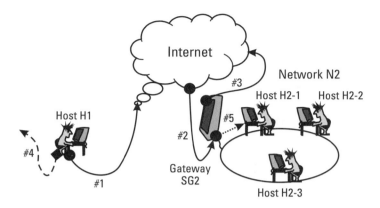

Figure 9.6 Road warrior communications.

and require the client to route all traffic through the gateway, as it would if the client physically resided on the network.

9.4 IPsec Policy Solutions

The current outlook is a little chaotic. A number of solutions have been proposed, each of which tackles one or more aspects of the IPsec policy thicket. It is not yet clear which of them, if any, will be the mandated solution. When and if specific approaches are officially blessed, it will be necessary to specify how the various pieces of the policy puzzle fit together and interact with each other. At that point, some approaches may be discarded. If the policy server approach is adopted, a separate gateway discovery process is not necessary. The policy server will be able to identify any intervening gateways in the inquiring host's domain and specify the gateways' security requirements.

A major unresolved issue is whether each aspect of the solution should be defined as an independent entity or whether some aspects should be combined in a unified protocol. For example, should the discovery aspects of policy (gateway or server discovery, peer policy discovery) be combined or separate? An obvious benefit to the combined approach is to limit the amount of preliminary policy-related traffic. However, developers are leery of a new complex and interlocking protocol. If multiple protocols are defined, changes to one need not affect the others. The same pluses and minuses apply to the bundling of policy discovery, exchange, and resolution. Unfortunately, too many separate pieces can well lead to confusion, ambiguity, and security holes.

The potential solutions currently on the table take several different forms: a model of the policy-handling process, a protocol for policy discovery, a data structure that can be used for policy configuration, and languages to handle several aspects of the problem. Some of the solutions appear fairly complicated and resource intensive, even for the most straightforward case. IKE has come under attack for its complexity; it remains to be seen what level of complexity will be acceptable in a pre-IKE protocol.

9.4.1   The IPsec Configuration Policy Model

The IPsec Configuration Policy Model [15] is an attempt to describe the policy aspects of IPsec in an abstract, conceptual, object-oriented manner. The model is not tied to any specification language or to any particular task-related aspect of policy but can be translated into the appropriate task-dependent specification language to facilitate the performance of a particular task, such as policy distribution, configuration, or resolution. This section does not attempt to describe the model in detail, but mention of select details will give the reader a sampling of its flavor.

The model consists of a hierarchical set of classes, each of which is characterized by one or more properties. The highest level classes of the model are taken from a general policy model, the Policy Core Information Model (PCIM). Those classes are Policy, PolicyGroup, PolicyRule, PolicyCondition, and PolicyAction. New IPsec-specific classes are derived from each of those classes. For example, PolicyRule has spawned the IPsec class SARule, which in turn contains two classes: IKERule and IPsecRule. In each PolicyGroup, the rules are defined in order of decreasing priority. The class PolicyGroup has two interesting properties: IKERuleOverridePoint and IPsecRuleOverridePoint. All rules above that priority must be enforced at all times; rules below the priority can be overriden by rules added by a local administrator. That enables the distribution of global policy guidelines, which can then be meshed with locally dictated rules.

Each PolicyRule has one or more conditions that lead to the application of one or more actions. However, all the rules do not have to take effect under the same circumstances. Each rule can be set in motion by a triggering event, which can be one of the following:

- System start-up;
- A user action;
- Traffic (inbound, outbound, or both) not covered by an existing SA;
- An IKE negotiation initiated by a peer.

There are two classes of actions: static and negotiated. The static actions are the following:

- *Bypass IPsec.* Do not require IPsec protection.
- *Discard traffic.* Do not allow this traffic to proceed further.
- *No IKE negotiation.* Do not allow an IKE negotiation for this traffic.
- *Manual.* Apply a manually established IPsec SA, using predefined algorithms and keys.

The negotiated actions are the following:

- Perform an IKE negotiation.
- Perform an IPsec Transport Mode negotiation.
- Perform an IPsec Tunnel Mode negotiation.

To leverage the usefulness of the model, it needs to be attached to more concrete solutions: protocols, languages, or both.

9.4.2   The IPsec Policy Information Base

The IPsec Policy Information Base (PIB) [16] consists of a series of tables that contain policy-related information. The tables are delivered to IPsec-enabled hosts from a policy server either in response to a direct request from the host or when the server sees fit to alter policy-related variables that affect the host; the recommended communications protocol is COPS-PR. The information can then be used by the host to construct its internal SPD. The information contained in the tables includes policy rules (selectors and actions), IKE and IPsec SA requirements, allowable cryptographic transforms, and SA lifetimes. The tables are designed to be consistent with the IPsec Configuration Policy Model.

9.4.3   The Security Policy Protocol

The Security Policy Protocol (SPP) [17] can be used to conduct gateway and policy discovery. It also can be used for certificate exchange. It predicates the use of policy servers for policy configuration and discovery and, optionally, for policy resolution. If a hierarchical policy structure is desirable within a policy domain, a chain of trust is established, consisting of a series of policy servers, each of which can cryptographically prove that it is responsible for the policy of the next policy server in the chain. SPP defines message formats that can be used for server-to-server policy exchange and host-to-server policy discovery.

All SPP messages require source address authentication and integrity protection. Within a policy domain, that can be provided through the use of IPsec; messages that traverse multiple policy domains carry a digital signature that covers the whole message. Each message also carries a timestamp, which can be used for anti-replay protection. That requires either an authoritative time source or time synchronization between the communicating entities.

The policy information carried in SPP messages can be used for policy resolution, either by individual hosts or by policy servers, but SPP does not define a resolution methodology. When a host requests policy information from a policy server, the host can specify whether the policy server should perform policy resolution for all or part of the chain of trust or whether the server should just deliver unresolved policy information. If policy resolution is required, the server merges or resolves policy received from the peer's policy server with any local policy requirements before responding to the host. Because any policy resolution is done either by the initiating host or by that host's policy server, the burden of this most demanding aspect of policy pre-negotiation is borne by the initiator. Thus, it cannot be used to mount a denial-of-service attack on the responder. On the other hand, if a peer does not monitor its policy-related traffic, flooding the peer with policy discovery inquiries could constitute a fairly effective denial-of-service attack.

To enhance the efficiency of the policy discovery process, SPP incorporates a number of features to facilitate the caching of policy information by policy servers. Cached information can eliminate the need for a policy server to request information from a policy server in another domain. However, care needs to be taken to ensure that the cached information still reflects the peer's up-to-date policy requirements. Policy information that is conveyed to a policy server includes a field that specifies how long that information can be cached. In addition, SPP messages carry flags that inform the policy server whether to use cached policy information for the current exchange and whether to cache policy information for future use.

Although the policies dispensed by the policy servers must be decorrelated, SPP does not specify how that should be performed. It also does not specify the method through which the policy servers are configured with their initial policies.

Six types of messages can appear in an SPP exchange.

- *Query.* A request for policy information sent to a policy server from a host, security gateway, or another policy server. It optionally can include policy information that will enable the policy server to narrow the scope of the information sent in response to the query. Three types of information can be requested:
  - *Security gateway.* The identities of all security gateways between the entity that sent the query and its potential peer;
  - *Communications security.* An indication of whether the potential peer will allow communications for traffic with specific selectors;
  - *Certificate.* The certificate of one or more of the parties to the communication or to the policy discovery process.
- *Reply.* Policy information sent by a policy server in response to a query message. The reply also echoes the original query to which it is responding. Alternatively, if the original query was problematic or erroneous, or if no satisfactory policy information can be found, the reply contains a diagnostic error code. Five types of information can be sent:
  - *Security gateway.* The identities of all security gateways, between the entity that sent the query and its potential peer, for which the queried policy server or those servers in its chain of trust are responsible.
  - *Communications security.* An indication of whether the potential peer will allow communications for traffic with the selectors specified in the query. The response is to permit unprotected traffic, deny all such traffic, or allow the traffic with IPsec protection.
  - *SA information.* The IPsec protection required by the peer for the specified selectors.
  - *Policy server.* The identity of the policy server responsible for the peer.
  - *Certificate.* the certificate that was requested in the query.
- *Policy.* Policy information sent to a policy server by a host, security gateway, or another policy server. The information is intended to be saved in the policy server's cache for future use.
- *Policy acknowledgment.* An acknowledgment by a policy server that it has received a policy message. This message also contains either an

acceptance of the policy information that was sent or a refusal together with the reason for the refusal.

- *Transfer.* Used for bulk policy information exchange between policy servers. SPP does not specify the format and the content of this information.

- *Keep-alive or heartbeat.* A periodic notification sent by a policy server to a security gateway. The notification informs the gateway that the policy server is still available to dispense policy information.

Figure 9.7 shows scenario 2 (see Chapter 1) reinforced by the addition of a policy server for each network. In this case, for host H1-1 to communicate with host H2-1, the SPP policy discovery procedure would work as follows.

1. Host H1-1 sends a policy query to PS1, the policy server for network N1.

2. If PS1 already has H2-1's relevant policy in its cache, it responds immediately to H1-1. Otherwise, PS1 sends a signed policy query to H2-1.

3. SG2 intercepts the query and forwards it to PS2, the policy server for network N2.

4. PS2 validates PS1's signature and then sends the policy response, signed with its private key, to PS1. The response includes the original query, the local policy information necessary to accomplish the

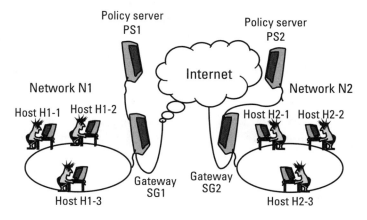

Figure 9.7 Scenario 2 with policy servers.

requested communication, and proof that PS2 is the authorized policy server for H2-1.

5. PS1 validates PS2's signature and verifies that PS2 is H2-1's authorized policy server. If the response enables caching, PS1 caches H2-1's policy for further use. If H1-1 has requested PS1 to resolve H2-1's policy with the local policy requirements, it does so. PS1 then sends the raw or the resolved policy to H1-1.

6. If required, H1-1 performs policy resolution. H1-1 is now ready to initiate an IKE negotiation with H2-1.

9.4.4 The Security Policy Specification Language

The Security Policy Specification Language (SPSL) [18] is a text-based language that a system administrator can use to perform policy-related tasks, such as policy configuration and resolution. It can also be used by a system for policy enforcement and by peer systems for interoperable policy exchange. However, no automated methodology has been identified for the former; no protocol or message format has been specified for the latter.

SPSL can be applied to node-based or domain-based policy. In node-based policy, each independent entity (host, security gateway, etc.) manages and enforces its own policy. For domain-based policy, a group of related nodes rely on one or more policy enforcement points (PEPs) for their policy enforcement. Each path leading into or out of the policy domain must contain a PEP. PEPs are extremely powerful entities that can force the establishment and use of IPsec tunnels. Policy servers and/or security gateways can be either co-located with the PEP or located separately.

Four classes of SPSL objects are currently identified. Each object consists of an ordered set of named attributes, some of which are mandatory and some optional; each attribute has one or more values. The order of attributes is significant only when the interpretation of one attribute is dependent on the value of another. However, if an object is digitally signed, reordering the attributes can cause object verification to fail. Within each class, the objects are differentiated by their first attribute, known as the key attribute, which must have a value that is unique relative to the other members of its class. The SPSL object classes are as follows.

- *Maintainer.* Maintainers are management agents that can create, delete, and change other SPSL objects. They are authenticated either through passwords or certificates that control the maintainer's access to and modification of other objects. Each maintainer has a public key certificate that is used to sign policies issued by the maintainer.

- *Certificate.* Certificates are also considered to be management agents. They are used to sign other SPSL objects.

- *Network entity.* An individual network entity, which can be a node, a gateway, or a policy server, is identified by its DNS name and its IP address. A collective network entity can be a set of nodes, a set of gateways, or a domain. The first two consist of a list of the appropriate class of individual network entities. A domain is a set of nodes, gateways, and policy servers. The gateways constitute the PEPs of the domain.

- *Policy.* An SPSL policy consists of a set of policy-related conditions and a related set of prioritized, alternative security actions. The selectors used in the policy conditions include the standard IPsec selectors, as well as additional, SPSL-specific selectors. Three of the extended SPSL selectors are IPv4 fragment, which selects a packet based on whether it is a fragment; IP header length; and IP version. Because policies in SPSL are not required to be decorrelated, the order of policy objects within a domain and the order of policies within a policy object are significant.

Every policy object is digitally signed with the private key of the policy's maintainer; that provides integrity protection and data origin authentication. SPSL policies can be expressed in a short, long, or combined form. Figure 9.8 is a sample SPSL policy object in the long form.

9.4.5   The KeyNote Trust Management System

We have already described the SPD processing and its relationship to the SAD; those steps constitute the original IPsec architectural approach, which considered only the local policy aspects as they affected the actual IPsec communications and key negotiation. A more policy-centric view can accomplish the same goal but in a manner that is at once more humanly understandable and intuitive and at the same time automates the process so that it becomes more of a "black box." The policy specifications and proposed communication are inserted into the box, the crank is turned, and out comes an acceptance, a denial, or a specification of further actions that need to be taken. That is the potential contribution of KeyNote [19–21] to IPsec policy.

```
ipsec-policy-name:      H11-H21-tunnel-long
association:            SG1
dst :                   H2-1
src :                   H1-1
ike-action:             ikemode  main \
                        auth  rsa  \
                        cipher des3 \
                        hash sha1 \
                        group-desc modp-1024 \
                        expiry seconds 3600
ike-action:             ikemode quick pfs true \
                        cipher des3 \
                        hash sha1 \
                        group-desc modp-1024 \
                        expiry seconds 900
ipsec-action:           esp req \
                        cipher des3 \
                        integrity hmacsha1 \
                        tunnel \
                        from SG1 \
                        to SG2
mnt-by:                 network-admin
changed:                network-admin 20010401
signature: network-admin admin-cert rsa-pkcs1 ABCDEFGHIJKLMNOP
```

Figure 9.8 Sample SPSL policy in the long form.

KeyNote, characterized by its authors as a trust management system, can be applied to a broad range of policy management and compliance checking problems. It includes a language that can be used to express policies and other policy-related entities. The language lends itself to automated processing via a KeyNote interpreter. KeyNote components, which resemble self-contained executable programs, can be authenticated indirectly through the use of traditional certificates, or directly through the use of digital signatures.

As applied to IPsec, KeyNote has four major components:

- *Packet filter language.* A language that lends itself to the efficient processing of inbound and outbound packets.

- *SA policy language.* A more elaborate language that can be used for policy discovery, exchange, and resolution and for compliance checking. Figure 9.9 is a sample KeyNote IPsec policy.

```
Authorizer: "POLICY"
  Licensees: "rsa-base64:ABCDEFGHIJKLMNOP"
  Conditions: app_domain == "IPsec policy" && doi == "ipsec"
          && pfs == "yes"
          && ah_present == "no" && esp_present == "yes"
          && esp_enc_alg == "3des" && esp_auth_alg == "hmac-sha"
          && esp_encapsulation == "tunnel"
          && remote_ike_address == "SG2";
  Signature: "sig-rsa-sha1-base64:QRSTUVWXYZ"
```

Figure 9.9 Sample KeyNote policy.

- *IPsec credentials.* A language and a procedure for ensuring that policy entities are authenticated and integrity protected.

- *Protocol.* Negotiates policy and performs compliance checking using KeyNote policies and credentials.

The languages are somewhat specified, but the IPsec-specific constructions most likely will need to be more explicitly defined. An automated general-purpose KeyNote compliance checker has been tested and applied to IPsec, but the protocol and its interactions with the KeyNote language need to be fleshed out.

It is not clear whether KeyNote will be an optional or a required element of IPsec policy management. The IPSP policy architecture requires that IPSP policies, when used for anything other than strictly local purposes, be expressed as KeyNote policies. In particular, it states that policies exchanged by SPP must be expressed as KeyNote credentials. The SPP draft has no such expectations.

9.4.6　An Overall Plan

Each approach is at best a partial solution to the IPsec policy problem space. It is essential to attempt a global, general, and unified approach. Such an approach should include packet formats and contents for each piece of the solution. If a different language is required for the node-based processing, such as decorrelation or policy resolution, it would be helpful to relate the language used to transport policy-related messages to the language used for single-node processing. Only when such steps are taken will it become clear whether the whole problem space has been satisfactorily resolved. As we have seen, a protocol such as SPP, which needs to take into account the needs of stand-alone hosts, domain-based hosts, security gateways, and policy servers, becomes fairly complex even for the least demanding and simplest example. It is possible that different policy-related solutions will be needed to address the needs of different communication models; capitalizing on the specifics of a particular segment of the problem can make a more streamlined approach possible.

9.5 Summary

Policy discovery, negotiation, and management make up a critical but not yet fully explored frontier. Currently, unless they are using the same proprietary implementation, peers need some prior policy-related knowledge before embarking on an IKE negotiation and subsequent IPsec communications. Security gateways must be known in advance, and IKE policies must be either somewhat generic or agreed on in advance. Once a more general policy-related infrastructure is defined, truly opportunistic IPsec communications can become a reality.

9.6 Further Reading

The IPSP group's approach is defined in an architecture document [1] and a requirements document [2]. There is also an alternative architecture document [3]. General policy terminology is defined in [5]. The protocols that can be used for delivery of policy configuration information are COPS-PR [7], SNMPCONF [8, 9], LDAP [10, 11], DHCP [12, 13], and SACRED [14]. The Configuration Policy Model is laid out in [15]; the PIB in [16]; SPP in [17]; SPSL in [18]; and KeyNote in [19–21]. The IPSP email list archive can be found at http://www.vpnc.org/ipsec-policy.

References

[1]   Blaze, M., et al., "IPsec Policy Architecture," <draft-ietf-ipsp-arch-00.txt>, July 2000.

[2]   Blaze, M., et al., "IPSP Requirements," <draft-ietf-ipsp-requirements-00.txt>, July 2000.

[3]   Cuervo, F., and A. Rayhan, "IPSEC Policy Architecture," <draft-cuervo-ipsp-arch-00.txt>, July 2000.

[4] Zao, J., "Semantic Model for IPsec Policy Interaction," <draft-zao-ipses-policy-semantics-00.txt>, Mar. 10, 2000.

[5] Westerinen, A., et al., "Policy Terminology," <draft-ietf-policy-terminology-00.txt>, July 2000.

[6] Kent, S., and R. Atkinson, *Security Architecture for the Internet Protocol*, RFC 2401, Nov. 1998.

[7] Chan, K., et al., "COPS Usage for Policy Provisioning (COPS-PR)," <draft-ietf-rap-pr-05.txt>, Oct. 2000.

[8] MacFaden, M., and J. Saperia, "Configuring Networks and Devices With SNMP," <draft-ietf-snmpconf-bcp-02.txt>, July 2000.

[9] Saperia, J., "Policy Configuration With SNMP," <draft-saperia-ipsp-spp-00.txt>, July 2000.

[10] Wahl, M., et al., *Authentication Methods for LDAP*, RFC 2829, May 2000.

[11] Wahl, M., T. Howes, and S. Kille, *Lightweight Directory Access Protocol (v3)*, RFC 2251, Dec. 1997.

[12] Droms, R., and W. Arbaugh, "Authentication for DHCP Messages," <draft-ietf-dhc-authentication-14.txt>, June 2000.

[13] Droms, R., *Dynamic Host Configuration Protocol*, RFC 2131, March 1997.

[14] Farrell, S., and M. Nystrom, "Securely Available Credentials," <draft-farrell-sacred-00.txt>, July 2000.

[15] Jason, J., "IPsec Configuration Policy Model," <draft-ietf-ipsp-config-policy-model-01.txt>, July 2000.

[16] Li, M., A. Doria, and J. Jason, "IPSec Policy Information Base," <draft-ietf-ipsp-ipsecpib-00.txt>, July 2000.

[17] Sanchez, L., and M. Condell, "Security Policy Protocol," <draft-ietf-ipsp-spp-00.txt>, July 2000.

[18] Condell, C., C. Lynn, and J. Zao, "Security Policy Specification Language," <draft-ietf-ipsp-spsl-00.txt>, Mar. 2000.

[19] Blaze, M., J. Ioannidis, and A. Keromytis, "Compliance Checking and IPSEC Policy Management," <draft-blaze-ipsp-trustmgt-00.txt>, Mar. 2000.

[20] Blaze, M., J. Ioannidis, and A. Keromytis, *DSA and RSA Key and Signature Encoding for the KeyNote Trust Management System*, RFC 2792, Mar. 2000.

[21] Blaze, M., et al., *The KeyNote Trust-Management System Version 2*, RFC 2704, Sep. 1999.

10

The Framework: Public Key Infrastructure (PKI)

> "When I use a word," Humpty Dumpty said, in rather a scornful tone, "it means just what I choose it to mean—neither more nor less." "The question is," said Alice, "whether you can make words mean so many different things." "The question is," said Humpty Dumpty, "which is to be master—that's all."
>
> *Lewis Carroll, Alice's Adventures in Wonderland*

Previous chapters examined mysterious objects called certificates in a number of contexts related to IPsec and IKE. Those objects are related to a larger edifice called the public key infrastructure (PKI). PKI and certificates rate several books on their own. This chapter attempts to present enough background on these subjects for the reader to understand their role, function, and significance within the framework of IPsec. Most technological areas develop their own jargon and acronyms, which serve as a sort of shorthand for the initiated. The PKI area has more than its share of both, with the interpretation of some acronyms buried three layers deep in a nested acronym tree. This chapter addresses the most common certificate contents, procedures, and jargon, resulting (one would hope) in PKI-literate users.

As we have seen, it is difficult to define a complex protocol in a complete and unambiguous manner. For PKI, the description and definition of certificates and certificate requests are scattered among a large number of non-IPsec documents. Agreeing on and pinning down the precise subset of this constantly developing information is a Herculean task. The most fruitful method for resolving those conflicts has been the ongoing series of IPsec interoperability workshops, during which many problems have surfaced and solutions have been hammered out.

In various aspects of IPsec, we have seen that authentication is required. A certificate provides assurance that the certificate's owner is what it claims to be. But what exactly is that? Many businesses use certificates as an electronic analog to an ID card. Certificates, then, verify a person's claim to be a trusted employee of the company. A certificate is a credential, just as a driver's license is a credential. A driver's license is trusted for two reasons: the photo ties the license to the owner in an easily verifiable manner, and the connection is backed by trust in the issuing government agency. Similarly, a certificate ties a public key to its owner, and the connection is backed by the digital signature of the certificate authority (CA), which is a trusted entity. Certificate verification requires the user to possess the CA's public key, which is used to verify the CA's digital signature. Once that has been done, the user can trust the contents of the certificate, including the owner's public key. Trust in the CA ensures that the owner's identity was sufficiently investigated before the certificate was issued.

The most common type of certificate in use today is the X.509 certificate [1], defined under the umbrella of the International Telecommunications Union (ITU). The IETF's Public Key Infrastructure X.509 (PKIX) group has developed a large number of documents that address the deployment of X.509 certificates for the full range of Internet applications and usage.

The deployment and effective use of a PKI infrastructure require the solution of a number of global issues and widespread agreement on many underlying assumptions. As is often the case, IPsec PKI interactions falter on many levels well below the global ones. It is the minutiae of keys and certificates that provide those stumbling blocks.

10.1　PKI Functional Components

Who are the players in the PKI process? The following components are necessary to enable the initial deployment of a PKI and the continued management and use of its certificates.

- *Certification authority* (CA). The entity that issues certificates. Each certificate is signed by the CA's private key, vouchsafing both its authenticity and the integrity of its data, including the certificate holder's public key and identity. In addition to issuing and signing the certificates, the CA is responsible for their continued maintenance. That involves reissuing the certificate when it expires or some other problem occurs, as well as revoking certificates that are no longer valid and publishing the information in a certificate revocation list (CRL) or its moral equivalent. The public-private key pair can be generated centrally by the CA or locally by the certificate owner. When the keys are not generated by the CA, the CA may require the applicant to prove that it actually possesses the private key. This is known as proof of possession (POP).

- *Registration authority* (RA). The RA is responsible for verifying the certificate holder's identity before the certificate is issued. The steps taken to fulfill that goal depend on the level of security provided by a certificate and the issuing policies of the CA. If the holder's identity is tied to an email address, the registration process can take place through an exchange of email messages, during which the candidate certificate holder exhibits the ability to originate mail from the relevant email address. If a round-trip Web-based exchange is deemed sufficient to verify the IP address of a device that is a potential certificate holder, a browser session can be used to register. For greater levels of security, an in-person interview or some other in-depth investigation may be required, and certificate usage might depend on the possession of a hardware token as well. In those cases, the RA not only consists of automated procedures, but human intervention is required. The RA can be a separate entity, or its functions can be performed by the CA.

- *Certificate holder or owner.* Referred to as end entity (EE) in the PKIX literature, the certificate holder is the object that is bound to the certificate's public key and that possesses the corresponding private key. It can be a person, an email address, a security gateway, or the like. For IPsec, we are currently interested in identity-based certificates, which are used to establish an entity's name or network address in one of the predefined formats listed in Chapter 2. Using some of the more restrictive SA selectors, such as port and protocol, can empower an IPsec certificate to be used for a finer level of access control as well.

Many people feel that a different approach should be taken. A certificate should not identify who you are but what role or functions you are authorized to perform. The PKIX group has begun to standardize a privilege management infrastructure (PMI), in which attribute certificates (ACs) are issued by attribute authorities (AAs). In this context, the traditional PKI certificates are referred to as public key certificates (PKCs). Multiple ACs can be tied to a single PKC; a single AC can be related to multiple PKCs; or ACs can be used as independent entities.

- *Certificate user.* Also known as clients in the e-commerce arena and as peers in the IPsec world, these entities need to transact business or to communicate with the certificate holder. They use the CA's public key to verify the signature on the certificate; after that, they are free to use the certificate holder's public key for its intended use, which can include verification of digital signatures or decryption of data that were encrypted with the certificate holder's private key.

- *Repository.* A database in which the certificates and CRLs are stored and from which they can be accessed by peers wishing to communicate with the certificate holders.

10.2   The PKI World View

A single CA generally issues certificates for a single enterprise, which might be a business, a government agency, or a department. How do we get from enterprisewide PKI to worldwide (or at least wider) deployment and use? Original proponents of PKI envisioned a *hierarchical,* inverted, tree-like structure with the root, or most trusted PKI, at the top and successive layers beneath it. Each CA would issue certificates, signed with its private key, to the CAs on the next lower level. Assume that two certificate holders, C1 and C2, hold certificates signed respectively by CA1 and CA2. To communicate, each would have to "walk" the PKI tree from the top-level CA to the peer. Figure 10.1 illustrates the tree. All trust stems from the mutually trusted top-level CA. In this case, C1 and C2 would have to find a certificate path from the top-level CA to the peer's certificate. Each would then have to verify the signatures on the chain of certificates from the peer's certificate up to the trusted CA. If two hierarchical PKIs had distinct root CAs, the roots would have to "cross-certify" each other to enable communications between holders of certificates of the two separate trees.

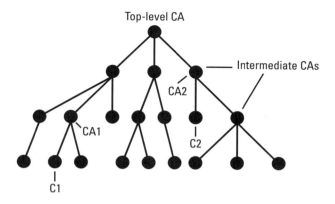

Figure 10.1 A hierarchical CA structure.

At some point, people realized that the world is not hierarchical. The hierarchical model might work within some limited domains, although trees with too many levels might require a substantial level of verification-related computations. An alternative PKI structure, the *meshed* model, more clearly models the real world. Arbitrarily complex relationships can result. The root CAs of several trees can cross-certify each other, but so can individual CAs within the trees.

What exactly does cross-certification mean? Let's say that CA1 has three levels of certificates: Level A is the least secure, level B is intermediate, and level C is the most secure. CA2 has four levels of certificates, ranging from level 1 (least secure) to level 4 (most secure). After comparing policies and procedures, it becomes apparent that CA1's level A certificates correspond to CA2's level 1 certificates; CA1's level B certificates are analogous to CA2's level 2 and 3 certificates; and CA1's level C certificates are comparable to CA2's level 4 certificates. If CA1 and CA2 cross-certify each other, holders of comparable certificates signed by one of the CAs can communicate with certificate holders of the other CA. To complicate things even more, cross-certification can flow in both directions or in only one direction. Thus, CA1 might accept CA2's certificates but CA2 might not accept CA1's certificates.

10.3   The Life Cycle of a Certificate

Communications between a certificate holder or an aspiring certificate holder and the CA or RA generally revolve around the following milestones in the certificate's life cycle.

- *Certificate establishment.* The certificate is issued by the CA, binding the public key to the certificate holder. This is generally set in motion when the potential certificate holder sends a CR to the CA.

- *Certificate publication.* The certificate is made available to potential users. This can take the form of publication in a directory, posting on a Web site, availability through email requests, or other methods agreed on by the community of certificate users.

- *Certificate update.* If a certificate is about to expire, but the key has not been used to excess and is considered still to have some useful life left, the certificate's life can be extended by updating its expiration date.

- *Key update.* If a certificate is about to expire, and issuing a new key is desirable, a replacement certificate can be issued with a new public key. The old certificate would then be revoked.

- *Certificate revocation.* The end of the certificate's useful life, which can occur as a natural part of the life cycle when the certificate's expiration date is reached. Alternatively, it can occur abruptly if the key is compromised or if the certificate holder is no longer entitled to the privileges conferred by the certificate. One common case is that of an employee who quits and is removed from the business's PKI. It can also occur at the request of the certificate's owner. In such a case, the CA generally requires the use of a previously established revocation password to ensure that the entity requesting the certificate's termination is in fact the certificate's owner.

10.4 PKI Protocol-Related Components

We now know the players that must cooperate for successful PKI establishment and deployment. But what are the requirements, in terms of operational protocols and data formats, that enable users from the same or different PKI domains to interoperate? The PKIX roadmap [2] identifies four such components.

- *Data content and formats.* The format and contents of certificates, CRs, and CRLs must be standardized. That includes a list of required fields and allowable values for those fields. The X.509 standard [1] defines the contents of public key certificates in an extremely broad and flexible manner. RSA defined a whole family of cryptography-related formats, known collectively as Public Key Cryptography Standards (PKCS); each member of the family has its own number, which is appended to the family name. In particular, PKCS #10 [3] defines the format for CRs, most often used by a hopeful certificate owner to ask a CA to create a certificate (that does not yet exist). Certificate requests can also be used by potential certificate users who want to access or download a specific certificate. In addition, they appear in IKE CR payloads to ask the peer to send one or more existing certificates. PKCS #7 [4] is a format that can be used for a number of cryptographic entities, including digitally signed certificates and digitally signed CRLs. It also can be used to send "digital envelopes," which consist of data encrypted with a symmetric key, along with the symmetric key encrypted with a public key. A newer specification, Certificate Request Message Format (CRMF), also can be used for CRs.

- *Operational protocols.* Potential peers of a certificate's holder need to be able to retrieve the certificate. They also need to check its current status, to ascertain whether it is still valid or has been revoked. Placing the certificates in an accessible directory is a good first step, but standardized protocols are necessary to accomplish the certificate-accessing and status-checking operations. Certificates and CRLs can be retrieved from a directory [5] using LDAP [6–8]. They also can be requested and obtained via FTP, HTTP, or email. An alternative to the use of static, periodically updated CRLs is an online query protocol known as Online Certificate Status Protocol (OCSP) [9], which allows a potential certificate user to check the up-to-the-minute status of a certificate.

- *Management protocols.* CAs and RAs require a different set of protocols than certificate users. CAs need to store, update, and remove certificates and CRLs. They also must be able to communicate with other CAs for the purpose of cross-certification and CA hierarchy establishment. Aspiring certificate holders need to be able to request a new certificate from the CA, securely provide the CA and RA with the necessary information, and possibly download the private key from the CA.

A number of competing protocols have been defined for certificate establishment and maintenance. Each has its own strengths and weaknesses, and each is currently used or planned for use by one or more commercial CAs or CA providers.

- *Certificate Management Protocol* (CMP) [10]. This is a full certificate life cycle management protocol, specifying all the necessary messages that could possibly be exchanged by the CA, RA, and certificate holder or any combination thereof. It is a heavy-duty protocol, especially because many alternative behaviors are allowed, and only a few mandatory ones are specified. For example, the RA is an optional entity, but if it exists, it can perform any or all of an array of functions, from user authentication to key generation. Any required functions not performed by the RA are assumed by the CA. The preferred message syntax is CRMF. For backward compatibility, CRs in PKCS#10 format are accepted, but strongly discouraged. This protocol is actively supported by Entrust Technologies and Baltimore Technologies.

- *Certificate Management Protocol Using CMS* (CMC) [11]. This is a recursive acronym; CMS stands for cryptographic message syntax. CMC is also a full-service protocol, lacking only the ability to perform cross-certification. Its messages can be encoded in multiple formats, including CRMF and PKCS. This protocol has been blessed by Verisign, Cisco, and Microsoft.

- *Simple Certificate Enrollment Protocol* (SCEP) [12]. This is a somewhat limited protocol, created to fill the need for a straightforward interactive protocol that can create certificates for network (specifically IPsec) devices. It was intended for rapid implementation and deployment while other more complicated and complete protocols worked their way through the standardization process. Web-based HTTP messages are exchanged to perform certificate issuing and revocation and to access certificates and CRLs. CRs are in PKCS#10 format; all messages are PKCS#7-encoded. There is no explicit facility for certificate renewal; to accomplish that, the certificate holder first must revoke the certificate and then request a new certificate. A number of vendors have announced their intentions to implement SCEP.

- *PKCS10 Plus Out of Band* (P10POUB). This method will not be found in any of the standard PKI literature. It was invented by members of the IPsec community, desperate to successfully interoperate in the absence of a global PKI infrastructure, and formally defined in the IKE PKI profile [13]. Communication with the CA takes place via email messages or through Web access, with the applicant filling out a form that constitutes the

CR. In either case, the CR is in PKCS#10 format, including the applicant's public key; the request also should include the desired alternative name and certificate extensions. (Certificate fields are examined later in this chapter.) The CA then sends back the newly minted certificate in one of a variety of formats.

- *Certificate policies and practices.* CAs need to specify and adhere to their individual certificate policy (CP) and certification practice statement (CPS) [14]. They relate to operational matters and security, including the methods used to verify potential certificate holders' identities, security of physical objects and personnel procedures, and revocation polices. They affect the level of trust that can be accorded to the CA's certificates.

10.5 Certificates and CRLs

A common repository for certificates and CRLs is an X.500 directory. The directory is a distributed database, which is capable of holding many different types of data. In the PKI world, it is used to hold certificates and CRLs. Those objects are often accessed via the Lightweight Directory Access Protocol [8] (LDAP), which permits directory objects to be downloaded. LDAP does allow for the use of optional access controls and confidentiality, but they generally are omitted for certificate and CRL retrieval. Because the certificates' and CRLs' contents are authenticated through the use of the CA's digital signature, they can be fetched using an insecure protocol. PKIX also has defined certificate and CRL access using FTP [15, 16], HTTP [15, 17], and email. For IKE, those methods suffice if certificates and CRLs are obtained before the IKE negotiation. IKE can then validate the certificate, ensuring that its CA is trusted and its contents have not been tampered with, before using the certificate's key as part of the peer authentication process. When the certificates are exchanged as part of the IKE phase 1 exchange with peer authentication through digital signatures, it is preferable to send the certificate in Main Mode message 5 or 6, when it can be encrypted and its integrity guaranteed by the authenticating hash. That maximizes the possibility that the exchange can proceed without sabotage by an attacker that could otherwise alter the certificate's contents.

CRLs can be stored and accessed in the same manner as certificates. CRLs generally are issued at fixed intervals. Certificate revocation can occur at any time; in particular, it can occur after one CRL has been issued but well before the next one. Thus, CRLs are not a foolproof method of ensuring the currency of a certificate. OCSP provides more up-to-the-minute information, but that protocol has its own complications for IKE, because an IKE negotiation can time out while waiting for an OCSP response.

10.6 Certificate Formats

For certificates and CRLs to be universally useful, it is important to establish a standard, unambiguous way in which to describe their components. Ideally, that is the function of Abstract Syntax Notation One [18, 19], generally referred to as ASN.1. It is a symbolic language, consisting of a series of rules that, together, definitively describe a composite object; in our case, the ultimate objects we want to define are certificates, CRs, and CRLs. That is accomplished in an iterative manner. The initial ASN.1 rule describes the highest level object in terms of a series of components. Successive rules refine the definition of each component in an increasingly concrete manner, until the lowest level, that of digits and characters, is reached.

Figure 10.2 shows the ASN.1 representation of two portions of a certificate. The first rule defines the general structure of a certificate, which consists of a "tbscertificate," the portion of the certificate that will be digitally signed, an identifier for the algorithm used to create the digital signature, and the signature itself. The second rule defines the time-related validity period of the certificate.

Now that we have an abstract way to describe certificates, we need to be able to translate this structure into an encoding that consists of bits and bytes. That is where basic encoding rules (BER) and distinguished encoding rules (DER) come in [20]. Each ASN.1 component is assigned a unique identifier, a numeric object identifier (OID). BER and DER are used to

```
Certificate   ::=   SEQUENCE  {
          tbsCertificate        TBSCertificate,
          signatureAlgorithm    AlgorithmIdentifier,
          signatureValue        BIT STRING  }

Validity ::= SEQUENCE {
          notBefore    Time,
          notAfter     Time }
```

Figure 10.2 Sample ASN.1 rules.

translate the abstract definition, using OIDs and the specific data appropriate to an individual case, into an encoded certificate. Figure 10.3 shows the DER encoding of a sample certificate field, the email address jdoe@bb.gov, along with two BER alternative encodings. The first example is the DER encoding; the second is an alternative BER encoding; and the third shows a BER encoding with the e-mail address broken up into three components: jdoe, @, and bb.gov.

Why two alternative encodings? The BER rules often allow the same object to be encoded in several different ways, while the DER rules define a single encoding for each case. BER can be more efficient to implement, because its alternative formats generally allow a program to encode or decode an object in a single pass, without the necessity to look ahead for coming attractions. Using DER may necessitate some lookahead, but a single standard encoding is essential to ensure that the verifying signature is computed over the same entity. Now that we have presented samples of ASN.1, DER, and BER for the reader's edification and mystification, we will not delve further into their minutiae.

Here's where it gets even more complicated, if possible. DER-encoded certificates need to be stored in repositories and transmitted over the network. Some transmission methods, such as email, cannot handle binary objects. That gave rise to the Privacy Enhanced Mail (PEM) [21], encoding of the DER encoding of an ASN.1 certificate. PEM-encoded certificates and CRLs thus can be sent as email attachments. PKCS#10 CRs and PKCS#7 cryptographic objects are defined over the DER format of a certificate. They can be transformed into, but are not equivalent to, the PEM-encoded versions. And let us not forget the PKCS#7-wrapped version of PKCS#10 objects. As if that were not confusing enough, the ASN.1 definitions and

```
16 0a
   6a 64 6f 65 40 62 62 2e 67 6f 76

16 81 0a
   6a 64 6f 65 40 62 62 2e 67 6f 76

36 13
   16 04
      6a 64 6f 65
   16 01
      40
   16 06
      62 62 2e 67 6f 76
```

Figure 10.3 Sample DER and BER encodings.

OIDs for various certificate pieces are defined in numerous documents, some intended for the universal PKI domain and some aimed at specific subsets of that domain.

IPsec implementers have tried to do an end run around some of this confusion by holding periodic IPsec interoperability workshops, also known as bake-offs. That allows developers to compare certificate contents and formats. At the end of each workshop, a list of issues that cropped up during the workshop is compiled. Solutions are discussed on the IPsec email list, and, once consensus is reached, those solutions are publicized in Internet Drafts. For vendors who are latecomers to the process, the email list archives supply a record of previously discussed issues, the array of proposed solutions, and the rationale behind the ultimate consensual solution.

10.7   Certificate Contents

For an end user of IPsec, it would be nice to treat certificates as opaque entities that merely serve as grist for the IPsec mill. If that were the case, the fortunate end user would not need to be aware of the fields and the data contained within the certificate. Unfortunately, the literature and standards are replete with quaint compound terms such as subjectAltName and Distinguished Name.

X.509 certificates consist of a number of basic fields found in all certificates and a number of optional extensions, added in X.509 version 3. In addition, communities of certificate users can agree on the definition, format, applicability, and use of other extensions. The basic fields are as follows.

- *Version.* Identifies whether the X.509 conventions used in the certificate conform to version 1, 2, or 3. For PKIX and IPsec, version 3 certificates are used.

- *Serial number.* A number assigned by the CA that is unique among all the CA's certificates.

- *Signature.* The identifier (OID) of the algorithms used by the CA to hash and digitally sign the certificate. Two examples mentioned in the IKE PKI profile are id-dsa-with-sha1 and sha-1WithRSAEncryption. The IKE PKIX profile suggests that all IKE implementations should be able to handle both RSA signatures and DSA signatures using the SHA-1 hash algorithm. As mentioned in Chapter 4, DSA can be computed only over a SHA-1 hash, but RSA can use a variety of hash algorithms, including MD5 and SHA-1.

- *Issuer.* The distinguished name (DN) of the CA. It generally is made up of a series of fields that uniquely characterize the CA. Figure 10.4 contains two DNs, the first of which could apply to a CA. Following are some of the fields that can be used within the DN and examples of their use.

  - Country (C): C = United States
  - Organization (O): O = Bureau of the Budget
  - Organizational unit (OU): OU = Red Ink Department

- *Validity.* The start and end dates that delineate the certificate's lifetime. If an IKE SA is authenticated via a certificate, or an IPsec SA is generated using this type of IKE SA, the IKE PKI profile does not allow either SA to expire any later than the certificate's expiration date. It also requires IKE to check that no certificates in the path from the peer's certificate up to the issuing CA have been revoked.

- *Subject.* The DN of the certificate's holder. The second distinguished name in Figure 10.4 could appear as a certificate's subject. All the fields shown for a CA's DN can also be used for a certificate holder's DN. Some additional DN fields appropriate only for the holder's DN are these:

  - Common name (CN): CN=Joe Smith
  - Surname (SN): SN=Smith
  - Given name (GN): GN=Joe
  - Personal name (PN): PN='SN=Smith, GN=Joe'

  The DN was originally intended to place its subject at a unique node in the X.500 directory information tree (DIT), which was supposed to organize the whole world into a uniform, hierarchical framework. Because a unified framework has not been established, this field is of dubious value, and some of its lesser used components (such as organizationalUnitName, localityName, and stateOr Province Name) are applied differently, if at all, in different domains.

- *Subject's public key information.* The public key algorithm to be used in conjunction with the certificate holder's public key and the key itself.

C=US, O="Bureau of the Budget", CN="Federal PKI", L=Baltimore

C=US, O="Bureau of the Budget", OU="Red Ink Department", CN="John Doe", L=Gaithersburg

Figure 10.4 Sample distinguished names (DNs).

- *Unique subject and issuer (CA) identifiers.* These fields are intended to ensure that a CA cannot issue multiple certificates that have the same owner's name but were actually issued to disparate entities. They also guard against the problem of multiple CAs with the same issuer name. PKIX disapproves of this approach and recommends careful use of issuer and subject namespace instead.

- *Signature algorithm.* The identifiers of the algorithms used by the CA to hash and digitally sign the certificate. This field is not cryptographically protected by the digital signature, to enable the certificate's users to verify the signature. It is duplicated in the signature field mentioned above, which is included in the digital signature; that ensures that an attacker cannot disable use of the certificate by altering this field.

- *Signature value.* A hash of the DER-encoded form of the certificate's contents, digitally signed with the CA's private key.

The X.509 data definitions include multiple extensions, some of which are necessary for Internet-related communications. To interoperate, there must be agreement on support for those extensions. The handling of optional extensions also must be defined. That is an important step toward the interoperation of two implementations, one of which includes optional extensions but does not necessarily expect the peer to process them, and the other of which can ignore those extensions without rejecting the peer's whole data object. Extensions to the basic certificate fields can be processed in several different ways. If they are marked as critical fields within the certificate, certificate users must be capable of processing and acting on the extension field's information; otherwise, the certificate must be ignored. Extension fields not marked as critical can be ignored by certificate users that do not accept or understand that particular extension. Some of the more commonly accepted extensions are the following.

- *CA.* This extension includes the cA bit, used to identify a CA's public key certificate, whose private key can be used to sign other certificates as well as its own. When this extension is used and the cA bit is on, the maximum nesting depth of lower-level CA certificates may be specified. This extension's official name is *basic constraints.* PKIX requires this extension to be present and to be marked as critical in all CA certificates. The cA bit cannot be on for certificates whose owner is not a CA.

- *Alternative name.* This GeneralName (GN) contains any identifying names of the certificate's holder that do not fit the DN format, for example, email address, fully qualified domain name (FQDN), IP address, or URL. If the certificate holder does not have a DN, this field must be present and is considered a critical field. The DN and any alternative names are the identities that are bound to the certificate's keys. This field is formally labeled subjectAltName, a term that is often found in the PKI literature and commonly used by PKI aficionados. To add to the confusion, PKI documents frequently refer to email addresses as RFC822 [22] names.

  For IKE, one of the names in the certificate must match exactly the peer's phase 1 ID payload; the ID types and content must be identical. For example, if the initiator's phase 1 ID is a DN, it must match the DN in the certificate presented to the responder. If the responder's phase 1 ID is an email address, one of the names that constitute the certificate's subjectAltName field must be the same email address.

  The IKE PKI profile allows (but does not require) an IKE participant to terminate an IKE negotiation if this field contains an IP address or DNS domain name that is deemed unacceptable in the context of the current negotiation. When a peer's certificate is accessed and examined prior to an IKE negotiation, that information can be used by an initiator to generate the appropriate proposals or by a responder to evaluate the initiator's proposals. If the certificate is sent as part of an IKE negotiation, an unfortunate situation can occur. In the digital signature mode, the certificates are exchanged after the protection suite has been negotiated. Thus, a proposal may have been proposed or accepted based on the IP address from which the peer sent the packet, which may not correspond to the address or other identity information found in the certificate. In the public key encryption modes, when a responder has multiple certificates, the relevant one is identified after the exchange of proposals, with the responder possibly facing the same dilemma as in the digital signature mode. In such a case, the only possible solution might be to terminate peremptorily the current phase 1 negotiation, optionally starting a new negotiation that takes into account the ID information that has been gleaned from the certificate.

- *Key usage.* Suggests or mandates the uses to which the certificate's public-private key pair can be put, including digital signature, key

encipherment (i.e., transport of symmetric session keys), data encipherment (i.e., encryption), and certificate signing (found only in a
CA's certificate). If this is a critical field, the key can be used only for
one of the designated purposes. To limit the exposure of the private
key, a single entity could have several certificates, each one used for
a different purpose. If this field is marked as critical, that speciali-
zation is enforced; otherwise, it is suggested but not enforced. The
PKIX profile requires the certificate signing bit to be in accord with
the basic constraints extension. For a CA, both the cA bit and the
certificate signing bit must be on; for a non-CA, both must be either
omitted or turned off.

- *Extended key usage.* In addition to the standardized key usage fields,
  additional ones may be defined for special-purpose use. One such is
  iKEIntermediate, proposed in the IKE PKI profile to designate a key
  that can be used for phase 1 IKE authentication. (In the early days of
  IKE, PKIX [23] listed several other IKE-related extended key usage
  values, but they were rejected by the proponents of IPsec.) This
  field also can be marked critical. If both the key usage field and the
  extended key usage fields are critical, the certificate's key can be used
  only in situations that satisfy both fields.

- *CRL distribution points.* A pointer to the location of the CRL. This is
  useful in cases where the CRLs are not colocated with the certificates.

There is a subtle interplay among flexibility, interoperability, and security
in the use and interpretation of many of the certificate fields [24], notably
the key usage and extended key usage bits. If an IKE implementation is
extremely demanding and limiting in the use, interpretation, and validation
of certificate fields, security is enhanced but interoperability may be impossible. At the other end of the spectrum, too much flexibility maximizes
interoperability at the expense of meaningful security.

A CR has the same format as a certificate, but the only fields that contain data are those whose values are required to be matched by the certificate
sent by the IKE peer or generated by the CA in response to the request. The
CRs format specification currently is up to version 2.

10.8   IKE and IPsec Considerations

Standards written for general certificate and PKI use do not always fulfill the
specific needs of IKE and IPsec users. Pieces of the solution are contained in

the PKIX roadmap [2], the PKIX profile [23], and the IKE PKI profile [13]. At times, the PKIX profile and the IKE PKI profile are at odds; in such a situation, IKE wins hands down. An IPsec PKI profile has not yet been written, so its relationship to its fellow travelers is as yet undefined. On the other hand, with continued use and experimentation, new issues continue to crop up.

In phase 1, peers' certificates can be requested through the use of a CR payload and transmitted using a certificate payload. In addition to the peer's certificate, the certificate payload can include the certificate of the CA whose private key was used to sign the peer's certificate; a whole chain of intermediate CA certificates used to sign and validate the peer's certificate; and/or the CA's latest CRL. Clearly, those payloads can contain data that would be of interest to an attacker. In particular, if the certificate's identity is not identical to the peer's ID address, revealing that information defeats IKE's phase 1 identity protection. Thus, the phase 1 messages in which it makes sense to include either CRs or certificates vary, depending on the type of phase 1 negotiation and the peer authentication method that is used.

When IKE peers use digital signatures for authentication, the certificate's public key is only needed by the initiator in Main Mode message 5 and by the responder in Main Mode message 6. Thus, to preserve identity protection, certificate payloads should be included only in Main Mode messages 5 or 6 if the identity is a value other than the peer's IP address or domain name. A CR can include a specific CA or certificate type, limiting the types of certificates that will be accepted by the requester. If an IKE initiator does not want to reveal this type of information, it can send its CR payload as part of an encrypted Main Mode message 5. Because the responder's only encrypted message is the last Main Mode message, message 6, there is no way for a responder to send a protected CR payload. In Aggressive Mode, because identity protection is not an issue, the CR payload can be part of message 1 or 2; in Base Mode it can appear in messages 1, 2, or 3. In those two modes, because the public key is used in only the last two messages, the certificate payload can appear in any message.

With preshared secret key authentication, certificates can be requested and exchanged for use in future PKI-based negotiations. The messages in which they can be used are identical for those in digital signature mode.

When the authentication method is public key encryption, the initiator and responder public keys are used in Main Mode messages 3 and 4, respectively; in Aggressive Mode and Base Mode, they are required in messages 1 and 2. Thus, for Aggressive Mode and Base Mode, CRs are not useful. The initiator must obtain the responder's certificate before the negotiation begins, but the initiator can preemptively send its certificate to the responder. In Main Mode, the CRs can be sent in messages 1 (initiator) and 2 (responder), and the resulting certificates can be exchanged in messages 2 (responder) and 3 (initiator). Needless to say, in such a case the CRs are not protected. The initiator's certificate can be protected with the peer's public key (original encryption mode) or the generated symmetric key (revised encryption mode), but the responder's certificate must be sent in the clear.

A CR can be used to request a single peer certificate or the whole chain of intermediate CA certificates; the chain may or may not include the top-level root certificate. The original IKE documents do not descend to this level of specificity, leading to numerous interoperability problems. The IKE PKI profile attempts to rectify that with an extra layer of detail gleaned from interoperability workshops. However, an implementation still has to be somewhat flexible in this area. A CR for a PKCS#7-wrapped certificate should be interpreted as a request for the whole chain of certificates, while a request for either a signature certificate or a key exchange certificate should result just in the return of the single peer certificate. If the CR identifies a specific CA, the resulting peer certificate ultimately should be rooted in the requested CA. In such a case, it is assumed that the requester already has the top-level CA certificate, and the returned certificate chain need include only the peer certificate and the intermediate CA certificates. If no CA is specified in the CR, the IKE PKI profile allows the receiver to return either a certificate chain or a single certificate rooted in a CA that the receiver believes will be trusted by the requester, if such a beast exists. A CRL request that lacks a CA and is not sent in conjunction with a CR should be ignored.

In the event that a CR asks for a certificate or a CRL that the receiver cannot provide, the IKE PKI profile recommends that no response to that request should be provided. On the other hand, there are conditions under which the receiver should send a notification message containing one of the IKE standard diagnostics. Those messages, which can apply to either erroneous CR payloads or erroneous certificate payloads, include the following.

- *Invalid key.* The public key is not the expected size.

- *Invalid ID.* The ID type is not a valid IKE ID type or is not supported by the peer's implementation.

- *Invalid certificate encoding.* Something about the format or encoding of the certificate or CR is unpalatable to the recipient.

- *Invalid certificate.* The payload contains invalid data or formatting.

- *Certificate type unsupported.* The encoding is valid but not supported by the peer's implementation.
- *Invalid CA.* The CA field is erroneous or invalid.
- *Invalid hash.* The signed hash is not the expected length.
- *Authentication failed.* The signature's value is not the expected one.
- *Invalid signature.* The signature is not the expected length.
- *Certificate unavailable.* The peer cannot send the requested certificate. The existence of this message seems to contradict the IKE PKI profile's recommendation not to send any diagnostic in such a situation.

10.9 Summary

Certificates are an essential element of a widespread, multivendor, interoperable IPsec. Although great strides have been made in PKI technology and products, the "killer app" for PKI has not yet surfaced. The knowledge to build PKI-enabled applications and the applications themselves are still in the early stages of development. Within the IPsec arena, many of the small details are not sufficiently specified to enable PKI deployment in any but a small-scale or controlled environment.

10.10 Further Reading

The IKE PKI profile is laid out in [13]. The PKIX roadmap [2] discusses PKIX history, defines terminology, discusses PKI requirements and players, and describes each current PKIX document. Each management protocol has its own defining document: CMP is defined in [10], which also has a good discussion about the functions of each player, the handling of each life cycle step, and the way each management message should be performed; CMC in [11]; and SCEP in [12]. OCSP's defining document is [9]. Message transport is described in [15–17]. Certificate policies and practices are laid out in RFC 2527 [14]. X.500 directories are defined in [5]. LDAP is defined in [8]; its use for X.500 directories is detailed in [7]; and its use within PKIX is further defined in [6]. The general description of X.509 certificates can be found in [1]; the more specific PKIX certificate description in [23]; and attribute certificates in [25]. For some really thrilling fare, ASN.1 is defined in [18]. However, any document that defines certificate or CRL extensions or modifications (e.g., [23]) generally includes the ASN.1 definitions for those objects. A more recent ASN.1 definition is in [19], but PKIX elected to stick with the previous version. DER and BER are elucidated in [20]; PEM in [21]; PKCS#7 in [4]; and PKCS#10 in [3]. [24] contains a humorous and informational description of each field in an X.509 certificate, along with a characterization of the idiosyncrasies of numerous current certificate implementations.

References

[1]   ITU-T Recommendation X.509, "The Directory: Authentication Framework," June 1997.

[2]   Arsenault, A., and S. Turner, "Internet X.509 Public Key Infrastructure: PKIX Roadmap," <draft-ietf-pkix-roadmap-05.txt>, Mar. 2000.

[3]   Nystrom, M., and B. Kaliski, *PKCS #10: Certification Request Syntax Version 1.7*, RFC 2986, Nov. 2000.

[4]   Kaliski, B., *PKCS #7: Cryptographic Message Syntax Version 1.5*, RFC 2315, Mar. 1998.

[5]   ITU-T Recommendation X.500, "The Directory: Overview of Concepts, Models and Service," 1993.

[6]   Chadwick, D., "Internet X.509 Public Key Infrastructure: Operational Protocols – LDAPv3," <draft-pkix-ldap-v3-03.txt>, Sep. 2000.

[7]   Wahl, M., *A Summary of the X.500(96) User Schema for Use With LDAPv3*, RFC 2256, Dec. 1997.

[8]   Wahl, M., T. Howes, and S. Kille, *Lightweight Directory Access Protocol (v3)*, RFC 2251, Dec. 1997.

[9]   Myers, M., *X.509 Internet Public Key Infrastructure: Online Certificate Status Protocol—OCSP*, RFC 2560, June 1999.

[10] Adams, C., and S. Farrell, "Internet X.509 Public Key Infrastructure: Certificate Management Protocols," <draft-ietf-pkix-rfc2510bis-01.txt>, July 2000.

[11] Myers, M., *Certificate Management Messages Over CMS*, RFC 2797, Apr. 2000.

[12] Liu, X., et al., "Cisco Systems' Simple Certificate Enrollment Protocol (SCEP)," <draft-nourse-scep-03.txt>, Aug. 2000.

[13] Thayer, R., C. Kunzinger, and P. Hoffman, "A PKIX Profile for IKE," <draft-ietf-ipsec-pki-req-05.txt>, July 2000.

[14] Chokhani, S., and W. Ford, *Internet X.509 Public Key Infrastructure: Certificate Policy and Certification Practices Framework*, RFC 2527, Mar. 1999.

[15]   Housley, R., and P. Hoffman, *Internet X.509 Public Key Infrastructure: Operational Protocols—FTP and HTTP*, RFC 2585, May 1999.

[16]   Kapoor, A., and R. TschalŠr, "Transport Protocols for CMP," <draft-ietf-pkix-cmp-transport-protocols-02.txt>, Oct. 2000.

[17]   Reddy, S., "WEB Based Certificate Access Protocol—WebCAP/1.0," <draft-skreddy-pkix-webcap-00.txt>, May 2000.

[18]   "CCITT Recommendation X.208: Specification of Abstract Syntax Notation One (ASN.1)," 1988.

[19]   ITU-T Recommendation X.680, "Abstract Syntax Notation One (ASN.1): Specification of Basic Notation," 1994.

[20]   ITU-T Recommendation X.690, "Specification of ASN.1 Encoding Rules: Basic Canonical, and Distinguished Encoding Rules," 1994.

[21]   Kent, S., *Privacy Enhancement for Internet Electronic Mail: Part II: Certificate-Based Key Management*, RFC 844, Feb. 1993.

[22]   Crocker, D., *Standard for the Format of ARPA Internet Text Messages*, RFC 822, Aug. 1982.

[23]   Housley, R., et al., "Internet X.509 Public Key Infrastructure: Certificate and CRL Profile," <draft-ietf-pkix-new-part1-02.txt>, July 2000.

[24]   Gutmann, P., *X.509 Style Guide*, http://www.cs.auckland.ac.nz/~pgut001/pubs/X509guide.txtOct. 2000.

[25]   Farrell, S., and R. Housley, "An Internet Attribute Certificate Profile for Authorization," <draft-ietf-pkix-ac509prof-05.txt>, Aug. 2000.

11

The Unsolved Puzzle: Secure IP Multicast

I would not join a group which would have me as a member.

Groucho Marx

The previous chapters discussed IP-layer security for unicast communications, which are messages sent by a source host to a single destination host. Sometimes, a message originator may want to send a single message to multiple recipients. A number of special Internet routing mechanisms allow that to be performed with minimal usage of network resources. One method is multicast, which carries traffic from a single source host to multiple destination hosts, often residing on numerous diverse networks.

Although multicast can be used for a wide variety of uses, an oft cited example is cable television, in which a single sender, the cable company, sends traffic consisting of video broadcasts to a preselected list of recipients, which constitutes the multicast group. The sender only has to process a single message, which is sent through a series of routers that form a tree structure; at the end of each terminal tree branch lie one or more group members. Figure 11.1 shows a sample multicast delivery tree, in which the branches are intermediate routers or switches and the leaves are the local routers that deliver the multicast messages to group members on their local network. The beauty of this approach is that the message has to be duplicated only when it

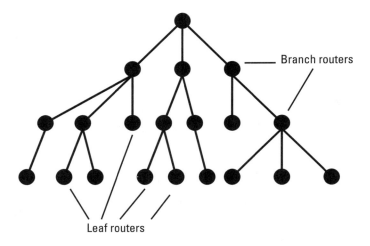

Figure 11.1 A sample multicast delivery tree.

reaches a branch in the tree structure. That minimizes the burden on both the sender and the network at large. When a new host requests to join a multicast group, a new multicast tree branch is established, if necessary, to the host's nearest router.

This type of traffic most decidedly can require security protection; the nature and severity of that requirement vary, based on the multicast group's purpose, characteristics, and membership. Internet standardization has not yet selected one or more official multicast security protocols. This chapter presents different approaches to the various challenges, along with their pluses and minuses, but does not describe specific groupings of the features that constitute particular protocols.

11.1   Some Examples

The most commonly mentioned example of a multicast group, involving a single sender and multiple recipients, is a video broadcast, either pay-per-view TV, cable TV, or a pay-TV station. Another class with multiple senders and recipients is a teleconference, which could take the form of a committee, corporate, or town hall meeting; a conference; or a chat group. There is also distance learning, involving either the one-way communication of a lecture or the two-way communication of a class. Groups can form to conduct a multiplayer video game or to collaborate on the production of a journal or a document. Members can sign up to receive periodic updates on the news, stock quotes, weather conditions, or seismic events. As time goes on, the categories of multicast groups undoubtedly will continue to increase.

11.2 Multicast Logistics

If security is not an issue, central management is not necessarily required, because multicast operations are handled mostly by multicast routers. The Internet Group Management Protocol (IGMP) [1] is used to establish and maintain membership in a multicast group. A host that wants to join a multicast group communicates the request to its local multicast router. The router maintains a list of multicast groups that have members among its local hosts.

The router periodically queries its local hosts regarding current multicast group membership. When a host wants to leave the multicast group, it does not have to notify the router. It simply waits until the next multicast query from the router and omits the abandoned multicast group from its response. The router then updates its internal multicast membership table. A local multicast group can be handled in this way by a single multicast router. For nonlocal groups, multicast routers share information; one of the numerous multicast routing protocols is used to build a multicast delivery tree or trees. In the best case, the only leaf routers that receive multicast messages are those that have group members within their local network. Each leaf router forwards the multicast messages it receives, which contain a multicast destination address that was assigned to the particular group, to all hosts on its network. Nonmember hosts filter out the unwanted packets either at the hardware level, using hardware filters, or at the IP level.

This mechanism does not require any one entity, host or router, to maintain a complete list of multicast group members. Each multicast branch router needs to know only the next multicast router or routers on the delivery tree; each multicast leaf router needs to know only whether any of its local hosts are members, but it does not need to know which specific local hosts belong. That works well in an ideal world, in which multicast resources are freely available to any host that desires to receive them and in which message integrity or secrecy is not necessary. If membership must be limited, due either to monetary considerations or to the secret or proprietary nature of the information, this model is not sufficient. That is the niche to be filled by multicast security.

11.3 Functional Requirements

There are a number of ways in which multicast groups can be characterized. One way is based on the external characteristics of the group [2–4]. Because those characteristics are numerous, and any individual group is a mix-and-match combination of them all, it is difficult to come up with a "typical" multicast group. The most commonly cited external characteristics are the following.

- *Group size.* A multicast group can range from a discussion group with tens of participants, to an interactive conference or class with thousands of members, to a video broadcast with millions of recipients. As with most networking technologies, scalability is an issue. An approach that may work well for a small group might not be feasible for a medium or large group.

- *Processing power.* Multicast group managers or controllers need to have considerably more processing power than ordinary members. But the members' processing power might affect the volume of traffic or the real-time capabilities of the group.

- *Group dynamics.* A multicast group could be a static group whose membership is known in advance or a dynamic group that is constantly gaining new members (referred to as *joins*) and losing old ones (referred to as *leaves*). The demands of handling membership changes also depend on the patterns of joins and leaves: Are they randomly distributed in time, or do they come in bursts? Do members generally stay in the group a long time (also a relative term), or are there constant changes? The nature of the group also might dictate the speed with which joins and leaves must be processed. For example, if a multichannel pay-TV server uses the Internet for its broadcasts, large numbers of members might join right before the showing of a popular program and leave immediately after it ends. If each channel constitutes a separate multicast group, rapid processing of joins and leaves would be essential, because changing channels would correspond to leaving one multicast group and joining another. On the other hand, a group that disseminates newspaper reports could allow more of a delay for both joins and leaves.

- *Composition of senders.* There are two broad categories of multicast groups. In one-to-many groups, a single member is always the sender, and the rest of the group just receives messages. In many-to-many groups, any member can send messages to the rest of the group. Even in many-to-many groups, the majority of the traffic might be sent by one member or by a relatively limited group of members. For example, in a distance learning class, to allow students to ask questions and make comments, any member can send a message; however, the majority of the traffic is generated by the teacher. Some multicast groups might even allow messages to originate from non-members, hosts that do not belong to the group.

- *Group lifetime.* Once formed, a multicast group could last for a few minutes or days, or it could continue indefinitely.

- *Traffic volume.* The number of messages can range from a few short messages to almost continuous, extremely large messages. An example of the former is news headlines or updates sent several times each day; an example of the latter is a cable TV broadcast.

- *Traffic requirements.* Some multicast traffic must be received rapidly and reliably; with other traffic, reliability is important but delay is acceptable. For example, it is difficult to take part in an online discussion if messages are dropped, received out of order, or not received until after the discussion has terminated. On the other hand, bulk data transfer can stand some delivery delay. The speed and reliability requirements placed on multicast traffic are independent of their frequency and volume. Video broadcasts generally are high volume and require rapid (real-time) delivery; audio broadcasts also demand real-time delivery but typically are lower volume; bulk data delivery is high volume but would not require real-time handling.

11.4 Security Requirements

What concerns us more than the external traits of a multicast group is its security requirements. Although those requirements stem from both the group's purpose and its external parameters, two groups can have the same membership, function, and characteristics but very different security-related needs.

When secure multicast is not required, no central authority needs to manage a multicast group or keep track of its membership. For secure multicast, which by its nature requires member authentication and secret keys, a more massive administrative infrastructure is required. The administrative work of managing a secure multicast group is performed by two entities: the group controller (GC) and the key server (KS). Those functions can be performed by a single host or be split between two or more hosts. The KS negotiates, manages, and updates the group's secret keys. The GC handles joins and leaves, ensuring that the multicast delivery tree is up-to-date. It also authenticates potential new members, possibly through the use of public key certificates. Numerous multicast protocols have been designed, some in a manner specific enough for implementation and others at a theoretical level. Each protocol uses its own terminology to indicate the entities that correspond to the GC and KS. Some approaches delegate or share some of the GC's and KS's responsibilities, either with trusted routers or with a select group of members. The trusted routers do not necessarily constitute or even lie on the multicast delivery path. In that way, the multicast routing protocol can be totally independent of the multicast security protocol. Some of the documents refer to these entities as a single body called KS+GC [5] or GCKS [6, 7]. That does not mean they have to be colocated. It is a method of deferring or avoiding the necessity to address the specifics of the protocol used for communications between the KS and the GC.

The rest of this section describes the major security requirements associated with multicast groups, along with a number of the methods that have been suggested to satisfy those needs.

11.4.1 Key Management

Two classes of keys are handled by the KS: individual member keys and the group key or keys. Once a potential group member is authenticated and approved for membership, the KS establishes a secure channel, including a unique symmetric key, with the member. That channel conceivably could be an IKE SA. Its key is used for administrative exchanges between the KS and the individual member; it also can be used to communicate group policies and security parameters to the member, as well as to encrypt the group key for secure delivery to the member. The group key is used to encrypt and authenticate the multicast group messages sent to the members. That could be the product of a special multicast key management protocol, resulting in a group security association (GSA). When the key of an IKE or IPsec SA is negotiated, both peers contribute portions of the keying material. In a multicast GSA, the key can be unilaterally dictated by the KS, or it could be established by the KS with input from one or more group members.

Obviously, using a single group key to deliver all multicast messages to the group can be problematic. If it is known to all the members, it may not remain secret; even if secrecy is not an issue, the key might need to be updated whenever a member joins or leaves. An update would be required to prevent a new member from accessing group messages sent prior to its entry and to prevent an ex-member from accessing group messages sent after its exit.

Embedding the group key in tamper-resistant hardware, such as a SmartCard or a set-top box, can help to restrict the key's use to authorized members without requiring constant updates. However, even those hardware solutions can be subject to key-guessing attacks, so that solution may not be sufficient for ultrasecure multicast communications.

Investing all key-related responsibilities in a single KS or GC also can be problematic. The existence of a single, critical point of failure in a security-related protocol is never ideal. In addition, the KS and GC can become overloaded at peak times. Some approaches delegate member authentication or key distribution to other entities, either trusted routers or select group members. That mitigates the processing burden but does not solve the problems related to a single group key. In this distributed approach, an additional group key is necessary to enable all the KSs and GCs to communicate in a secure manner.

Other multicast protocols use a tree-based key approach, in which the KS establishes a group key with a group of intermediate KSs. The intermediate KSs each establish a group key with a designated subset of the group members or, for a tree with multiple layers, with the next intermediate KS in the tree. That spreads the workload and reduces the number of members that need to be rekeyed as a result of joins and leaves; however, it does require each message to be decrypted and reencrypted by each intermediate KS in its path. The replacement of an intermediate KS involves a significant amount of processing and additional network traffic. An interesting side effect of this delegation of responsibility, whether or not it involves multiple group keys, is that different subtrees can employ different multicast protocols, both for key establishment and for message delivery. In that way, the higher level KSs can select one or more protocols that are optimized for intradomain applications, and the lower level KSs can use protocols that address interdomain issues. However, that would appear to necessitate an interaction between the multicast security protocol and the multicast routing infrastructure. Another factor that should be taken into consideration is the nature of the differences between protocols. A single KS conceivably could handle multiple disparate multicast security protocols, but it would be unreasonable to expect that of a single host that just wants to participate in multiple multicast groups.

11.4.2 Secrecy

Multicast traffic can require protection from eavesdroppers for different reasons. If a group charges subscribers for membership, secrecy is required to prevent nonsubscribers from accessing the messages. That would apply to groups that furnish traffic as diverse as cable TV broadcasts and up-to-the-minute stock quotes. Alternatively, a group's messages might require secrecy because they contain confidential or proprietary information. That could apply to interactive meetings or discussions.

Apart from the purpose served by secrecy, there are wide variations in the required time limitations during which the secrecy must remain in effect. Ephemeral, or short-lived, secrecy is sufficient for stock quotes, which will shortly enter the domain of public knowledge; for that purpose, it suffices if the secrecy guarantees only delayed access by nonmembers. Long-lasting secrecy would be required for confidential or proprietary information. In addition, PFS might be desirable, to limit the damage that could result from the compromise of a single key.

Because the logical way to provide secrecy is through message encryption with a symmetric key, secrecy is subject to all the issues related to key management and distribution.

11.4.3 Data Integrity

Even when secrecy is not required, data integrity may be necessary for multicast traffic. An example is a sensor that sends seismic data to a multicast group. The data must arrive accurate and unaltered. In addition, when messages are encrypted, ensuring data integrity is critical. If that integrity is provided with a shared group key, it can be relied on only if all group members can be trusted. Otherwise, any group member could use the group key to modify the data without the knowledge of the rest of the group.

Once a group key or keys have been established, both encryption and data integrity could be provided through the use of IPsec headers. However, it seems likely that multicast IPsec will require alterations to the classic IPsec headers as well.

11.4.4 Source Authentication

When all the members share a single group key, the source authentication that can be provided through the use of that key and its associated SA differs from source authentication in unicast traffic. Knowledge of the group key is sufficient to prove to the recipient that the message was sent by a member of the group; that is different from proof that the message's originator was a specific member of the group.

If individual authentication is required, each message could be digitally signed by the sender. However, digital signing and verification are expensive operations. A number of digital signature variations are more efficient than the standard RSA or DSS signatures. For example, a batch variant of RSA, in which multiple messages can be signed without significantly more processing than that required for a single message, could be appropriate for broadcast-type multicast groups. Other approaches include [8] stream signatures, flow signatures, hybrid signatures, timed MACs, and asymmetric MACs. The KS might need to distribute the individual public keys used to verify the digital signatures.

11.4.5 Order of Cryptographic Operations

In unicast IPsec, when both authentication and encryption are applied in the ESP header, the data are first encrypted and then authenticated. That enables recipients to head off attempted denial-of-service attacks in the form of bogus IPsec-protected packets. If the authentication fails, the packet is discarded; the more expensive decryption operation is not attempted. In multicast IPsec, the order of operations might depend on the multicast security protocol. If group authentication and encryption are required, protection against denial of service would mandate encrypting first and then authenticating. However, if the protocol involves intermediate routers that perform a series of decryptions followed by reencryption, performing the group authentication first would eliminate the necessity to recalculate the authenticating MAC multiple times as well. If individual source authentication is used, it should be applied first if nonrepudiation also is required. Thus, unlike unicast ESP, the order of cryptographic operations for multicast ESP might depend on the nature of the multicast group and on which multicast keying protocol is used.

11.4.6 Membership Management

Processing joins and leaves requires alterations to the multicast delivery tree, but that is not a major bottleneck, because it is not performed by a central KS. Authenticating a new member in a timely and efficient manner, especially if new membership requests arrive in clumps, or bursts, can be a problem for the KS.

11.4.7 Access-Related Issues

In some cases, timely updating of the multicast delivery tree is required just as an expedient measure. Nonmembers do not want to be unnecessarily bothered with unwanted messages, the network should not be burdened with unnecessary traffic, and new members want to receive messages as soon as possible.

In other cases, not only is timely update required, but encryption may be used to enforce group membership and exclusion. Groups may need to ensure that a new member does not have access to traffic that predated the member's join and that an ex-member cannot access traffic that occurred after the member's leave. In the case of subscription-based services, such as video broadcasts, monetary loss can result, but the message contents themselves are not compromised by the inclusion of nonmembers. For confidential or proprietary teleconferences, exposure to recipients who are not current members can jeopardize the enterprise itself.

An additional access-related issue is whether nonmembers are allowed to send messages to the group.

11.4.8 Policy Determination

Multicast policy issues are even thornier than those that face the as-yet-unresolved unicast model. In addition to the issues of policy representation and determination across multiple domains, different policies may govern communication between each member and the GC than those that apply to the group communications. Before the group is set up, those policies must be set in place. They can be dictated by the GC or negotiated. Negotiated policies can take the form of policies that are acceptable to all members, or some sort of weighted voting system can be used. Once the policies have been established, a member should not join the group until it is fully cognizant of all policy ramifications. Any members that cannot accept the group's security-related policies have the option of not joining.

11.4.9 Anonymity

A multicast group may be constituted to provide three different types of anonymity to its members: keeping group members' identities secret from other members, keeping them secret from nonmembers, or not revealing the identity of the sender of some or all of the messages. That may be an impossible goal if the multicast traffic is susceptible to traffic analysis, because examination of the packets will reveal the sender's IP address. In addition, monitoring the multicast delivery tree will pinpoint the location of the recipients, if not their exact identities.

11.4.10   Nonrepudiation

In some cases, the opposite of anonymity may be required. It might be desirable for a recipient to be able to prove that a specific member was the source of a particular multicast message.

11.4.11   Service Availability

If the multicast traffic is critically important to its recipients, extra resistance to active attacks may be required. Such attacks might take the form of network flooding or clogging or denial-of-service attacks aimed at the group, the KS, or the GC.

11.4.12   Firewall Traversal

For a host that is protected by a firewall to participate in a multicast group, the firewall must allow several types of relevant traffic to traverse the firewall: join and leave messages from the host to the GC; management traffic from the GC to the host; key negotiation and update messages in both directions; and the multicast traffic itself.

11.4.13   Piracy

Although most security threats to a multicast group come from nonmembers, piracy is a threat posed by group members who are willing to reveal either the group key or unencrypted group messages to nonmembers.

11.5   Whither IP Multicast Security?

Unicast IPsec is a thorny problem that has a partial universally acknowledged solution, along with other pieces that are in the process of taking shape. Numerous secure multicast protocols have been proposed. Some are applicable to any multicast group but are computationally feasible or reasonably scalable only under certain restrictions; some are optimized for the characteristics of a particular group. Some have been tested under wide-scale deployment; some are still experimental or theoretical. Developing a secure multicast protocol is not an insurmountable problem; finding a single multicast protocol that is computationally feasible and scalable for all groups, all senders, and all receivers is. On the other hand, allowing the solution to encompass too many protocols would be equally harmful, because it would impose the burden of dealing with the disparate requirements not only on the GC and KS but also on the individual members.

Recognizing that this problem required further investigation, in 1998 the Internet Society commissioned a research group under the umbrella of the Internet Research Task Force (IRTF). That group, the Secure Multicast Group (SMuG), recently released a number of documents [2, 5–11] setting out the problems and issues inherent in secure IP multicast, alternative approaches to resolve them, and components or building blocks that can be defined separately and then combined to surmount the obstacles. Some of the documents suggest pieces of protocols and message formats, but that level of detail most likely will be defined by a different group within the IETF. That will happen once this topic is considered sufficiently analyzed and understood to be defined at the operational level.

11.6 Summary

Different multicast groups can have very different characteristics, which affect the functional and operational priorities on which a multicast security protocol is based. Because those characteristics generally are closely tied to the functions and purpose of the group, it is conceivable that multiple multicast key management protocols will be necessary, each with its own specific advantages and disadvantages. The initiator or manager of the group can then select the optimal protocol before the group is formed; potential members will have to fall in line with that selection if they want to join.

The advantage of multicast is that each message, although destined for multiple destinations, is processed only once by the originator. A single packet leaves the source and travels through the network until the first routing branch. For both the sender and the network, the amounts of processing and traffic are several orders of magnitude less than they would be if each recipient's message was processed and sent individually.

11.7 Further Reading

The sources on this topic all stem from IETF and IRTF working groups. Most IETF Internet drafts are written in the context of a somewhat understood problem. Because multicast security is still a research topic, a number of Internet drafts fully describe the issues, along with the pros and cons of alternative solutions. They also cite numerous other sources of information. There is a considerable amount of overlap among these documents. A single, modular, and consistent approach is planned but has not yet been completely laid out. Two treasure troves of multicast information and analysis are [2] and [4]. IGMP is described in [1]. [5] defines several problem areas related to multicast security and suggests a series of building blocks that could constitute the solution and the interrelationships among those components. [7] contains a conceptual definition of multicast SAs (GSAs) and the KS. [6] describes three types of GSAs that could satisfy the multicast requirements, along with additional payloads and exchanges used for their establishment. [8] suggests an approach to multicast ESP (MESP), including the requirements for special-purpose algorithms. [9] describes a multicast key management scheme for large, dynamic groups. [3] lays out a framework along with key management approaches for the intradomain trunk region as well as for the interdomain leaf region. [10] further defines the key management protocol for the leaf region. [11] elucidates the issues connected with multicast policy.

References

[1]   Fenner, W., *Internet Group Management Protocol, Version 2*, RFC 2236, Nov. 1997.

[2]   Canetti, R., and B. Pinkas, "A Taxonomy of Multicast Security Issues (Updated Version)," <draft-irtf-smug-taxonomy-01.txt>, Aug. 2000.

[3]   Hardjono, T., B. Cain, and N. Doraswamy, "A Framework for Group Key Management for Multicast Security," <draft-ietf-ipsec-gkmframework-03.txt>, Aug. 2000.

[4]   Wallner, D., E. Harder, and R. Agee, *Key Management for Multicast: Issues and Architectures*, RFC 2627, June 1999.

[5]   Hardjono, T., et al., "Secure IP Multicast: Problem Areas, Framework, and Building Blocks," <draft-irtf-smug-framework-01.txt>, Sep. 2000.

[6]   Baugher, M., T. Hardjono, and B. Weis, "Group Domain of Interpretation for ISAKMP," <draft-irtf-smug-gdoi-00.txt>, Sep. 2000.

[7]   Harney, H., M. Baugher, and T. Hardjono, "GKM Building Block: Group Security Association (GSA) Definition," <draft-irtf-smug-gkmbb-gsadef-01.txt>, Sep. 2000.

[8]   Canetti, R., P. Rohatgi, and P. Cheng, "Multicast Data Security Transformations: Requirements, Considerations, and Proposed Design," <draft-irtf-smug-data-transforms-00.txt>, June 2000.

[9]   Balenson, D., D. McGrew, and A. Sherman, "Key Management for Large Dynamic Groups: One-Way Function Trees and Amortized Initialization," <draft-ietf-smug-groupkeymgmt-oft-00.txt>, Aug. 2000.

[10]   Hardjono, T., B. Cainm, and I. Monga, "Intra-Domain Group Key Management Protocol," <draft-irtf-smug-intragkm-00.txt>, Sep. 2000.

[11]   McDaniel, P., et al., "Multicast Security Policy," <draft-irtf-smug-mcast-policy-00.txt>, May 2000.

12

The Whole Puzzle: Is IPsec the Correct Solution?

בן בג בג אומר: הפוך בה והפוך בה, דכולה בה.
פרקי אבות ה:כו

Ben Bag Bag says: Turn it over and turn it over, for all is contained within it.

Mishnah Avot 5:26

We have now described the various facets of IPsec. Some of them are mature in both definition and implementation, some are still in the testing stage, and others as yet have not been fully fleshed out. It is now time to summarize the pluses and minuses of IPsec, its major competitors, and its future.

We have seen that IPsec has the potential to add a needed layer of security to Internet traffic. The protections that it can provide include source authentication, message integrity and confidentiality, replay protection, some protection from traffic analysis, and some types of access control. Those protections qualify IPsec to be used in the creation of VPNs. A fully fleshed-out and agreed-on IPsec could be used to protect not only Internet traffic but the Internet's infrastructure.

When a protocol is used extensively to protect infinite variations on multiple axes (configuration, policy, types of users, etc.), it risks two opposing types of failure. One is that it will become so complex that it cannot possibly be implemented correctly, let alone in a secure manner. The other is that it will not meet the needs of so many of its proponents that they will be forced to add nonstandard or proprietary extensions. That is the tightrope walked by IPsec.

12.1 Advantages of IPsec

What are the pluses of IPsec protection? The level at which it is provided, the IP layer, is a major advantage. That means all types of Internet traffic can be IPsec protected, independent of the specific applications that conduct the communications. The applications do not need to be aware of the protection and do not need to be altered in any way to enable it. It also means that the granularity of protection can vary widely: A single SA can protect all communications between two hosts or two networks, just specific types of traffic, a single application-specific session, or many intermediate gradations of coverage. The level and type of IPsec protection to be applied, as well as the keys to provide that protection, are both flexible and negotiable.

Just as specific applications do not have to be IPsec aware, so too users can be protected in spite of themselves. A network administrator can determine and enforce either networkwide or host-specific policies. Individual users can be prevented from altering those policies; they can be allowed to strengthen the preset policies but be forbidden from diluting or weakening them; or they can be afforded total control over their own individual domain.

A distinct advantage of IPsec is that it can be deployed incrementally; unlike other network-related protocols or technologies, it is not an all-or-nothing proposition. A business that leases private communication lines to link multiple sites can replace one of those lines with an IPsec-protected VPN connecting two sites. Once the kinks are worked out on that relatively limited segment, the private lines can gradually be replaced by IPsec VPNs linking all the sites. IPsec can be easily applied to create various flavors of VPNs: intranets, extranets, and multiple combinations. But IPsec is not limited to enterprisewide use. A road warrior who accesses a PC, located either at home or at work, from a laptop can decide to use IPsec to protect those communications. If the PC is at a business location protected by a firewall, the firewall must allow these strange new packet headers to pass through the firewall's defenses.

Thus, the flexibility and the power of IPsec are its strongest advocates.

12.2 Disadvantages of IPsec

What are some of the minuses? The use of IPsec carries a cost: additional processing and increased packet size. That includes the IKE traffic that precedes the IPsec-protected communications, as well as the additional information added to each IPsec-protected packet. Moreover, IPsec as it exists today is not for the faint of heart. It can require quite a bit of network-level tinkering. Those who install IPsec but are not sufficiently knowledgeable about the options not only risk disruption of network communications but serious security breaches. Like any entity that has been designed through a consensus process, IPsec is not always as streamlined or as consistent as it might have been. But, on balance, even its detractors have great hopes and expectations for its future expansion and use.

12.3 Alternatives to IPsec

For businesses or individuals looking to improve their Internet security, a number of alternatives to IPsec are currently in widespread use.

12.3.1 Transport Layer Security Protocol

Originally developed by Netscape and known as the Secure Sockets Layer (SSL), the Transport Layer Security (TLS) [1] Protocol was subsequently adopted, renamed, and slightly modified by the IETF. It is a session-oriented protocol that provides security at the transport layer, a higher layer in the TCP/IP protocol stack than IP. It can more easily provide individual user-level access protection than the current IPsec. However, that comes at a price: Applications that use TLS must be modified for the purpose, and each individual session must establish its own TLS protection. Moreover, TLS can protect only applications that run over TCP. TLS is currently used to protect browser traffic and quite possibly could continue to be used for that purpose even after IPsec has been more universally deployed.

12.3.2 Layer 2 Tunneling Protocol

The Layer 2 Tunneling Protocol (L2TP) [2] is an extension of the Point-to-Point Protocol (PPP) [3], which was developed to incorporate dial-up traffic into an IP network. PPP allows a dial-up user to connect with its destination and authenticate through the use of a protocol such as RADIUS. It then creates a PPP tunnel, encapsulating the phone link in an IP packet, enabling the non-IP phone traffic to act like any other Internet traffic. That is useful if the user is dialing into a network via a local call. With the advent of ISPs, an additional leg was added: The first leg, handled by PPP, is from the user to the ISP's modem; the new leg, from the ISP's modem to the network entry point, is handled by IP. L2TP creates an extended tunnel that includes the PPP tunnel and the new leg and extends from the dial-up user to the network entry point. That enables the user to authenticate directly to the network rather than to the ISP. Once it is established, an L2TP tunnel contains both control-type messages and the data traffic itself. L2TP allows for authentication of the tunnel endpoints via any of the PPP authentication mechanisms. However, it does not include any mechanism for the encryption of either control or data packets or for data packet integrity.

A number of schemes have been suggested [4–6] for the protection of L2TP traffic by IPsec, thus providing the facilities of a secure VPN [7, 8]. Like IP, PPP and L2TP were designed to maximize communications with minimal security protections. The purists are opposed to dependence on inherently insecure protocols, while the pragmatists oppose the redefinition of extensive machinery that is already part of existing protocols. This is another debate that most likely will be resolved in the marketplace. In the short term, the warring parties have agreed to disagree, and a number of different variations have been fielded. For opportunistic, multidomain, interoperable IPsec to be a reality, a unified solution would be preferable. In the longer term, there most likely will be a shakeout, and one approach will triumph.

There is another substantive objection to the use of L2TP over IPsec. IPsec's tunnel mode is intimately and intricately connected to other aspects of the protocol, including the tunnel and policy selectors. That is not possible when IPsec is used in conjunction with another type of tunneling; security- or policy-related controls are sacrificed in such a case. The IPsec processing cannot take into account the specific nature of the L2TP-encapsulated traffic that is protected by IPsec. By the time the traffic is examined, the IPsec processing has been completed; thus, fields that should be used as selectors are not accessible to IPsec.

The use of L2TP also has been suggested to fill in nonstandardized areas within IPsec, such as the exchange of policy or configuration information between a road warrior and a gateway. The L2TP messages could be tunneled using a previously negotiated ISAKMP SA. This approach has been suggested by the "use existing technology and do not reinvent the wheel" camp. However, that is vociferously countered by the "do not layer protocols that were defined with no security features on top of a secure protocol" proponents. So far, there has been no meeting of the minds, and the volume of the debate continues to escalate.

12.3.3 Point-to-Point Tunneling Protocol

The Point-to-Point Tunneling Protocol (PPTP) [9] is a predecessor of L2TP that shares L2TP's major goals. A version of PPTP, with proprietary Microsoft extensions, is found in most Microsoft Windows operating systems. Thus, it is an attractive and widely accessible vehicle for the creation of VPNs. Bruce Schneier has criticized the underlying security of Microsoft's original PPTP implementation [10] and an improved version [11] and suggests IPsec as a preferable choice.

12.4 IPsec Today

Some of IPsec's components, including the security headers (ESP and AH) and IKE, are specified in sufficient detail to enable a reasonable level of interoperability, following some experimentation. That is all that is required to establish a VPN between disparate domains under two preconditions. To enable IKE negotiation, either each domain must trust the other's root CA or preshared secrets must be established in advance. In addition, the policy requirements must be known and agreed on in advance. Some limited opportunistic IPsec is possible, if the policy requirements of the participants are either extremely flexible or somewhat standardized and if mutual certificate recognition is possible. IPsec, with proprietary extensions for policy handling and road warrior configuration, is widely used today to field VPNs.

12.5 The Future of IPsec

IPsec is at times reminiscent of the venerable elephant joke. Several people encounter an elephant in a dark place, necessitating their discovery of the nature of the beast only through their sense of touch. The person who encounters the elephant's leg pictures an entity resembling a tree trunk. The one who finds one of the elephant's ears thinks it is a fan. The person touching the elephant's trunk is sure it is a rope. And the person who leans against the elephant's side knows it is like a wall. Several aspects of IPsec are plagued by the elephant problem. Making certain assumptions about specific uses and users of IPsec enables the solution to be more elegant, efficient, or secure. But defining a one-size-fits-all garment when we are not too sure of the elephant's size or shape presents major problems and leads to unending and sometimes unresolvable debates regarding the correct approach.

At a recent conference whose sole focus was IPsec[1], a panel of experts was convened to answer these questions: Where are we now? What are the most pressing issues? What changes can we expect to see? It was agreed that IPsec and IKE interoperate and that it is possible to create a working IPsec VPN using the products of any two different vendors. Three or more vendors in an operational (as opposed to experimental or research) environment is still a tricky business. The consensus was that the following features remain to be addressed:

- Transparent interoperability among the IPsec implementations of more than two vendors.

- Simple, failsafe configuration of IPsec devices.

- Secure, user-friendly VPN management and administration.

- A nonproprietary uniform approach to IPsec remote access, including authentication that crosses administrative boundaries.

- Interdomain and intradomain policy issues: nonproprietary policy configuration that is applicable to a wide range of devices (wireless devices, palm pilots, household appliances); a secure policy distribution mechanism; gateway discovery.

- Facilitation of IPsec-based VPNs managed by ISPs. Adding accounting, auditing, and billing capabilities to IPsec devices will allow ISPs to provide different levels of service to different customers. It also will allow customers to include quality of service as a criterion for satisfactory VPN management.

- The inclusion of high availability, backup capability, and resiliency in IPsec devices.

- The seamless integration of IPsec as an integral part of the networking infrastructure.

- Additional issues that doubtless will crop up as a result of the widespread deployment of IPsec and the increased installation of very high-speed networks.

---

1. IPsec2000, Paris Le Defense, October 25–27, 2000, http://www.upperside.fr/baipsec2.html.

When asked whether IPsec should and would be simplified, Steve Kent, one of the main architects of IPsec and the author of many Internet Drafts, replied that everyone connected with IPsec agrees that it is too complex. However, when polled on essential features versus expendable ones, there is no agreement. A feature labeled as extraneous and overly complex by one person appears as essential and nonnegotiable on another person's list.

12.6 Summary

Now that the IPsec puzzle has been assembled, what is it good for? Will it suffer the fate of numerous standards-based solutions: to be hung on the wall or shoved into the closet? Nowadays, even as an incomplete solution, IPsec has a number of very useful applications. It is no longer an esoteric topic relegated to experimental uses. It is deployed and used in a large number of diverse networks, providing remote access security, VPN capabilities, and general IP-level protection. Once the policy and PKI components are more fully fleshed out, the use of IPsec may well expand into every facet of Internet communications and infrastructure protection. Its use will spread and diversify as universal solutions are developed that remove the remaining barriers to its widespread deployment.

12.7 Further Reading

General discussions of VPN frameworks and requirements can be found in [7] and [8]. Each of IPsec's rivals is defined in its own RFC: TLS in RFC 2246 [1], L2TP in RFC 2661 [2], and PPTP in RFC 2637 [9]. PPP is described in RFC 1661 [3]. Schneier's critique of Microsoft's PPTP appears in [10, 11]. Differing approaches to the marriage of L2TP and IPsec can be found in [4] and [5]. An IPsec VPN that uses IP tunnels is proposed in [6].

References

[1]   Dierks, T., and C. Allen, *The TLS Protocol: Version 1.0*, RFC 2246, Jan. 1999.

[2]   Townsley, W., *Layer Two Tunneling Protocol (L2TP)*, RFC 2661, Aug. 1999.

[3]   Simpson, W., *The Point-to-Point Protocol (PPP)*, RFC 1661, July 1994.

[4]   Patel, B., et al., "Securing L2TP Using IPsec," <draft-ietf-l2tpext-security-01.txt>, Aug. 2000.

[5]   Srisurech, P., *Secure Remote Access With L2TP*, RFC 2888, Aug. 2000.

[6]   Touch, J., and L. Eggert, "Use of IPsec Transport Mode for Virtual Networks," <draft-touch-ipsec-vpn-00.txt>, Mar. 2000.

[7]   Gleeson, B., et al., *A Framework for IP Based Virtual Private Networks*, RFC 2764, Feb. 2000.

[8]   Yu, J., "Criteria for Evaluating VPN Implementation Mechanisms," <draft-yu-vpn-criteria-00.txt>, July 2000.

[9]   Hamzeh, K., *Point-to-Point Tunneling Protocol (PPTP)*, RFC 2637, July 1999.

[10] Schneier, B., and Mudge, "Cryptanalysis of Microsoft's Point-to-Point Tunneling Protocol (PPTP)," *Proc. 5th ACM Conference on Communications and Computer Security*, ACM Press, Nov. 1998, http://www.counterpane.com/pptp.{pdf, ps, zip}

[11] Schneier, B., Mudge, and D. Wagner, "Cryptanalysis of Microsoft's PPTP Authentication Extensions (MS-CHAPv2)," *CQRE '99*, Springer-Verlag, Heidelberg, Germany, 1999, pp. 192–203, http://www.counterpane.com/pptpv2.{pdf, ps, zip}.

List of Acronyms and Abbreviations

AA   attribute authority

AC   attribute certificate

AES   Advanced Encryption Standard

AH   Authentication Header

AM   Aggressive Mode

API   Application Programming Interface

ASN.1   Abstract Syntax Notation One

BER   basic encoding rules

BITS   bump in the stack

BITW   bump in the wire

BM   Base Mode

CA   certification authority

CAST   Carlisle Adams/Stafford Tavares

CBC   cipher block chaining

CFB   cipher feedback

CHAP   Challenge Handshake Authentication Protocol

CMC   Certificate Management using CMS

CMP   Certificate Management Protocol

CMS   cryptographic message syntax

CN   common name

COPS   Common Open Policy Service Protocol

COPS-PR   COPS Usage for Policy Provisioning

CP   certificate policy

CPS   certificate practice statement

CR   certificate request

CRACK   challenge/response for authenticated cryptographic keys

CRL   certificate revocation list

CRMF   Certificate Request Message Format

DER   distinguished encoding rules

DES   Data Encryption Standard

DF   don't/may fragment flag

DH   Diffie-Hellman

DHCP   Dynamic Host Configuration Protocol

DIT   directory information tree

DN   distinguished name

DNS   Domain Naming System

DOI   domain of interpretation

DSA   digital signature algorithm

DSS   Digital Signature Standard

EAP   Extensible Authentication Protocol

ECB   electronic codebook

EE   end entity

ESP   Encapsulating Security Protocol

FIPS   Federal Information Processing Standard

FQDN   fully qualified domain name

FTP   File Transfer Protocol

GC   group controller

GN   general name

GSA   group security association

H   host

HTML   Hyper Text Markup Language

HTTP   Hyper Text Transfer Protocol

IAB   Internet Architecture Board

iaPCBC   integrity-aware plaintext-ciphertext block chaining

ICMP   Internet Control Message Protocol

ICV   integrity check value

ID   identity *or* identifier

IDEA   International Data Encryption Algorithm

IETF   Internet Engineering Task Force

IGMP   Internet Group Management Protocol

IKE   Internet Key Exchange

IMAP   Internet Message Access Protocol

IP   Internet Protocol

IPCOMP   IP compression

IPsec   Internet Protocol Security

IPSP   IP Security Policy

IPsra   IP Security Remote Access

IPv4   Internet Protocol version 4

IPv6   Internet Protocol version 6

IRTF   Internet Research Task Force

ISAKMP   Internet Security Association and Key Management Protocol

ISP   Internet service provider

ITU   International Telecommunication Union

ITU-T   International Telecommunication Standardization Sector

IV   initialization value (or vector)

KS   key server

L2TP   Layer 2 Tunneling Protocol

LDAP   Lightweight Directory Access Protocol

MAC   message authentication code

MD   message digest

MESP   Multicast Encapsulating Security Protocol

MF   more/last fragment

MIB   Management Information Base

MM   Main Mode

MODP   modular exponentiation

MTU   maximum transmission unit

N   Network

NAT   network address translation

NSA   National Security Agency

OCSP   Online Certificate Status Protocol

OFB   output feedback

OID   object identifier

OTP   one-time password

P10POUB   PKCS 10 Plus Out of Band

PAP   Password Authentication Protocol

PCBC   Plaintext-Cyphertext Block Chaining

PCIM   Policy Core Information Model

PEM   privacy enhanced mail

PEP   policy enforcement point

PF   protocol family

PFS   perfect forward secrecy

PIB   policy information base

PIC   Pre-IKE Credential Provisioning

PID   Process Identifier

PIN   Personal Identification Number

PKC   public key certificate

PKCS   Public Key Cryptography Standards

PKI   public key infrastructure

PKIX   Public Key Infrastructure X.509

PMI   Privilege Management Infrastructure

PMTU   path maximum transmission unit

POP　post office protocol or proof of possession or point of presence

PPP　Point-to-Point Protocol

PPTP　Point-to-Point Tunneling Protocol

PRF　Pseudo-Random Function

PS　policy server

QM　Quick Mode

QOS　quality of service

RA　registration authority

RADIUS　remote authentication dial-in user service

RFC　Request for Comments

RIP　Routing Information Protocol

RIPEMD　Race Integrity Primitives Evaluation Message Digest

RSA　Rivest/Shamir/Adelman

RSIP　Realm-Specific Internet Protocol

SA　security association

SACRED　securely available credentials

SAD *and* SADB　security association database

SCEP　Simple Certificate Enrollment Protocol

SG　security gateway

SHA　Secure Hash Algorithm

SKIP   Simple Key Management for Internet Protocol

SMTP   Simple Mail Transfer Protocol

SMuG   Secure Multicast Group

SN   sequence number

SNMP   Simple Network Management Protocol

SNMPCONF   Configuration Management with Simple Network Management Protocol

SPD   security policy database

SPI   security parameters index

SPP   Security Policy Protocol

SPSL   Security Policy Specification Language

SSL   secure sockets layer

TCP   Transmission Control Protocol

TCP/IP   Transmission Control Protocol/Internet Protocol

TFESP   Transport-Friendly Encapsulating Security Protocol

TLS   transport layer security

TOS   type of service

TTL   time to live

UDP   User Datagram Protocol

ULA   user-level authentication

URI   Universal Resource Identifier

URL Uniform Resource Locator

VPN virtual private network

WINS Windows Internet Naming Service

WWW World Wide Web

XAUTH extended authentication

XOR exclusive Or

About the Author

Sheila Frankel is a senior computer scientist at the National Institute of Standards and Technology (NIST). She is currently responsible for the technical development of NIST's IPsec and IKE reference implementations, Cerberus and PlutoPlus; and NIST's interactive Web-based IPsec interoperability tester, IPsec-WIT. She remembers when it was possible to have absolute computer security: The computer was behind glass, and the operator handed you a printout. In those days, she contributed to the development of IBM's optimizing Fortran compilers. She holds a B.A. in mathematics from Yeshiva University and an M.S. in computer science from New York University's Courant Institute of Mathematics. Married and the mother of five children, she resides in Silver Spring, Maryland.

Index

Recent Titles in the Artech House Computing Library

Advanced ANSI SQL Data Modeling and Structure Processing,
Michael M. David

Advanced Database Technology and Design, Mario Piattini
and Oscar Díaz, editors

*Business Process Implementation for IT Professionals and
Managers,* Robert B. Walford

*Configuration Management: The Missing Link in Web
Engineering,* Susan Dart

Data Modeling and Design for Today's Architectures,
Angelo Bobak

Demystifying the IPsec Puzzle, Sheila Frankel

Electronic Payment Systems, Donal O'Mahony, Michael Peirce,
and Hitesh Tewari

Fundamentals of Network Security, John E. Canavan

*Future Codes: Essays in Advanced Computer Technology and
the Law,* Curtis E. A. Karnow

Global Distributed Applications with Windows® DNA, Enrique
Madrona

A Guide to Software Configuration Management, Alexis Leon

*Guide to Standards and Specifications for Designing Web
Software,* Stan Magee and Leonard L. Tripp

*Information Hiding Techniques for Steganography and Digital
Watermarking,* Stefan Katzenbeisser and
Fabien A. P. Petitcolas, editors

Internet Commerce Development, Craig Standing

Internet and Intranet Security, Rolf Oppliger

*Managing Computer Networks: A Case-Based Reasoning
Approach,* Lundy Lewis

Metadata Management for Information Control and Business Success, Guy Tozer

Multimedia Database Management Systems, Guojun Lu

Practical Guide to Software Quality Management, John W. Horch

Practical Process Simulation Using Object-Oriented Techniques and C++, José Garrido

Secure Messaging with PGP and S/MIME, Rolf Oppliger

Security Fundamentals for E-Commerce, Vesna Hassler

Security Technologies for the World Wide Web, Rolf Oppliger

Software Verification and Validation: A Practitioner's Guide, Steven R. Rakitin

Strategic Software Production with Domain-Oriented Reuse, Paolo Predonzani, Giancarlo Succi, and Tullio Vernazza

Systems Modeling for Business Process Improvement, David Bustard, Peter Kawalek, and Mark Norris, editors

User-Centered Information Design for Improved Software Usability, Pradeep Henry

Workflow Modeling: Tools for Process Improvement and Application Development, Alec Sharp and Patrick McDermott

For further information on these and other Artech House titles, including previously considered out-of-print books now available through our In-Print-Forever® (IPF®) program, contact:

Artech House	Artech House
685 Canton Street	46 Gillingham Street
Norwood, MA 02062	London SW1V 1AH UK
Phone: 781-769-9750	Phone: +44 (0)20 7596-8750
Fax: 781-769-6334	Fax: +44 (0)20 7630-0166
e-mail: artech@artechhouse.com	e-mail: artech-uk@artechhouse.com

Find us on the World Wide Web at:
www.artechhouse.com